The
Supreme Court
Yearbook
1992-1993

President Bill Clinton poses with the members of the Supreme Court, October 1, 1993, the day his appointee, Ruth Bader Ginsburg, signed her judicial oath. From left, Justices Antonin Scalia, Ginsburg, Anthony M. Kennedy, John Paul Stevens, Chief Justice William H. Rehnquist, the president, Justices Harry A. Blackmun, Sandra Day O'Connor, David H. Souter, and Clarence Thomas.

The
Supreme Court
Yearbook
1992-1993

Kenneth Jost

With a Foreword by Joan Biskupic

Congressional Quarterly Inc.
Washington, D.C.

JAN 2 4 1994

Congressional Quarterly Inc.

Congressional Quarterly Inc., an editorial research service and publishing company, serves clients in the fields of news, education, business, and government. It combines specific coverage of Congress, government, and politics contained in the *Congressional Quarterly Weekly Report* with the more general subject range of an affiliated publication, *CQ Researcher.*

Congressional Quarterly publishes a variety of books, including college political science textbooks under the CQ Press imprint and public affairs paperbacks on developing issues and events. CQ also develops information directories and reference books on the federal government, national elections, and politics, such as the *Guide to the Presidency,* the *Guide to Congress,* the *Guide to the U.S. Supreme Court,* the *Guide to U.S. Elections,* and *Politics in America.* The *CQ Almanac,* a compendium of legislation for one session of Congress, is published each year. *Congress and the Nation,* a record of government for a presidential term, is published every four years. *CQ's Encyclopedia of American Government* is a three-volume reference work providing essential information about the U.S. government.

CQ publishes the *Congressional Monitor,* a daily report of late-breaking news and committee schedules, and *Congressional Insight,* a weekly newsletter of analysis. The CQ FaxReport is a daily update available every afternoon when Congress is in session. An electronic online information system, Washington Alert, provides immediate access to CQ's databases of legislative action, votes, schedules, profiles, and analyses.

Cover design: Julie Booth/P. Eloise Fuller

Photo credits: cover, R. Michael Jenkins; frontispiece, 12, Ken Heinen for the Supreme Court; 3, Rick T. Wilking, Reuter; 28, U.S. Coast Guard; 31, Bruce McClelland, *Arizona Daily Star;* 37, Public Information Office, Texas Department of Criminal Justice; 38, *Kenosha News;* 216, Courtesy of Luke Records; 217, AP Laser Photo.

Published in the United States of America

ISBN 0-87187-796-1
ISBN 0-87187-795-3 (pbk)
ISSN 1054-2701

Contents

Preface

With this volume, the *Supreme Court Yearbook* goes through a changing of the guard. Joan Biskupic, who developed the idea for the book and wrote the first three books in the series, moved from Congressional Quarterly to the *Washington Post* and, reluctantly, decided to relinquish the additional work of preparing the Yearbook. Joan's reporting on the Court has been the model of clarity, insight, and objectivity. I am honored to follow her and grateful for her Foreword to this volume.

Along with a new author, the 1992-1993 Yearbook reflects other changes aimed at making the material more accessible and useful. We have added charts and tables with statistical analyses of the Court's decisions and the justices' votes. In the listing of Court decisions, we have reorganized the subject-matter categories somewhat to highlight certain areas—such as First Amendment cases—and to tie together other subjects—as in the new category, Courts and Procedure. We have included illustrations of current cases to emphasize that the Court deals not just with legal principles but also with real people whose lives are directly affected by its decisions.

The book largely follows its previous organization. Chapter 1 gives an overview of the Court's term and the major "news" of the year, the nomination and confirmation of Justice Ruth Bader Ginsburg. Chapter 2 examines the Court's major decisions from the past term. Chapter 3 contains the comprehensive listing of the Court's decisions from the past term. Chapter 4 consists of excerpts from ten of the Court's major rulings. Chapter 5 provides a preview of the 1993-1994 term. The Appendix contains the description of the Court's operations, brief biographies of the justices, a glossary of legal terms, and the U.S. Constitution.

At Congressional Quarterly, my thanks go to Dave Tarr for inviting me to take over the book and to Carolyn Goldinger for improving my manuscript with skillful editing. I also thank Sandra Stencel, who gave me the time to work on the book, and Robert Merry, who has been a supporter and friend throughout my association with CQ.

Finally, I thank Katie for her constant love and encouragement and Nicole and Andrew for the special joy they have brought to our lives.

Foreword

On Ruth Bader Ginsburg's first visit to the Supreme Court after her Senate confirmation, she was measured for the customary, high-back black leather chair that would become hers as the Court's newest justice. The diminutive Ginsburg, who in August 1993 became the Court's 107th justice and the second woman to serve, was not the usual appointee for whom the Court fashions a chair. Yet, in many ways the ninth chair was waiting for Ginsburg.

Her moderate judicial approach matched that of important, swing-vote justices. And the combination of her fixed views on the role of judges in society and steady confidence positioned Ginsburg for influence beyond that of the usual freshman justice.

President Bill Clinton said he chose Ginsburg, a federal appeals court judge, because she would bring a new harmony to what in the early 1990s was an often fractured, idiosyncratic Court. The first Democratic appointment in twenty-six years followed a series of nominations by Presidents Ronald Reagan and George Bush who specifically sought candidates who were conservative. The Republican presidents believed their nominees would help sweep aside the remains of liberal activism identified with the Court under Earl Warren (1953-1969) and, to a lesser extent, Warren E. Burger (1969-1986).

Ginsburg's view, a nexus of conservatism and liberalism, was that the Court "generally follows, it does not lead, changes taking place elsewhere in society." "But," she immediately added, "without taking giant strides and thereby risking a backlash, the Court, through constitutional adjudication can moderately accelerate the pace of change." During Senate confirmation hearings, she said, "When political avenues become dead-end streets, judicial intervention in the politics of the people may be essential in order to have effective politics."

By 1993, when Ginsburg was chosen, the Court under Chief Justice William H. Rehnquist had acquired its own signature. It had moved beyond simple contrasts with the Warren era, when the Court struck down the separate-but-equal doctrine and broadened individual rights, or the Burger Court, when the justices made abortion legal nationwide and sanctioned affirmative action. In the sweep of rulings since the 1988-1989 term, when a conservative majority first formed, trends were apparent. The Court deferred to elected officials on social problems. The majority, for example, continually voted to give state lawmakers greater ability to regulate abortion, as well as, in 1990, an individual's "right to die." At the same time, the Court interpreted statutes narrowly, demanding that elected officials be explicit about what rights and obligations they want in the law.

And while the Court applied the brakes to the "activist" liberal social agenda identified with the Warren and Burger eras, it refused to become the engine of a conservative political agenda. To the dismay of many Republicans, abortion rights prevailed and school prayer was not held constitutional under the conservative majority.

Indicative of the conflicts on the Court, a majority of justices who were on the Court through the 1992-1993 term had said at times that *Roe v. Wade,* which made abortion legal nationwide, should be overruled and the wall of separation between church and state should be lowered. But they could not summon enough votes among themselves to actually reverse the laws people had lived with for twenty years. In a 1992 ruling upholding abortion rights, Justices Sandra Day O'Connor, Anthony M. Kennedy, and David H. Souter wrote in an unusual joint opinion that while they might individually oppose abortion, adherence to precedent and the Court's integrity were overriding. They said overturning *Roe,* which both Reagan and Bush had sought, would have serious social repercussions.

Beyond that landmark decision in *Planned Parenthood of Southeastern Pennsylvania v. Casey,* Justices O'Connor, Kennedy, and Souter at times chafed at the conservatism that had defined the Court in the late 1980s. But their inclinations and alliances in any given case were unpredictable.

The balance of power changed from term to term. For example, in the most controversial, closely decided disputes during the 1991-1992 session, Justices O'Connor, Kennedy, and Souter prevailed as a bloc in most of the cases. Chief Justice Rehnquist was mostly on the losing side of 5-4 rulings. But just one term later, in the cases decided by a one-vote difference, Rehnquist held sway. The chief, who was joined often by Kennedy, also dominated in cases decided by 6-3 votes. Conversely, Souter ended up on the losing side in most close cases in the 1992-1993 term. In 5-4 cases, he was in the dissent more often than any other justice. Justice O'Connor remained ensconced in the middle. Overall, it was clear in 1993 that pivotal justices were dissatisfied with earlier alliances and conflicted over judicial approaches.

Generally, a "conservative" justice maintains that the courts should not become involved in social problems that are the realm of legislators. Conservatism also connotes a penchant to side with a governmental interest over individual rights, as well as a traditional social conservatism. Judicial "liberals," conversely, are more apt to broadly interpret constitutional guarantees, irrespective of the will of elected officials.

Chief Justice Rehnquist and Justices Antonin Scalia and Clarence Thomas consistently voted conservative. Although Kennedy earlier had indicated he might pursue a more moderate course, in the 1992-1993 term he voted with those conservative justices about 90 percent of the time. O'Connor, while still leaning to conservatism, voted less with Rehnquist and tended to seek a middle ground. Souter was to the left of O'Connor. In the 1992-1993 term, he sided in the most controversial cases with the Court's two remaining liberally disposed justices, Harry A. Blackmun and John Paul Stevens. And they were typically in the dissent.

Ginsburg, who is liberal in her personal views—supporting abortion rights and disdaining discrimination on the basis of sexual orientation—yet restrained in her judging, confounds traditional labels. If she were to instigate a new swing bloc, it would most likely be with Justices Souter and O'Connor.

Throughout his thirty-one years on the Court, Justice Byron R. White, whom Ginsburg succeeded, was often a swing vote. But White's overall record was more conservative than the record Ginsburg accumulated as a judge for thirteen years on the U.S. Court of Appeals for the District of Columbia Circuit.

Before she was appointed to the federal bench by President Jimmy Carter, Ginsburg was director of the American Civil Liberties Union's Women's Rights Project. In that position and since, she has advocated a broader reading of the constitutional guarantee of equal protection. During her confirmation hearing she endorsed an equal rights amendment, at least for its "symbolic" value.

Ultimately, any shift away from conservatism because of Ginsburg is likely to be incremental. "Measured motions seem to me right, in the main, for constitutional as well as common law adjudication," she has written.

Ginsburg also declared that as a justice she intended to be beholden only to the law. "A judge is not a politician," she said during her confirmation hearings. "If [a decision] is legally right, it's a decision the judge should render." No matter what the "home crowd" wants, Ginsburg often added. In asserting that she would march to no one, Ginsburg may have made it more likely that the other justices march to her.

Joan Biskupic

1 | A New Justice

Twenty-six years had passed since the last time a Democratic president appointed a member of the United States Supreme Court. The politics of the country—and the Court—had changed dramatically since Lyndon B. Johnson selected Thurgood Marshall in 1967 as the first African American to sit on the nation's highest court. The era of liberal activism under Chief Justice Earl Warren had ended, and the Court had shifted to the right under two Republican-appointed chief justices, Warren E. Burger and William H. Rehnquist. The retirement of William J. Brennan, Jr., in 1990 and Marshall in 1991 left the Court with no consistent liberals. Justices appointed by Presidents Ronald Reagan and George Bush formed a conservative majority on many of the most controversial issues before the Court.

In 1993 the retirement of Justice Byron R. White gave the new Democratic president, Bill Clinton, a chance to begin remaking the Court in a different image. White, appointed by Democrat John F. Kennedy in 1962, usually voted with the Court's conservative bloc, but he timed his departure so that the first Democrat in the White House in twelve years could choose his successor. By announcing his plan to step down in mid-March, White gave Clinton and the Democratic-controlled Senate ample time to nominate and confirm a new justice before the Court reconvened in October.

What would Clinton do? He promised during his campaign to appoint justices who were pro-choice on abortion and who took "an expansive view of the Constitution and the Bill of Rights." On March 19, the day of White's announcement, Clinton told reporters that he would look for a justice with experience, judgment, and "a big heart." His search lasted eighty-seven days—far longer than either Reagan or Bush had taken in making any of their appointments to the Court.

At the outset, aides said Clinton was interested in picking a politician instead of a sitting judge. That criterion seemed to lead to New York's cerebral and often enigmatic three-term governor, Mario Cuomo. But Cuomo surprised the White House in early April by telling Clinton that he did not want to be considered.

Over the next two months, White House aides assembled dossiers on some forty-two candidates, who were vetted by a team of seventy-five outside lawyers and legal experts. In early June, Clinton was said to be leaning toward Secretary of the Interior Bruce Babbitt, a former Arizona governor with no judicial experience and a record of fiscal conservatism combined with liberal views on the environment and social policy. Babbitt's candidacy, however, touched off a storm of protest from the environmental community, which wanted to keep him as a strong ally within the administration.

The pressure forced Clinton to reconsider Babbitt's candidacy and turn instead to a highly regarded federal judge, Stephen G. Breyer, the chief judge of the First U.S. Circuit Court of Appeals in Boston. Breyer, a former aide to Sen. Edward M. Kennedy, D-Mass., had solid ties to senators from both parties from his work on the Judiciary Committee, where he had advocated economic deregulation and helped craft the tough federal sentencing guidelines. White House aides described Breyer as the all-but-certain choice as they prepared for Clinton to meet him for the first time in a face-to-face interview. But Clinton left the interview dissatisfied and secretly ordered his aides to give him another candidate even while news reports continued to describe Breyer as the president's choice.

Ruth Bader Ginsburg had been high on the list of possible nominees since the beginning of the selection process. She had many strengths. She pioneered legal advocacy for women's rights in major Supreme Court cases during the 1970s and then earned a respected record as a judicial moderate since her appointment to the U.S. Court of Appeals for the District of Columbia in 1980. Her age—sixty—counted against her, but her appointment would be a "two-fer" in terms of diversity. She would be the second woman on the Court, joining Reagan's first appointee, Sandra Day O'Connor; and she would be the first Jewish justice since Abe Fortas resigned in 1969.

As White House aides later recounted Ginsburg's selection, however, Clinton made his decision from the heart rather than from a yellow legal pad. In a ninety-minute Sunday morning meeting in the White House, Clinton was moved by Ginsburg's life story. Aides said that he was especially impressed with the way that Ginsburg had overcome the legal profession's entrenched discrimination against women and gone on to establish important legal precedents guaranteeing equal rights for women and men before the law. A White House team spent the afternoon poring over Ginsburg's financial records, but found nothing like the unpaid Social Security taxes on domestic help that sank Zoë Baird, Clinton's first choice for attorney general, at the start of his presidency. With that assurance, Clinton telephoned Ginsburg late Sunday night to tell her she had been picked.

In the Rose Garden the next day, June 14, Clinton said that Ginsburg had "genuinely distinguished herself as one of our nation's best judges, progressive in outlook, wise in judgment, balanced and fair in her opinions." He cited her "truly historic record of achievement" on women's rights. Finally, he said, "I believe that in the years ahead, she will be able

President Bill Clinton listening to the remarks of Judge Ruth Bader Ginsburg, his nominee to the Supreme Court. Clinton announced June 14, 1993, that Ginsburg was his choice to fill the seat of Justice Byron R. White, who announced his retirement in March.

to be a force for consensus-building on the Supreme Court, just as she has been on the Court of Appeals, so that our judges can become an instrument of our common unity in the expression of their fidelity to the Constitution."

As for the nominee's judicial philosophy, Clinton said, "Ruth Bader Ginsburg cannot be called a liberal or a conservative. She has proved herself too thoughtful for such labels."

In her turn, Ginsburg delivered a moving, personal account of the advances she had seen for women in the law. She recalled that she had been one of fewer than ten women in a law school class of five hundred students. Now, she said, few law schools had less than 40 percent female enrollment. In 1976, Ginsburg said, only one woman served on the federal appeals courts. Today, she said, "close to twenty-five" women held appellate court seats in the federal system. For herself, Ginsburg recalled that her daughter Jane had written in her high school yearbook that her ambition was "to see her mother appointed to the Supreme Court."

Ginsburg closed with a tribute to her family, in particular, to her mother, who died of cancer when Ginsburg was fifteen. "I pray that I may be all that she would have been," Ginsburg said, "had she lived in an age when women could aspire and achieve and daughters are cherished as much as sons."

In the days after Clinton's announcement, Ginsburg won wide praise, but there was wariness from some quarters. Some conservative legal groups expressed concern that she would adopt more activist views once on the Supreme Court. Antiabortion groups assailed her record of supporting abortion rights. In the opposing camps, abortion rights forces expressed concern about Ginsburg's views that the Supreme Court had acted too quickly in overturning state abortion laws in its 1973 ruling, *Roe v. Wade*. And some liberal commentators worried that Ginsburg was too much the legal technician and cautious jurist to help reverse the Court's two decades of conservative tilt.

The skeptics were in a distinct minority, however. The consensus on Capitol Hill and in other political and legal circles was that Clinton had achieved his desire of hitting a home run with his choice. Barring any misstep in her appearance before the Senate Judiciary Committee, Ruth Bader Ginsburg seemed assured of becoming the Supreme Court's 107th justice.

A Conservative Term

As Ginsburg prepared for her confirmation hearings, the Court was nearing the end of a somewhat lackluster term. It was continuing to decide fewer cases, just 107 signed opinions—well below the average of 139 opinions issued in the 1980s *(Figure 1-1)*. As in its previous term, the Court did not have enough cases to fill its calendar for the final two weeks of arguments in April.

The term's most notable characteristic was the renewed strength of its conservative majority. The Court's most conservative members led the end-of-term statistics in voting in the majority. Justice Anthony M. Kennedy, appointed by Reagan in 1988, dissented least often—in only 7 of 107 signed opinions. He was followed closely by fellow Reagan appointee Antonin Scalia with nine dissents, Chief Justice Rehnquist with ten, and Bush appointee Clarence Thomas with twelve *(See Table 1-1)*.

In a telling indication of the conservative bloc's clout, Rehnquist, Scalia, and Thomas were outvoted only one time in cases where the three voted together. Put differently, with one exception, the Court's few "liberal" rulings of the 1992-1993 term always had at least one of the Court's three most conservative members voting in the majority. In the Court's twenty 5-4 decisions, the conservatives had enviable success. Rehnquist, Scalia, and Kennedy dissented in only five of those rulings; Thomas in six.

A year earlier, the buzz around the Court had been very different. Three Reagan-Bush appointees—O'Connor, Kennedy, and David H. Souter—had come together in 1992 on a handful of sensitive issues to forge a sort of centrist bloc with the votes to form a majority behind moderate stands that rankled conservatives and comforted liberals. The trio, most dramatically, joined to write the end-of-term abortion ruling, *Planned Parenthood of Southeastern Pennsylvania v. Casey,* that reaffirmed the constitutional right to abortion while giving states somewhat more leeway to regulate abortion procedures.

In the 1992-1993 term, however, talk of a centrist bloc faded as O'Connor, Kennedy, and Souter split apart. They divided in thirty-three of the Court's sixty-one non-unanimous opinions. Most significant, they voted together in none of the Court's 5-4 decisions.

Kennedy heartened conservatives by moving back to the right. He voted with Rehnquist, for example, 88 percent of the time. That record was more akin to Kennedy's record in his first two terms than to the figures from the 1991-1992 term, when his alignment with Rehnquist fell to 76 percent.

For his part, Souter, appointed by Bush in 1990, encouraged liberals by moving to the left. He still voted with the conservative justices more than 70 percent of the time. But in the Court's most closely divided decisions, Souter aligned himself most often with what remained of the Court's liberal wing: Justices Harry A. Blackmun and John Paul Stevens. Of twenty 5-4 rulings, Souter agreed with Blackmun and Stevens fourteen times—eleven times in dissent and just three times in the majority.

Meanwhile, O'Connor continued to defy easy categorization. Typi-

Figure 1-1 Supreme Court Caseload, 1960 Term -1992 Term

Total cases on docket

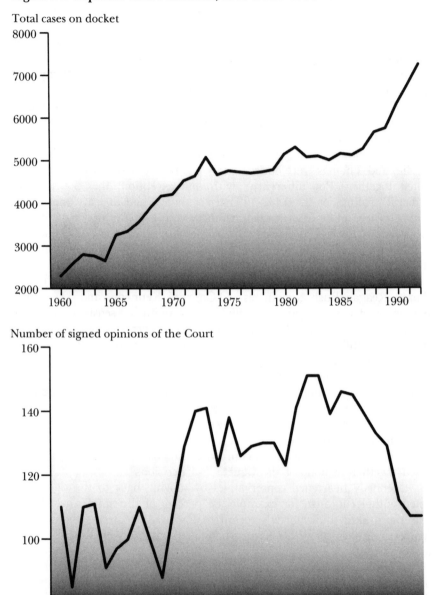

Number of signed opinions of the Court

Table 1-1   Justices in Dissent, 1992-1993 Term

Justice	Dissented[a]	Percentage
Rehnquist	10	9.3
White	17	15.9
Blackmun	33	30.8
Stevens	37	34.6
O'Connor	18	16.8
Scalia	9	8.4
Kennedy	7	6.5
Souter	22	20.6
Thomas	12	11.2

Note: There were 107 signed opinions during the 1992-1993 term.

[a] Dissented in whole or in part

cally, she lined up with the Court's conservative bloc, voting with Rehnquist, Scalia, and Thomas each more than 80 percent of the time. But in 5-4 decisions, she sided with Blackmun and Stevens eight times—twice in the majority and six times in dissent.

Blackmun, a 1970 Nixon appointee, and Stevens, President Gerald Ford's sole appointee to the Court in 1975, saw their power dwindle during the term. They voted together 80 percent of the time. They dissented in just over half of the Court's sixty-two divided decisions: Stevens, thirty-seven times; Blackmun, thirty-three. Each was in the minority in twelve of the Court's twenty 5-4 rulings.

As for White, he closed his tenure as a justice much as he had begun it in the early 1960s—as a supporter of government in criminal law cases and an ally of civil rights causes. He voted most often, 86 percent of the time, with Chief Justice Rehnquist and provided a critical fifth vote for conservative rulings in six 5-4 decisions. But he parted company with the conservative bloc in other 5-4 rulings, including two decisions in the Court's final days that raised the burden of proof for plaintiffs in job discrimination suits and opened the door to challenges by white voters to racially drawn legislative or congressional districts. *(See Table 1-2 for justices' voting alignment.)*

Underlying the conservatives' general alignment was a subtle, but sometimes significant, difference. Rehnquist and Kennedy on occasion adopted a pragmatic approach that divided them from the stricter ideological stance of Thomas and Scalia. Thomas, in his second term, continued a close alignment with Scalia, who had adopted an uncompromising conservative stance since his appointment in 1986. They voted together 90 percent of the time, the highest degree of alignment between any pair of justices for the term.

Table 1-2   Justices' Alignment, 1992-1993 Term

This chart shows the percentage of decisions in which each justice agreed with each of the other members of the Court. Of the 107 signed decisions for the 1992-1993 term, 46—or 43 percent—were unanimous.

The Court's four most conservative members—Chief Justice Rehnquist and Associate Justices Scalia, Kennedy, and Thomas—were closely aligned during the term. Each of the justices agreed with each of the other three in more than 85 percent of the signed decisions. Scalia and Thomas had the closest alignment of any pair of justices, just below 90 percent.

Liberal justices Blackmun and Stevens were not quite so closely aligned as the conservatives. They agreed with each other just over 80 percent of the time.

Of the three justices who took more centrist positions during the term, White and O'Connor had the highest degree of alignment with justices in the conservative bloc. Souter aligned himself in pivotal cases with the liberal justices, but overall he agreed more often with the conservatives than he did with Blackmun or Stevens.

	Rehnquist	White	Blackmun	Stevens	O'Connor	Scalia	Kennedy	Souter	Thomas
Rehnquist		75.4	32.8	29.5	67.2	75.4	78.7	54.1	77.0
		86.0	61.7	59.8	81.3	86.0	87.8	73.8	86.9
White	75.4		47.5	41.0	55.7	60.7	67.2	65.6	59.0
	86.0		70.1	66.4	74.8	77.6	81.3	80.4	76.6
Blackmun	32.8	47.5		65.6	45.9	31.1	44.3	52.5	36.1
	61.7	70.1		80.4	69.2	60.7	68.2	72.9	63.6
Stevens	29.5	41.0	65.6		36.1	31.1	37.7	45.9	26.2
	59.8	66.4	80.4		63.6	60.7	64.5	69.2	58.0
O'Connor	67.2	55.7	45.9	36.1		65.6	62.3	60.7	70.5
	81.3	74.8	69.2	63.6		80.4	78.5	77.6	83.2
Scalia	75.4	60.7	31.1	31.1	65.6		80.3	65.6	82.0
	86.0	77.6	60.7	60.7	80.4		88.8	80.4	89.7
Kennedy	78.7	67.2	44.3	37.7	62.3	80.3		62.3	78.7
	87.8	81.3	68.2	64.5	78.5	88.8		78.5	87.8
Souter	54.1	65.6	52.5	45.9	60.7	65.6	62.3		54.1
	73.8	80.4	72.9	69.2	77.6	80.4	78.5		73.8
Thomas	77.0	59.0	36.1	26.2	70.5	82.0	78.7	54.1	
	86.9	76.6	63.6	58.0	83.2	89.7	87.8	73.8	

Note: The first number in each cell represents the percentage of agreement in divided cases. The second number represents the percentage of agreement in all signed opinions.

The differences between the two pairs of conservatives produced results that were not always easy to predict. Scalia and Thomas, for example, sided with the "liberal" majority in a 6-3 decision that limited the federal drug forfeiture law, while Rehnquist, Kennedy, and White dissented. But when the Court voted 7-2 to permit prisoners to sue over exposure to second-hand tobacco smoke, Scalia and Thomas dissented while Rehnquist and Kennedy joined the majority.

The four conservatives also broke apart when the Court tried but failed to find a majority position on the issue of reviewing punitive damage awards. Rehnquist and Kennedy saw a limited role for the Court in ensuring that punitive damages were not unreasonable or arbitrary. Scalia and Thomas, on the other hand, insisted that federal courts had no role in evaluating damage awards except to ensure that proper procedures had been followed. In a similar vein, Scalia and Thomas argued, in a closely watched capital punishment case, for closing the door completely to federal court review of late claims of innocence by death row inmates. Rehnquist and Kennedy left that door ever so slightly ajar.

The fissures among the conservatives and the movements by the centrist-leaning justices made it difficult to sum up the Court's term or to make predictions for the future. To many, the Court's decisions seemed highly specific, its opinions often narrow and technical. "They seem to decide cases on very narrow points, so that they leave the substantive controversies unresolved," said Douglas Kmiec, a constitutional law expert at the University of Notre Dame law school.

Liberals, however, took some comfort from this trend. "The Court is much more cautious in its judicial temperament than it was a couple of years ago," said Steven Shapiro, associate legal director for the American Civil Liberties Union. "It's moved from radically conservative to a much more traditionally conservative posture."

Ginsburg may make categorizations and predictions all the more difficult. Despite her liberal background, a 1988 study showed she voted on the D.C. Circuit more often with Republican-appointed judges than with her Democratic-appointed colleagues. She pleased conservatives by praising the virtues of judicial restraint and disconcerted liberals with her critique of *Roe v. Wade*. She sided with conservatives in some criminal and business-related cases, but hewed to more liberal stands on issues relating to civil rights, civil liberties, and access to courts.

A Quick Confirmation

By early July, Ginsburg's nomination was continuing to win wide acclaim. She had gained endorsements from Democrats and from important Republicans, including Senate Minority Leader Bob Dole of Kansas and Utah's Orrin Hatch, the GOP's ranking member on the Judiciary Committee. Despite the seeming assurance of confirmation, senators said they would explore her legal views in detail. With or without fireworks, Ginsburg's confirmation hearings were to provide the only public opportunity to examine—and cross-examine—her positions before her anticipated accession to a lifetime position on the nation's highest court.

For the Senate Judiciary Committee, Ginsburg's nomination presented a chance to improve its image after three contentious and, in many respects, unsatisfying Supreme Court confirmation battles in the past six years. "Welcome," the committee's chairman, Democrat Joseph R. Biden, Jr., of Delaware, said as he greeted Ginsburg at the panel's opening session July 20. "And, believe me, you are welcome this morning."

If the committee wanted to avoid the ideological strife that had marred the recent hearings, Ginsburg's challenge was to avoid either of the problems that the previous nominees had experienced: saying too much or saying too little. Robert Bork, the conservative federal judge nominated by Reagan in 1987, had engaged in an intellectual wrestling match with the committee's Democrats. His comments on abortion, privacy, and equal protection helped Democratic senators depict him as outside the legal and political mainstream. The Senate rejected the nomination, 58-42.

President Bush's two nominees—Souter in 1990 and Thomas in 1991—gave the Judiciary Committee fewer openings for attacks. In particular, both nominees refused to give any hint how they would vote on preserving *Roe v. Wade*. Thomas went so far as to say that he had never "debated" the issue in the two decades since the ruling—producing incredulity among Democratic senators. Both went on to win confirmation—Souter by a wide margin and Thomas, damaged by charges of sexual harassment, by a bare 52-48 majority. Afterwards, Biden publicly vowed to oppose any future Court nominee who refused to answer the committee's questions on legal issues.

Ginsburg's solution was to tell the committee that she would respond fully to questions about views she had previously expressed during her work with the American Civil Liberties Union's women's rights project or on the federal bench. But she said she would give "no forecasts, no hints" of how she would vote on future cases. Her ground rules set the stage for three days of testing and probing by committee Democrats and Republicans alike.

Ginsburg depicted herself as an advocate—and a practitioner—of judicial restraint. "My approach is neither liberal or conservative," she said in an opening statement delivered with the deliberate cadence she was to use throughout the hearings. "Rather, it is rooted in the place of the judiciary, of judges in our democratic society." Judges, she said, should be "above the political fray." She promised that she would not write her own convictions into the Constitution and described the judicial process as one of gradual change. Quoting Justice Benjamin N. Cardozo, Ginsburg said that judges should remember that "justice is not to be taken by storm. She is to be wooed by slow advances."

In her second day, however, Ginsburg specified that courts did have a role in forcing social changes when groups are "shut out of the political process." As examples, she cited the Court's rulings on racial discrimination and reapportionment. And she strongly defended the Court's power to decide constitutional issues. "I prize the institution of judicial review for constitutionality," she said. "I think we have become a model for the world in that respect."

Ginsburg also reassured more liberal supporters with a ringing endorsement of abortion rights. When the issue was first raised, she had somewhat minimized her earlier criticism that the Court had acted too quickly in overturning all state abortion laws in *Roe v. Wade,* depicting it as "speculation" and "my view of what-if." When the issue came up again, she made clear that she viewed abortion as a fundamental issue of women's rights whether based on equal protection principles, as she had advocated, or on privacy grounds, as the Court decided. "This is something central to a woman's life, to her dignity," Ginsburg said. "It's a decision that she must make for herself. And when government controls that decision for her, she's being treated as less than a fully adult human responsible for her choices."

Ginsburg also had no hesitation in endorsing a constitutional right to privacy, linked to the Fourth Amendment's limit on government searches of one's home or office and to "the notion of personal autonomy: the government shall not make my decisions for me." Biden noted later that two previous nominees—referring to Bork and Thomas—had refused to endorse a constitutional right to privacy in their confirmation hearings.

To Democratic senators, Ginsburg also made a positive impression with strong support for women's rights. As a lawyer, Ginsburg in the 1970s had won the first rulings from the Court establishing special constitutional scrutiny of laws that treated men and women differently. Now, as a Supreme Court nominee, she made clear that she would continue to regard differential treatment for men and women as legally suspect. And she added an explicit endorsement of the Equal Rights Amendment, saying that the Constitution should include "a clarion call that women and men are equal before the law."

In their turn, Republican senators focused on the death penalty, producing the hearing's only major conflict between the nominee and her questioners. As a judge, Ginsburg had never handled a capital punishment case because the District of Columbia does not have the death penalty. But Pennsylvania's Arlen Specter, a former prosecutor, and Utah's Hatch both tried to pin her down on the issue.

"I will be scrupulous in applying the law on the basis of legislation

Ruth Bader Ginsburg signs the judical oath, the final step in the process of becoming a member of the United States Supreme Court. Chief Justice William H. Rehnquist looks on.

and precedent," Ginsburg said. But unlike Souter three years earlier, she refused to say whether she agreed with rulings that had held capital punishment to be constitutional. "If you want me to take a pledge that there is one position that I'm not going to take," she told Hatch, "I . . . that is what you must not ask a judge to do."

On other hot-button issues, Ginsburg evinced agreement with affirmative action, but said she was opposed to "rigid quotas." She reaffirmed a statement she made in 1979 opposing discrimination against homosexuals, but only in general terms. "I think rank discrimination against anyone is against the tradition of the United States and is to be deplored," she said. She sounded like a separationist on church-state issues. "We are a pluralistic society," she declared, and signaled that she was disinclined to scrap the existing, strict standard limiting government involvement with religion.

Ginsburg lived up to her promise to give no significant hints of her views on a host of other issues. She ducked questions on—to name a few subjects—gun control, habeas corpus, private school tuition vouchers, property rights, and racial gerrymandering. "I don't confuse my own predilections with what is the law," she said as the third day of hearings ended.

Ginsburg reinforced her image as a judicial moderate with references to the Court's history. As her judicial heroes, she cited Chief Justice John Marshall, Oliver Wendell Holmes, Jr., Louis F. Brandeis, Benjamin Cardozo, and two moderate-conservative justices of more recent times: John Marshall Harlan (1955-1971) and Lewis F. Powell, Jr. (1971-1987). For landmark Court decisions, she pointed to *Marbury v. Madison* (1803), which established the principle of judicial review; *Gibbons v. Ogden* (1825), which confirmed Congress's power to regulate interstate commerce; Holmes's and Brandeis's free-speech dissents from the 1920s; and *Brown v. Board of Education*, the 1954 school desegregation ruling. She made no mention of any of the Warren Court's rulings expanding the rights of criminal suspects and defendants.

On some contemporary issues, however, Ginsburg's comments—although guarded—made clear her differences with judicial conservatives, especially her former colleague on the D.C. Circuit, Antonin Scalia. Scalia strongly opposed using legislative history to help interpret congressional statutes, but Ginsburg told one senator that the Court's job was "to interpret the laws as you intended for them to be interpreted." Scalia also opposed recognizing new constitutional rights under the rubric of due process unless they were supported by historical practice. When asked about that issue, Ginsburg cited opinions written by Harlan and Powell that endorsed the use of contemporary standards to evaluate new claims of individual liberties.

The committee's fourth day of hearings included a brief, closed session under a new procedure for reviewing accusations of misconduct against Supreme Court nominees. The committee adopted the procedure to respond to criticisms that it had mishandled the sexual harassment charges against Clarence Thomas—first, by failing to convene the full committee to hear the evidence and, then, by conducting the investigation in public once the charges leaked. Although the topics of the closed session were supposed to remain secret, the *New York Times* quoted an official present at the meeting as saying that the main topic was one already explored in the open hearing: Ginsburg's failure in the early 1980s to list on her financial disclosure form a Washington country club's waiver of the $25,000 initiation fee for membership in the club. Ginsburg said she regretted failing to disclose the waived fee, a practice that the club routinely extended to members of the federal bench.

With no gaffes and few fireworks, the committee's hearings ended with Ginsburg assured confirmation. The committee approved the nomination by an 18-0 vote on July 29 with only scattered complaints about her reluctance to answer some of the panel's questions. Biden said he was satisfied that Ginsburg had been sufficiently forthcoming.

The Senate's debate on August 2 and 3 was also short and largely sweet. Sen. Jesse Helms, R-N.C., began the debate by entering into the record a conservative group's report sharply criticizing Ginsburg as "a judicial activist" with "a social vision that is extremely liberal." But every other senator who spoke endorsed the nomination. Democrats praised Ginsburg as a courageous advocate of women's rights and a brilliant judge who combined respect for judicial restraint with a continuing commitment to equal rights and justice. Some Republicans voiced reservations about her judicial philosophy, but most promptly added praise for Ginsburg's integrity, temperament, and judgment.

With the speeches over, Ginsburg won confirmation, 96-3. Three conservative Republicans cast the only negative votes. Helms focused on Ginsburg's record on abortion rights and speculated she would also support gay rights. New Hampshire's Robert C. Smith complained of Ginsburg's refusal to detail her views on the death penalty. Oklahoma's Don Nickles said he feared Ginsburg would prove to be a judicial activist. "I hope I am wrong," Nickles said, "but only time will tell."

Ginsburg's journey from nomination to confirmation in just under two months was the quickest since O'Connor won the Senate's nod one month after her selection in 1981. Reagan's and Bush's other nominees had averaged about three months each.

In swearing-in ceremonies at the White House a week later, Ginsburg again avoided any discussion of specific legal issues. But she returned to the theme of advancing opportunities for women, looking ahead to the day when there would be still more women on the bench. "A system of justice will be richer for a diversity of background and experience," she said.

Clinton followed, again stressing Ginsburg's personal accomplishments in overcoming gender discrimination and protecting rights rights for all women. He closed by predicting that now Justice Ginsburg would be "a guardian of liberty of all and an ensurer of equal justice under law."

2 | *The 1992-1993 Term*

As the Supreme Court neared the end of its 1992-1993 term, the justices were getting bad reviews for keeping up audience interest. "The Court is treading water," Burt Neuborne, a law professor at New York University Law School, told a gathering of federal judges in late June. "It's a boring term."

On their last day, however, the justices managed to produce a bit of drama. They opened the door for white voters to challenge "racial gerrymandering" in legislative and congressional districts. They set a constitutional limit on the government's power to seize money and property from criminals. They told federal judges to screen out unreliable scientific evidence from trials. And, for good measure, they threw out a three-year-old precedent on the constitutional ban on double jeopardy to ease somewhat the rule against multiple prosecutions.

The flurry of late-term rulings showed once again the justices' special power in the U.S. constitutional system. In the redistricting case, the Court rejected the legal views of the previous, Republican administration and, to some extent, cast doubt on the racial line-drawing that had resulted in the election of a record number of African Americans and Hispanics to Congress in 1992. The supposedly conservative Court dealt a blow to law enforcement by discovering in the Eighth Amendment's Excessive Fines Clause a limit on the use of recently toughened forfeiture laws in drug cases.

The Court flexed its supervisory muscles when it instructed lower court federal judges on how to evaluate scientific evidence that was often critical in major personal injury and environmental suits. In the double jeopardy case—the Court's third decision of the term scrapping its own prior rulings—the justices showed that a new majority can throw out a precedent so recent that it had yet to be published in the official volumes of Supreme Court decisions. *(See Table 2-1.)*

Nevertheless, the Court's power was easy to exaggerate. The justices returned the racial gerrymandering and forfeiture cases to lower courts with little guidance on how to enforce the newly declared constitutional rights. Some observers voiced doubts that either would prove to have great impact in the long run. The scientific evidence ruling could be read many different ways—and, with more than 700 judges in the federal system, undoubtedly would be.

On these, and many other hotly contested legal issues, the Court's word was often less final than it appeared. Nearly forty years earlier, the

Table 2-1   Reversals of Earlier Rulings

The Supreme Court issued three decisions during the 1992-1993 term that reversed previous rulings by the Court, either explicitly or in effect. The rulings brought the total number of such reversals in the Court's history to 207.

New Decision	Overruled Decision	New Holding
United States v. Dixon (1993) [p. 60]	*Grady v. Corbin* (1990)	Eases bar against double jeopardy
St. Mary's Honor Center v. Hicks (1993) [p. 88]	*Texas Dept. of Community Affairs v. Burdine* (1981); *McDonnell Douglas Corp. v. Green* (1973)	Raises plaintiff's burden of proof in job-bias suits
Harper v. Virginia Department of Taxation (1993) [p. 94]	*Chevron Oil Co. v. Huson* (1971)	New Supreme Court rulings normally to be applied retroactively

Source: Johnny Killian, American Law Division, Congressional Research Service, Library of Congress.

Court had declared segregated public schools unconstitutional. But the Court was continuing to grapple with legal issues on how to implement the ruling. Twenty years earlier, the Court had declared a constitutional right to abortion. But a political backlash brought about a partial retreat as the justices upheld new laws limiting public funding of abortions and regulating abortion procedures.

Several thoughtful Supreme Court observers have used these and other examples to draw a more accurate picture of the Court as only one of several actors in a continuing constitutional dialogue. These scholars, such as Vanderbilt University law professor Barry Friedman, emphasize that the Court's rulings are often shaped over time by new laws passed by Congress, changes in policy by the president, and shifts in public opinion. A dramatic decision by the Court is only the beginning of a political process to be played out in many other forums, with results that the justices cannot control. "Courts play a prominent role," Friedman writes, "but theirs is assuredly not the only voice in the dialogue."

In the 1992-1993 term, the Rehnquist Court for the most part seemed to be lowering its voice in this public dialogue. The Court took on fewer cases and shunned some volatile issues, such as renewed disputes over state abortion laws and school prayer. It issued more unanimous decisions than in its previous term. Except for the ruling on forfeitures, the justices had little new to say about criminal law. They again rejected pleas by business interests to limit the use of punitive damages in state courts. The Court refused to weaken protections for commercial speech or to scrap a controversial decision limiting government involvement with religion. And it overturned no laws passed by Congress and struck down only four state or local laws on constitutional grounds.

The Court showed its conservative bent most strongly in criminal cases. The Court ruled for the government in twenty of the term's thirty criminal law decisions, including four of five capital punishment cases. On the same day they limited forfeiture power under the Eighth Amendment, the justices voted 5-4 to uphold a draconian use of the federal antiracketeering law to seize a convicted pornographer's $25 million chain of adult bookstores and destroy the entire inventory. The Court also upheld state "hate crime" laws imposing longer sentences for offenses committed because of a victim's race, religion, or ethnic origin.

Against these rulings, the few decisions favoring criminal defendants were mostly minor. Except for the forfeiture ruling, the most notable victory was a 5-4 decision that merely preserved the power of federal courts in habeas corpus cases to throw out state court convictions because of violations of the *Miranda* interrogation rules. But in two other habeas corpus cases, the Court made it harder for inmates to challenge their convictions because of constitutional errors at trial and virtually shut the door on death row inmates seeking to block executions with new evidence that they may be innocent.

The Court also showed a conservative orientation in many of its rulings on individual rights. It refused to allow an 1871 federal civil rights law to be used to prevent illegal blockades of abortion clinics. It raised the burden of proof for plaintiffs in employment discrimination suits and refused to open federal courts to human rights suits against foreign governments. In a Kentucky case, the justices turned away an effort to require heightened scrutiny of laws affecting the mentally ill. And in a trio of decisions, the Court upheld restrictive federal immigration policies, including a presidential order to stop Haitian refugees at sea and return them to their home country.

Civil rights and civil liberties interests, however, could count some limited victories. The Court permitted prison inmates to sue over involuntary exposure to second-hand tobacco smoke, although the decision set a difficult standard to win such a case. The Court also reduced the legal protections for prosecutors from private damage suits. And, in a significant procedural ruling, the justices unanimously rebuffed federal courts that had imposed more difficult pleading requirements on plaintiffs in civil rights suits against state or local governments.

When the Court opened its term, many observers looked for significant developments in one of the most contentious areas involving individual freedoms: church and state. But the Court's rulings left groups that wanted to lower the barriers to government involvement with religion somewhat disappointed. The Court upheld the right of religious groups to use public school buildings on an equal basis with secular organizations, but in an opinion that glancingly cited a strict church-state ruling that conservatives had hoped to throw out. The Court also upheld government funding for a sign-language interpreter for a deaf student in a parochial school, but many observers doubted that the ruling would invite broader government aid to such schools.

In a third decision, the justices cheered religious conservatives and traditional civil libertarians alike by striking down a local law banning ritual animal sacrifice aimed at the followers of a small Afro-Cuban religion. The ruling strengthened the First Amendment's Free Exercise of Religion Clause after a controversial ruling three years earlier. In the 1990 case, the Court overrode free-exercise arguments by allowing the enforcement of a state drug law against a Native American religion that used peyote in worship services. In striking down the animal sacrifice law, however, the Court saw no need to reconsider the previous ruling—despite separate opinions joined by three of the justices calling for a re-examination.

One traditionally conservative constituency—business—continued to be disappointed by the Rehnquist Court in the past term. Most signifi-cant, the Court turned away—for the fifth time since 1981—business groups' pleas to set meaningful constitutional limits on punitive damage awards in state courts. The scientific evidence ruling gave some encour-agement to critics of the civil justice system, but the effects of the decision remained to be seen. The Court continued to reject many efforts to claim federal preemption to override state laws that were sometimes more protective of labor and consumer interests than federal provisions. And the Court backed workers' interests in many of the term's labor law cases, including a high-stakes decision that refused to bar union hiring agree-ments on state government public works projects.

Business groups took some comfort from antitrust rulings that seemed to return to a narrower approach after a pair of broader decisions in 1992. They also cheered a ruling that, for the first time, limited the scope of the federal antiracketeering law in civil damage suits. Some businesses stood to gain tax writeoffs from a ruling that allowed a depreciation deduction for the purchase of customer lists. And home mortgage lenders were helped by a pair of bankruptcy law rulings that rejected debtors' efforts to reduce their agreed-upon payments.

In a mixed ruling, the Court kept alive a major antitrust suit against the nation's biggest insurance companies. But the standards crafted by the Court's most conservative justices made it difficult for the states that brought the suit to win.

The biggest winners in the term appeared to be state and federal lawmakers and officials. Time and again, the Court made clear its reluctance to second-guess decisions by the "political branches" of government. Before handing down its end-of-term decision on racial gerrymandering, the Court had twice—unanimously—signaled a preference for staying out of disputes over legislative redistricting. It used a dispute over regulation of cable television systems to reemphasize its nearly absolute refusal to use the Equal Protection Clause to strike down social or economic legislation. And, except in four First Amendment cases, the Court rejected all other constitutional attacks on federal laws, state statutes, or local ordinances.

Conservatives saw in this record admirable judicial restraint. "More often than not, this Court tries to act more like a court than a legislature," said Thomas Jipping, director of the Judicial Selection Monitoring Project of the Free Congress Foundation's Center for Law and Democracy. But conservatives also chafed at what they regarded as lingering signs of liberal judicial activism. As one example, Jipping cited the Court's willingness to apply the Eighth Amendment to prison conditions. The Court's two staunchest conservatives, Scalia and Thomas, have called for overruling the doctrine, first announced in a 1976 decision.

For their part, liberals complained that the Court was turning its back on its role of safeguarding individual rights. "This Court takes a more cramped view of the Constitution, the Bill of Rights, and the role of the Court in protecting individual rights," said Steven Shapiro of the American Civil Liberties Union (ACLU). But Shapiro said the Court had retreated from what he called "an aggressive ideological agenda" of several years earlier and was now placing "greater stock in precedent and judicial stability." He and many other observers expected Justice Ginsburg's arrival to further blunt any movement toward renewed judicial activism by the Court's conservative bloc.

The mixed assessments outside the Court reflected the mixed views and changing alignments within the Court. As Notre Dame's Douglas Kmiec said, "The Court has no middle, or it may have multiple middles." In the 5-4 decisions of the past term, each of the more centrist justices—White, O'Connor, Kennedy, and Souter—paired off a nearly equal number of times with each of the other three. Ginsburg's arrival in White's seat may move the Court's middle more to the left. But unless Ginsburg lined up consistently on the left, the three-justice conservative bloc would continue to have the advantage over the two justices of the Court's liberal wing.

The strength of the Court's conservative bloc was reflected in the Court's most important rulings of the term. In ten major rulings, conservatives could claim substantial victory in eight cases and partial success in a ninth. Some liberal groups sided with conservatives in two of the cases: the unanimous decisions upholding state laws that enhance the penalty for a hate crime and protecting religious groups' access to school buildings. The only other liberal victory in the list was also unanimous: the decision limiting forfeiture laws.

Redistricting and Reapportionment

White Voters Can Contest "Irregular" Districts

Shaw v. Reno, Attorney General, decided by a 5-4 vote, June 28, 1993; O'Connor wrote the opinion; White, Blackmun, Stevens, and Souter dissented.

When North Carolina gained a new congressional seat after the 1990 census, the Democratic-controlled legislature drew a plan with a majority black population in one of the state's twelve districts. But the U.S. Justice Department, scrutinizing the plan under the federal Voting Rights Act's "preclearance" procedure, objected. It said that North Carolina, where African Americans comprised about 20 percent of the population, should create two majority black districts, not just one.

Legislators wanted to ward off a potential court challenge by the Justice Department, but they faced problems. The state's black population was relatively dispersed, so a compact district with a majority black population was difficult to draw. In addition, incumbent members of Congress wanted to preserve some of the areas of their political strength. With some ingenious mapmaking, however, the state's new Twelfth District was drawn to be about 57 percent black.

The resulting district won approval from the Justice Department, but it became the symbol of what political conservatives and other critics called racial gerrymandering. The district wound around in snakelike fashion for about 160 miles in the central part of the state, picking up black neighborhoods in four metropolitan areas. In places, the district was no wider than an interstate highway corridor.

The plan accomplished its electoral purpose. In 1992 North Carolina elected two African Americans to the House of Representatives: Eva Clayton from the First District and Melvin Watt from the Twelfth. But the plan also drew court challenges first from the state's Republican party and then from a group of white voters. The suit by the voters contended that the plan set up "a racially discriminatory voting process" and deprived them of the right to vote in "a color-blind" election.

A three-judge federal district court rejected the challenge in a split decision. When the Supreme Court agreed to review the case, the stakes were high. Civil rights advocates credited the reapportionment process with the election to Congress of thirteen additional African Americans and six Hispanics. They feared that a broad ruling limiting the use of race in

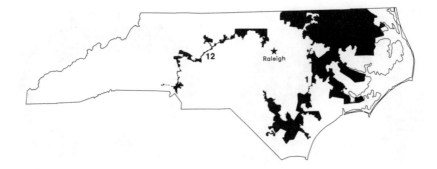

The First and Twelfth Congressional Districts of North Carolina. The Justice Department approved the redistricting plan, but it was challenged as a "racial gerrymander."

drawing district lines would jeopardize those gains. Critics, however, insisted that the bizarre shapes of many of the "majority-minority" districts had established a racial quota system in violation of white voters' rights.

The Court's decision—on the last day of its 1992-1993 term—gave the critics a limited, but important, victory. In a 5-4 ruling the justices held that white voters could challenge racially drawn districts as a violation of the Fourteenth Amendment's Equal Protection Clause if the districts were "highly irregular" in shape and "lacked sufficient justification."

Writing for the Court, Justice O'Connor acknowledged that racial considerations could not be excluded from the reapportionment process. But she said that in "some exceptional cases," a plan could be "so highly irregular that, on its face, it rationally cannot be understood as anything other than an effort to segregate voters on the basis of race." "Put differently, we believe that reapportionment is one area in which appearances do matter," O'Connor continued. A district that ignores geographical and political boundaries in order to concentrate members of a particular race, she said, "bears an uncomfortable resemblance to political apartheid" and risks perpetuating "the very patterns of racial bloc voting that majority-minority districting is sometimes said to counteract."

The decision returned the case to the lower court for further hearings. O'Connor said the panel should determine whether the reapportionment plan met the "strict scrutiny" test used in other racial challenges: whether it was narrowly tailored to serve a compelling government interest. O'Connor noted that the state had argued the plan was needed both to comply with the Voting Rights Act and to eradicate the effects of

Eva Clayton and Melvin Watt were elected to represent North Carolina's First and Twelfth Congressional Districts, respectively. White voters challenged the remapping of the state that created two "majority-minority" districts.

past racial discrimination. But she indicated doubts whether either consideration would meet that standard.

The Court's four most conservative members joined in the opinion: Chief Justice Rehnquist and Justices Scalia, Kennedy and Thomas. Dissenting were Justices White, Blackmun, Stevens, and Souter.

In the main dissenting opinion, White complained that the majority had never identified the harm that the state's white voters had suffered because of the plan. Whites constituted about 79 percent of the voting age population in the state, he said, but still had a majority in ten (or 83 percent) of the twelve congressional districts. "Though they might be dissatisfied at the prospect of casting a vote for a losing candidate," White said, "surely they cannot complain of discriminatory treatment."

Blackmun and Stevens both joined White's opinion and wrote shorter opinions of their own with tart rejoinders to the majority. Blackmun said it was "ironic" that the Court's ruling came after North Carolina had elected its first black members of Congress since Reconstruction. Stevens called it "perverse" to permit redistricting plans drawn to provide adequate representation for other groups—mentioning rural voters, union members, Hasidic Jews, Polish Americans, and Republicans—but not for blacks.

In his dissent, Souter limited himself to the issue of how to judge racially drawn district lines. He said the majority had "no justification" for adopting the strict scrutiny test. Instead, he said, the Court should have stuck with previous decisions that required proof of a discriminatory intent and effect to invalidate a district plan because of racial considerations.

Predictions about the impact of the Court's decision differed. In their dissents, White and Souter suggested the criteria described by the majority would be met rarely, if ever. The ruling, Souter said, "may wind up as an aberration." Watt and Clayton, the two black representatives elected under the plan, echoed that view. In a joint statement, they said the decision "will have little, if any, value in terms of establishing a precedent for other cases."

Advocates on both sides of the case, however, said the decision cast doubt on the entire theory of creating majority-minority districts. North Carolina attorney general Michael Easley, a white Democrat and one of the defendants, said the ruling "opens up every district to judicial attack."

More litigation seemed likely. Political observers of the reapportionment process identified irregularly shaped congressional districts in at least five other states that were vulnerable to challenge as racial gerrymanders. Moreover, the Court put another case involving racially drawn district lines on next term's docket. *(See preview of 1993-1994 term, p. 215.)*

Abortion

"Klan" Act Does Not Cover Clinic Blockades

Bray v. Alexandria Women's Health Clinic, decided by votes of 6-3 and 5-4, January 13, 1993; Scalia wrote the opinion; Souter dissented in part; Stevens, Blackmun, and O'Connor dissented.

Beginning in the late 1980s a militant antiabortion group calling itself Operation Rescue adopted the strategy of physically blockading clinics where abortions were performed. Patients and clinic workers were harassed and taunted. Demonstrators sometimes forced their way into clinics and smashed equipment. Clinics often were forced to close.

Abortion rights groups responded by bringing trespassing or harassment charges in state courts against the participants in the blockades. When those efforts failed to slow the confrontations, however, they turned to an obscure legal weapon: an 1871 civil rights law that Congress passed to protect African Americans from the Ku Klux Klan. The act authorized a civil suit in federal court against conspiracies aimed at "depriving . . . any person or class of persons of the equal protection of the laws" or "preventing or hindering [state or local authorities] from giving or securing to all persons . . . the equal protection of the laws."

The law was largely ignored after the Reconstruction era, but in 1971 the Supreme Court breathed new life into the statute by permitting its use in a violent attack against civil rights workers in the South. To avoid a broad expansion of federal tort law, however, the Court limited the law to conspiracies motivated by "a class-based, invidiously discriminatory animus." A second limitation required that the conspiracies be aimed only at those rights that were protected from infringement by private individuals, such as the right to vote or the right to interstate travel.

Despite those limitations, abortion rights groups succeeded in using the law to win injunctions from several federal courts against blockades by Operation Rescue or other groups. Other federal courts, however, rejected such suits. The Supreme Court agreed to resolve the conflict in 1991 in a case involving Operation Rescue blockades against several abortion clinics in northern Virginia.

The case was argued in October 1991 before Justice Clarence Thomas joined the Court. At the end of the 1991-1992 term, the Court announced the case would be reargued the next term—apparently indicating that the justices were evenly divided. When the case was reargued to a full Court in October 1992, antiabortion groups, backed by the Bush administration, argued that the law did not apply to the abortion protests. Abortion rights groups countered that blockades aimed at women exercising a constitutional right fell precisely within the terms of the law.

Just three months later, the Court agreed with the narrow view of the law. Women seeking an abortion did not constitute a "class of persons" for purposes of the law, Scalia said. Nor did the demonstrators' opposition to abortion reflect "an animus against women in general." "[O]pposition to voluntary abortion cannot possibly be considered . . . an irrational surrogate for opposition to (or paternalism towards) women," Scalia wrote. Moreover, Scalia said, the suit failed because the demonstrators' actions were not aimed at preventing women from traveling between states. The right to an abortion, he said, was not protected from infringement by individuals as opposed to government action.

The Court did not to rule on the applicability of the Klan Act's second provision—the "hindrance" or "prevention" clause. Scalia said the issue had not been properly raised in lower courts, but went on to say that such a claim also would require a racial or class-based motive.

Souter, bowing to precedent, concurred with the majority on the deprivation-clause issue, but said he would prefer to remand the case for further hearings on the prevention clause. He said that provision could apply when a conspiracy was "intended to hobble or overwhelm" the ability of authorities to protect equal rights. Under that clause, Souter said, plaintiffs need not prove the conspiracy was motivated by racial or other class-based prejudice.

The other dissenting justices took sharper issue with what Stevens called the majority's "parsimonious interpretation of an important federal statute." In her dissent, O'Connor complained that the majority had limited the law on the basis of a requirement not contained in the statute itself but imposed by a Court case a century later. "This case is not about abortion," O'Connor wrote. "[R]ather, this case is about whether a private conspiracy to deprive members of a protected class of legally protected interests gives rise to a federal cause of action. In my view, it does." Stevens and O'Connor said that either of the act's two clauses could be invoked against the blockades. Blackmun joined both dissents.

The Court's ruling did not end the debate. Abortion rights groups urged Congress to pass a bill establishing federal penalties for blocking access to abortion clinics. The Clinton administration in April urged a federal appeals court to settle the issue left open by the Court and interpret the Klan Act's "hindrance clause" to apply to antiabortion blockades.

The Court had another abortion-related case on its docket for the 1993-1994 term. The justices agreed to decide whether the powerful federal antiracketeering law known as RICO could be applied to abortion clinic blockades. *(See preview of 1993-1994 term, p. 215.)*

Job Discrimination

Employer's "Pretext" Does Not Prove Bias

St. Mary's Honor Center v. Hicks, decided by a 5-4 vote, June 25, 1993; Scalia wrote the opinion; Souter, White, Blackmun, and Stevens dissented.

When the Supreme Court handed down a series of decisions in 1989 narrowing the legal remedies in job discrimination cases, it touched off a long battle on Capitol Hill. Democrats in Congress argued that the Court's conservative majority had misread federal civil rights law and made job discrimination suits—already difficult to win—even more difficult. After a bitter struggle with the Bush administration, lawmakers in 1991 pushed through a compromise measure aimed at overturning the Court rulings.

In the 1992-1993 term, a conservative majority on the Court once again raised the hurdles for plaintiffs with job discrimination claims. As before, the issue was obscure: a seemingly technical debate about burdens of proof. But employment law experts said the stakes were real.

The case involved a suit by Melvin Hicks, an African American man who was demoted and then fired from his job as a correctional officer at the St. Mary's Honor Center in St. Louis. Hicks, who had worked at the minimum-security prison since 1978, clashed repeatedly with new supervisors in the first few months of 1984. After a series of disciplinary actions, he was fired in June and replaced by a white man.

Hicks went to court, claiming that the demotion and discharge amounted to racial discrimination in violation of Title VII of the 1964 Civil Rights Act. After a full trial, the judge in the case rejected the prison officials' explanations of Hicks' dismissal. But he also ruled that Hicks had failed to show he had been fired because of his race. Hicks proved there had been "a crusade to terminate him," the judge said, but did not show the crusade was "racially rather than personally motivated."

On appeal, the Eighth U.S. Circuit Court of Appeals said Hicks was entitled to win the case once the judge had rejected the prison officials' testimony. In a 5-4 decision, however, the Supreme Court said the appeals court was wrong.

The legal issue involved dissection of earlier Court decisions structuring the burden of proof in Title VII claims. The Court in 1973 held that once a plaintiff made out a "prima facie" case of discrimination, the employer had to offer a legitimate, nondiscriminatory reason for the unfavorable job action. If the employer met that burden, the plaintiff could then try to show that the reasons were not true, but were a pretext for discrimination.

Writing for the majority, Scalia said the appellate court had improperly shifted the burden of proof in the case. "By producing *evidence* (whether ultimately persuasive or not) of nondiscriminatory reasons, [prison officials] sustained their burden of production," Scalia wrote. The appeals court's holding, he said, "ignores our repeated admonition that the Title VII plaintiff at all times bears the ultimate burden of persuasion."

In a vigorous dissent, Souter said the ruling would be "unfair and unworkable" because plaintiffs would have "the burden of either producing direct evidence of discrimination or eliminating the entire universe of possible nondiscriminatory reasons for a personnel decision." In addition, Souter said, the ruling would reward employers for lying. "[C]ommon experience tells us that it is more likely than not that the employer who lies is simply trying to cover up the illegality alleged by the plaintiff," he said.

In a rejoinder, Scalia mocked what he called "the dissent's notion of judgment-for-lying." "Title VII is not a cause of action for perjury," Scalia wrote. In any event, Scalia continued, an employer's false explanation could "permit the trier of fact to infer the ultimate fact of discrimination," even if that alone was not necessarily enough.

Civil rights lawyers said the ruling would affect many job discrimination suits. The impact was hard to gauge, however, because of the new provision in the 1991 civil rights act for jury trials in Title VII cases. Some observers speculated that jurors who found an employer's defenses unbelievable would be inclined to rule for plaintiffs whatever the legal rules of proof were. Scalia anticipated that concern in his opinion. With the use of jury trials, he said, "Clarity regarding the requisite elements of proof becomes all the more important."

Immigration Law

Government May Return Haitian Refugees

Sale, Acting Commissioner, Immigration and Naturalization Service v. Haitian Centers Council, Inc., decided by an 8-1 vote, June 21, 1993; Stevens wrote the opinion; Blackmun dissented.

For most of its modern history, Haiti has known nothing but abject poverty and political dictatorship. Hopes for democracy rose in December 1990 when the Caribbean island nation chose its first democratically elected president: Jean-Bertrand Aristide. Those hopes were dashed in October 1991, however, when a military coup ousted Aristide and a new wave of political persecution began.

Many Haitians turned their eyes to the United States in hopes of escape. About 40,000 set out in boats—many of them ramshackle—on a long and perilous sea journey, hoping to reach a better life on U.S. soil.

For the United States, the "boat people" posed a difficult political and legal problem. Federal immigration law guaranteed foreigners fleeing political persecution a chance to apply for asylum as refugees. By spring 1992, however, the human flood had overwhelmed the camp for screening Haitian refugees that the Bush administration set up at the U.S. naval base at Guantamo Bay, Cuba.

In May the administration turned to a new strategy to control immigration and deter Haitians from embarking on the dangerous journey. President Bush ordered the Coast Guard to stop Haitians on the high seas and return them to Haiti without giving them the chance to apply for refugee status.

Bush's Democratic opponent, Bill Clinton, criticized the "interdiction" policy as cruel and illegal. Haitian refugee groups also challenged the policy in federal courts. They argued that it violated refugee protection provisions contained in U.S. immigration law and a 1951 international treaty, the United Nations Convention on the Status of Refugees.

Although he criticized the Bush administration for interdicting boatloads of Haitian refugees at sea, President Clinton continued the policy. The Supreme Court rejected a challenge to the practice.

Two federal appeals courts divided on the issue, and the Supreme Court agreed to settle the dispute. By the time the case was argued in March, however, Clinton, now president, had shifted his position. Clinton maintained the policy was the best way to protect Haitians from death on the seas and directed the Justice Department to continue defending the policy before the Supreme Court. Two months later, the Court gave the administration a legal victory. In an 8-1 ruling, the Court held that the interdiction policy did not violate immigration law or the UN treaty on refugees because neither of those laws applied outside U.S. borders.

The Court's central holding involved the Immigration and Nationality Act, passed in 1952 and amended by the Refugee Act of 1980. As amended, the law provided that the attorney general "shall not deport or return any alien" to a country if he determines that "such alien's life or freedom would be threatened . . . on account of race, religion, nationality, membership in a particular social group, or political opinion."

The refugee groups emphasized that the 1980 amendment mandated protection for refugees, broadened the kinds of persecution that could be raised, and removed the phrase "within the United States" to describe aliens covered by the law. On that basis, they argued the law was meant to protect refugees whether or not they had reached the United States. The Court rejected that argument. Justice Stevens said federal laws usually do not apply outside U.S. borders and there was "no affirmative evidence" that Congress meant for the 1980 law to do so. Instead, Stevens said, the change merely guaranteed protection for aliens in deportation proceedings if they were in the United States or in "exclusion" hearings if they were at U.S. borders.

Stevens similarly narrowed the impact of the UN treaty, which provided that nations not "expel or return" refugees to a country where they faced persecution. Despite what he called "the moral weight" of the argument for a broad interpretation, Stevens said that the treaty also "was not intended to have extraterritorial effect."

In a lone dissent, Justice Blackmun sharply criticized the Court's legal reasoning, saying that both the law and the treaty were "unambiguous" in prohibiting the return of "[v]ulnerable refugees." "What is extraordinary in this case," Blackmun wrote, "is that the Executive, in disregard of the law, would take to the seas to intercept fleeing refugees and force them back to their persecutors—and that the Court would strain to sanction such conduct."

Church and State

Aid Permitted for Deaf Student at Church School

Zobrest v. Catalina Foothills School District, decided by a 5-4 vote, June 18, 1993; Rehnquist wrote the opinion; Blackmun, Stevens, O'Connor, and Souter dissented.

Since the 1920s the Supreme Court has recognized a constitutional right for parents to send children to church-related schools. But the Court also has ruled that separation of church and state limits the assistance that government can provide parochial schools. The justices have struggled, however, to draw a clear line between permissible and impermissible aid. The Court has approved tuition tax credits, but not direct tuition reimbursements. It has approved textbook loans, but not reimbursement for field trips. Many observers have voiced frustration with these hair-splitting distinctions. Sen. Daniel Patrick Moynihan, D-N.Y., once quipped that if textbooks were permitted but not maps, "what about atlases, or books of maps?"

The issue returned to the Court this term in a case with a new twist. A deaf student in Tucson, Arizona, claimed that the federal Individuals With Disabilities Education Act *required* school authorities to furnish a sign-language interpreter to accompany him in his Roman Catholic high school. But the Catalina Foothills School District and the Arizona state attorney general rejected the request, saying it would violate the First Amendment's prohibition against establishment of religion.

The student, James Zobrest, and his parents took the issue to federal court. They argued that the interpreter's role was purely mechanical and therefore would not result in impermissible government involvement with religion. Their arguments were rejected first by a district court judge and then by a divided panel of the Ninth U.S. Circuit Court of Appeals. The appeals court said that furnishing the sign-language interpreter "would have the primary effect of advancing religion and thus would run afoul of the Establishment Clause." The Zobrests appealed that decision to the Supreme Court, where they gained support from the Bush administration and an array of religious groups.

In a 5-4 decision, the Court ruled in their favor. "The [federal law] creates a neutral government program dispensing aid not to schools but to individual handicapped children," Chief Justice Rehnquist said in an opinion joined by Justices White, Scalia, Kennedy, and Thomas. "If a handicapped child chooses to enroll in a sectarian school, we hold that the Establishment Clause does not prevent the school district from furnishing him with a sign-language interpreter there in order to facilitate his education."

Rehnquist distinguished previous Court decisions limiting aid to parochial schools by saying that in this case, the government would not be relieving Zobrest's school of costs that it would have incurred anyway. And he also agreed that the interpreter would not advance the school's sectarian mission. "Nothing in this record suggests that a sign-language interpreter would do more than accurately interpret whatever material is presented to the class as a whole," Rehnquist wrote.

Justices Blackmun, Stevens, O'Connor, and Souter dissented. All four agreed that the Court had improperly rushed to decide the constitutional issue. They said the Court should first have decided whether the federal law required the school district to pay for the interpreter or, alternatively, whether a federal regulation implementing the law prohibited it.

In his opinion, Rehnquist answered the dissenters. He said the two lower federal courts had focused solely on the constitutional issue. "Given the posture of this case," Rehnquist said, "we think the prudential rule of avoiding constitutional questions has no application."

James Zobrest, right, using sign language with his parents. In a close decision, the Supreme Court said the state should pay for the deaf student's sign-language interpreter even though he attended a religious high school.

Two of the dissenting justices—Blackmun and Souter—went further. They directly challenged the majority's position as contrary to the Court's precedents on aid to church schools. "[O]ur cases consistently have rejected the provision by government of any resource capable of advancing a school's religious mission," Blackmun wrote. Under this ruling, he continued, "it is beyond question that a state-employed sign-language interpreter would serve as the conduit for [Zobrest's] religious education, thereby assisting [the school] in its mission of religious indoctrination."

By the time the Court reached its decision, Jim Zobrest had finished high school. But after the ruling, the school district reimbursed the Zobrests $36,982 for their costs in hiring an interpreter for his four years in the Catholic school.

Religious Groups May Use School Buildings

Lamb's Chapel v. Center Moriches Union Free School District, decided by a 9-0 vote, June 7, 1993; White wrote the opinion.

Minority religious groups have played a major part in enforcing the First Amendment's protection for religious freedom. Jehovah's Witnesses won a series of Supreme Court decisions in the late 1930s and early 1940s striking down laws that restricted religious proselytizing. In the 1970s an Amish family won a Court ruling reinforcing the right of parents to choose a religious education for their children. A new test of religious freedom reached the Court this term in a case involving a small evangelical Christian church in a town in eastern Long Island. The Court's unanimous ruling reaffirmed that the government cannot arbitrarily deny free speech rights to religious groups.

The dispute began in 1990 when Lamb's Chapel asked the town of Center Moriches for permission to use school buildings after hours to show a six-part film series on family and child-rearing issues. The pastor of the 150-member church described the films as containing "a Christian perspective." The school board rejected the request on the basis of rules that permitted after-hours use of school buildings for social, civic, and recreational purposes, but specifically prohibited use by any group for religious purposes. A New York state law regulating use of school property also had been interpreted by the courts as barring meetings for religious purposes.

Lamb's Chapel challenged the refusal in federal court, arguing that the school buildings were a "public forum" that must be opened to all groups without discrimination. But a district court judge and the Second U.S. Circuit Court of Appeals both upheld the policy. The appeals court ruled that public school buildings were "a limited public forum" that could be opened only for designated purposes as long as the restrictions were reasonable and viewpoint-neutral.

The Supreme Court dispatched that argument in just twelve pages. Justice White agreed that the schools did not have to be open for public meetings, but he said access rules could not discriminate on the basis of the identity or viewpoint of the speaker. "The principle that has emerged from our cases is that the First Amendment forbids the government to regulate speech in ways that favor some viewpoints or ideas at the expense of others," White said, citing an earlier decision. In this case, he said, Lamb's Chapel had been denied permission "solely because the film dealt with the subject from a religious standpoint."

White also called "unfounded" the argument that permitting religious groups to use school property would be an unconstitutional establishment of religion. "The showing of this film would not have been during school hours, would not have been sponsored by the school, and would have been open to the public, not just to church members," White wrote. Under those circumstances, he said, the school board would not be "endorsing religion" or violating the test the Court has used for determining when government becomes too closely involved with religion.

White's opinion was joined in full by Chief Justice Rehnquist and Justices Blackmun, Stevens, O'Connor, and Souter and in part by Justice Kennedy.

Kennedy and Justice Scalia wrote separately, however, to fault White for citing the relatively strict test on separation of church and state established in a 1971 ruling, *Lemon v. Kurtzman.* That test permits government aid to religious schools only if the assistance has a secular purpose and effect and does not result in excessive "entanglement" with administration of the schools. Scalia, joined by Thomas, mocked the *Lemon* test as being like "some ghoul in a late-night horror movie that repeatedly sits up in its grave and shuffles abroad, after being repeatedly killed and buried." He noted that five of the current justices—including White—"have, in their own opinions, personally driven pencils through the creature's heart," and a sixth, Thomas, joined an opinion criticizing the test in the previous term. Kennedy also criticized White's use of the *Lemon* test, calling it "unnecessary and unsettling."

The ruling left open the question whether religious groups could use school facilities for religious services. Lamb's Chapel also had been denied permission to conduct Sunday morning worship services, but it did not press that issue in its appeal.

Forfeitures

Seizure of Criminals' Assets Is Limited

Austin v. United States, decided by a 9-0 vote, June 28, 1993; Blackmun wrote the opinion.

Frustrated in the fight against drug trafficking and other lucrative crimes, law enforcement officials decided in the 1980s to hit sophisticated criminal operations where it hurt most: in the pocketbook. They won enactment of new laws at the federal and state levels to make it easier for the government to seize money, goods, or property from criminal defendants or suspects.

These beefed-up forfeiture laws produced a whopping payoff. In the first five years of the federal asset forfeiture program, the Justice Department reported that it confiscated $2.4 billion in cash and property. But the aggressive use of forfeiture laws also provoked controversy. Criminal defense attorneys and civil liberties groups accused the government of confiscating tainted money or property not only from criminals but also from people with no knowledge that they had received proceeds of criminal activities. Critics also charged that sometimes the value of the property seized far outweighed the seriousness of the offenses.

For several years, the Supreme Court showed no great interest in the issue. In 1989, for example, the Court found no constitutional violation in seizing racketeering-tainted funds from criminal defendants even if they were left with no money to hire a lawyer. In a series of rulings this term, however, the justices reined in the government's forfeiture power. The most important decisions—a pair of rulings announced the last day of the term—held that the Eighth Amendment's little-used ban on "excessive fines" limits the power to confiscate money or property as part of a criminal prosecution or in separate civil forfeiture actions. A civil forfeiture can be ordered in a so-called *in rem* action, a lawsuit technically brought against property used in a crime or the proceeds of a crime. It does not require a prior criminal conviction.

The Court's ruling on civil forfeitures came in the case of a South Dakota man, Richard Austin, whose mobile home and auto body shop were taken after his state court conviction for selling two grams of cocaine to an undercover agent. To seize the property, the federal government used a 1984 drug law that authorized forfeiture of "all real property . . . used, or intended to be used, in any manner or part, to commit, or to facilitate the commission of" a drug offense.

A three-judge panel of the Eighth U.S. Circuit Court of Appeals "reluctantly" upheld the seizure of Austin's home and business, valued together at about $38,000, along with about $4,700 in cash. "In this case, it does appear that the Government is exacting too high a penalty in relation to the offense committed," the appeals court said. But the court said that a 1974 Supreme Court decision appeared to preclude any requirement of "proportionality" in judging forfeitures.

After the Supreme Court agreed to review the case, the Justice Department used a variety of arguments to prevent any constitutional limits on forfeitures. Government lawyers argued that the Eighth Amendment applied only to criminal cases, not to civil forfeiture actions. In addition, they said, drug forfeiture laws served a remedial purpose by removing the tools of drug trade and by compensating government for the costs of dealing with crime.

The Court unanimously rejected those arguments. Although they differed slightly in their reasoning, all nine justices agreed that the civil forfeitures amounted to punishment and were subject to the Eighth Amendment's prohibition on excessive fines. "[W]e cannot conclude that forfeiture under [the drug law provisions] serves solely a remedial purpose," Justice Blackmun wrote for the Court. "We therefore conclude that forfeiture under these provisions . . . is subject to the limitations of the Eighth Amendment's Excessive Fines Clause."

Justices White, Stevens, O'Connor, and Souter joined Blackmun's opinion. Blackmun based his opinion in part on his conclusion that forfeiture laws had historically been viewed as punishment in both English and American law. In separate opinions, Justices Scalia and Kennedy both questioned Blackmun's reading of history, but agreed that the drug forfeiture laws did constitute punishment. Chief Justice Rehnquist and Justice Thomas joined Kennedy's opinion.

Blackmun left unanswered what standard should be used to determine when a forfeiture is "excessive," saying the issue should be left initially to the lower federal courts. In his opinion, Scalia offered a suggestion. Instead of looking at the value of the property to be seized, Scalia said, a court should examine the connection between the property and the crime. "The question is not *how much* the confiscated property is worth, but *whether* the confiscated property has a close enough relationship to the offense," Scalia said.

Separately, the Court also applied the Eighth Amendment to forfeitures in criminal cases. The decision in *Alexander v. United States* involved the seizure of a $25 million pornography business following a conviction under the federal antiracketeering law. Chief Justice Rehnquist said the forfeiture was "clearly a form of monetary punishment" for purposes of the Excessive Fines Clause. The Court voted 5-4 in the case to reject a First Amendment challenge to the forfeiture, but returned the case to lower courts for hearings on the Eighth Amendment issue. *(See entry, p. 61.)*

Together, the Court's two rulings set the stage for a host of legal battles to be fought in federal and state courts. In addition, the Court agreed to resolve another forfeiture issue in its next term: whether the government can seize property used in drug crimes without first giving the owner notice and a hearing to challenge the seizure. *(See preview of 1993-1994 term, p. 215.)*

Capital Punishment

Late Innocence Claim No Bar to Execution

Herrera v. Collins, Director, Texas Department of Criminal Justice, Institutional Division, decided by a 6-3 vote, January 25, 1993; Rehnquist wrote the opinion; Blackmun, Stevens, and Souter dissented.

Does the Constitution permit the government to execute an innocent person? The answer seems self-evident, but the legal safeguards needed to ensure that no innocent person is put to death are less certain.

That issue reached the Supreme Court this term in the case of a Texas prisoner who, long after his 1982 conviction for killing a police officer, claimed that newly discovered evidence showed he was not guilty of the crime. Leonel Herrera filed a petition for federal habeas corpus relief in 1992 seeking a hearing on the evidence and a stay of execution in the meantime.

A federal district court judge—acting out of what he called "a sense of fairness and due process"—granted Herrera's request. But the Eleventh U.S. Circuit Court of Appeals ordered Herrera's petition dismissed. The appeals court said Herrera's claim of "actual innocence" did not entitle him to federal habeas relief unless he proved some other constitutional error in his state court proceedings. In a 6-3 decision, the Supreme Court agreed.

As Chief Justice Rehnquist described the case, Herrera had already pursued an array of challenges after his conviction and death sentence in a jury trial. The evidence at trial was strong: an eyewitness identification, blood stains on Herrera's belongings, and a letter by Herrera strongly implying he shot the officer because of a dispute over drug dealing. The next year, Herrera also pleaded guilty to killing a second officer in the incident.

Texas appellate courts affirmed the convictions in 1984. A federal habeas corpus petition also failed. Then, in 1990, Herrera filed a habeas petition in state court claiming that new evidence showed that his brother, Raul Herrera, Sr., had actually killed the first officer. Raul Herrera died in 1984. The state court judge dismissed the petition, but in 1992 Herrera filed another habeas petition in federal court. This one included additional affidavits, including one from Raul Herrera, Jr., saying that he had seen his father commit the killing. Raul, Jr., was nine at the time of the slaying.

Whatever weight the evidence carried, Herrera faced two legal hurdles. First, Texas rules of criminal procedure required that new evidence be presented within thirty days after sentencing. Second, federal courts in habeas corpus cases normally do not consider questions of guilt or innocence, but only violations of constitutional rights in state courts.

In his opinion, Rehnquist reiterated that federal habeas relief was limited to constitutional issues, citing a 1963 decision written by Chief Justice Earl Warren. Rehnquist went on to say that none of the Court's death penalty cases applying the Eighth Amendment's ban on cruel and unusual punishment entitled Herrera to a new hearing on guilt or innocence either. Rehnquist also rejected Herrera's claim that Texas's thirty-day limit on new evidence violated the Fourteenth Amendment's Due Process Clause. He noted that the Court had set a two-year deadline for federal courts while two-thirds of the states had limits of three years or under.

Moreover, Rehnquist said, Herrera could still seek a commutation from the governor. "Executive clemency has provided the 'fail safe' in our criminal justice system," he wrote.

Rehnquist ended, however, by assuming—"for the sake of argument in deciding this case"—that "a truly persuasive demonstration of actual innocence" in a capital case "would render the execution of a defendant unconstitutional, and warrant federal habeas relief if there were no state avenue open to process such a claim." But, he said, because of the "very disruptive effect" on state court systems, the threshold for such a showing "would necessarily be extraordinarily high." Herrera's evidence, he concluded, fell "far short."

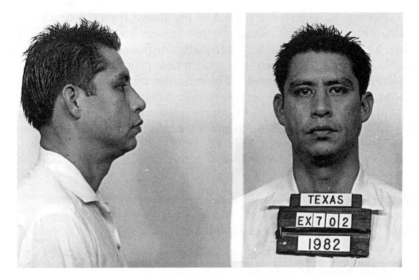

Leonel Herrera, who was convicted for murder in 1982, claimed to have new evidence proving his innocence. On January 25, 1993, the Supreme Court said he was not entitled to habeas corpus relief, and he was executed May 12.

Justices O'Connor, Scalia, Kennedy, and Thomas joined Rehnquist's opinion. But they paired off in separate opinions to offer different views of the issue left open by the ruling.

O'Connor, joined by Kennedy, said the Court was correct not to settle what she called the "difficult question" of whether a federal court could ever entertain a "convincing claim" of innocence. But Scalia, joined by Thomas, said the Court should have firmly shut the door to such claims. "There is no basis in text, tradition, or even in contemporary practice ... for finding in the Constitution a right to demand judicial consideration of newly discovered evidence of innocence brought forward after conviction," Scalia wrote.

White, concurring only in the judgment, explicitly said that a "persuasive showing of actual innocence" would render a prisoner's execution unconstitutional. He said he would permit such a claim if the evidence showed that "no rational trier of fact" could have found the prisoner guilty. But he too said Herrera did not meet the test.

The dissenting justices—Blackmun, Stevens, and Souter—argued that a condemned prisoner should be given a hearing if he could prove that he was "probably innocent." They also complained that the Court's ruling left the states "uncertain" about what postconviction procedures were required in capital cases.

Blackmun, who read a portion of his dissent from the bench, ended with an especially blunt paragraph that Stevens and Souter did not join. "Just as an execution without adequate safeguards is unacceptable, so, too, is an execution when the condemned prisoner can prove he is innocent," Blackmun declared. "The execution of a person who can show that he is innocent comes perilously close to simple murder."

In her written opinion, O'Connor answered that point with equal bluntness. Herrera, she said, "is not innocent, in any sense of the word."

Herrera was executed May 12, 1993.

Sentencing

Hate Crime Penalty Laws Upheld

Wisconsin v. Mitchell, decided by a 9-0 vote, June 11, 1993; Rehnquist wrote the opinion.

The United States in the 1980s experienced an apparent increase in assaults and other crimes against victims targeted because of their race, religion, ethnic origin, or sexual orientation. Law enforcement and minority civil rights groups counted more and more attacks, in particular, against blacks, Jews, Asian-Americans, and homosexuals. In response, more than half the states passed laws providing for longer sentences in "hate crime" cases.

Gregory Reddick, a white teenager in Kenosha, Wisconsin, became the victim of a hate crime on the evening of October 7, 1989. A group of black youths, angry after having watched a movie about the mistreatment of blacks during the 1950s and 1960s, saw Reddick as he was walking along a street. "There goes a white boy," Todd Mitchell, then nineteen, said to his friends. "Go get him."

Reddick was beaten into unconsciousness; he stayed in a coma for four days. Mitchell, the only adult in the group, was charged under Wisconsin's hate crime law.

Todd Mitchell

The statute allowed judges to add up to five years when sentencing a defendant who "intentionally selects" his or her victim on the basis of race, religion, ethnic origin, disability, or sexual orientation.

A jury convicted Mitchell of aggravated battery, and the judge imposed the maximum two-year sentence for the offense and an additional two-year term under the hate crime law. The Wisconsin Supreme Court invalidated the sentence, saying the state law "violates the First Amendment by punishing what the Legislature has deemed to be offensive thought." In a unanimous ruling, however, the U.S. Supreme Court upheld the law. The decision cleared a legal cloud over statutes on the books in twenty-six other states and the District of Columbia.

The Court had raised doubts about the hate crime penalty enhancement laws with a controversial decision just one year earlier. In that case, *R. A. V. v. City of St. Paul* (1992), the Court struck down a local ordinance that prohibited the use of "fighting words" that "insult or provoke violence" based on race, religion, or gender. The Court held that the First Amendment prohibited government from singling out specific types of "hate speech" for criminal punishment. State and federal governments and a coalition of civil rights groups argued that the hate crime laws were different. The penalty enhancement measures were aimed at conduct, not speech, these groups told the Court.

The Court agreed. Chief Justice Rehnquist's opinion upholding the hate crime penalty law was brief and straightforward, with little rhetoric and no footnotes. Judges traditionally have been permitted to consider "a wide variety of factors" in sentencing a defendant, including the motive for the crime, Rehnquist said. Courts cannot consider a defendant's "abstract beliefs," he acknowledged, but they can take racial bias or other prejudice into account when that is part of the motive for the offense.

Turning to the free speech issue, Rehnquist said that the law "is aimed at conduct unprotected by the First Amendment." Wisconsin lawmakers passed the measure, he said, because "bias-inspired conduct ... is thought to inflict greater individual and societal harm," including "distinct emotional harms" for victims and the possibility of provoking retaliation or inciting community unrest. "The State's desire to redress these perceived harms provides an adequate explanation for its penalty-enhancement provisions over and above mere disagreement with offenders' belief or biases," Rehnquist wrote.

Nor could the law be deemed to have a chilling effect on free speech rights, Rehnquist said. The likelihood that someone would suppress "his bigoted beliefs" because his views could be used against him later in a criminal trial was "too speculative" to support the contention that the law was unconstitutionally overbroad, Rehnquist said.

The Court spoke with one voice in upholding the law. None of the other justices wrote a separate opinion in the case—seemingly to prevent confusion or uncertainty about the meaning of the decision. And the Court largely ignored potentially knotty questions about how judges should conduct hate crime trials. Rehnquist said only that evidence about a defendant's previous statements "is commonly admitted" in trials, "subject to evidentiary rules dealing with relevancy, reliability, and the like."

Evidence

Judges Told to Screen Scientific Evidence

Daubert v. Merrell Dow Pharmaceuticals Co., decided by votes of 9-0 and 7-2, June 28, 1993; Blackmun wrote the opinion; Rehnquist and Stevens dissented in part.

For more than two decades, doctors prescribed the drug Bendectin for pregnant women to control the common, and sometimes serious, problem of nausea—"morning sickness." Then, in 1979, an Australian gynecologist claimed to have discovered that Bendectin caused birth defects in babies born to women who used the drug. The allegations led to a wave of lawsuits in U.S. courts. The maker of the drug, Merrell Dow Pharmaceuticals, won most of them. But despite its victories, the company decided in 1983 to pull the drug from the market, saying the cost of defending the suits was too great.

The Bendectin litigation became an important example for critics of the civil justice system to attack what they called "junk science" in the courtroom. These critics maintained that plaintiffs' lawyers often used unreliable evidence from scientists of dubious credentials to bring baseless suits and, sometimes, win unjustified awards or settlements. They wanted judges to apply stricter standards to keep the evidence out of court and away from juries. Plaintiffs' and consumer groups countered that juries were perfectly capable of deciding scientific issues fairly. More broadly, they insisted that the legal system could not wait for scientists to reach certain conclusions in cases that could affect public health and safety.

The Supreme Court agreed to review the legal issue in a pair of Bendectin suits from California. Lower federal courts had used a strict seventy-year-old evidentiary rule to exclude studies linking Bendectin to birth defects. The courts then threw out the suits brought by parents of children born with deformed arms and legs after the mothers had taken the drug.

The Court's ruling gave something to both sides of the debate. For plaintiffs, the Court unanimously threw out the widely used test first set out in a 1923 case called *Frye v. United States*. In that ruling, the federal appeals court for the District of Columbia said that scientific evidence could be used only if it had achieved "general acceptance" within the scientific community.

The Supreme Court ruled, however, that *Frye* had been superseded by the more liberal Federal Rules of Evidence, adopted in 1975. Those rules generally provide that "all relevant evidence" is admissible in court. In addition, Rule 702 specifically allows testimony by "expert" witnesses if "scientific, technical, or other specialized knowledge will assist the trier of fact to understand the evidence or to determine a fact in issue."

"Nothing in the text of this Rule," Justice Blackmun wrote for the Court, "establishes 'general acceptance' as an absolute prerequisite to admissibility."

In a second—and longer—part of the opinion, however, the Court assigned federal judges an active role in screening scientific evidence. "[T]he trial judge must ensure that any and all scientific testimony or evidence is not only relevant, but reliable," Blackmun wrote. In order to qualify as "scientific knowledge" under Rule 702, he said, evidence "must be derived by the scientific method." He rejected arguments by industry groups for an absolute rule that studies first be reviewed by other scientists and published in journals to be admitted as evidence. But he said peer review and publication were one "relevant" factor. In addition, Blackmun said, "general acceptance" may still "have a bearing" on the use of evidence. "Widespread acceptance" counts as a plus, he made clear, while studies with "minimal support" among scientists "may properly be viewed with skepticism."

Rehnquist, joined by Stevens, concurred in scrapping the *Frye* test, but dissented from the Court's instructions to judges. Rehnquist accused the majority of creating a new requirement of "reliability" for expert testimony only by "parsing the language" of Rule 702. He ended by arguing that judges were being given too broad a role with too little guidance. "I do not doubt that Rule 702 confides to the judge some gatekeeping responsibility in deciding questions of the admissibility of proffered testimony," Rehnquist said. "But I do not think it imposes on them either the obligation or the authority to become amateur scientists in order to perform that role."

3 | *Case Summaries*

Throughout his thirty-one years on the Supreme Court, Justice Byron R. White was considered a workhorse. His former clerks recalled with admiration and amazement that he was always at work before them in the morning and outlasted them during the day.

White also prodded his colleagues to keep up the pace, often dissenting from decisions to deny review in cases brought to the Court. White's votes did not always indicate a particular point of view on the issue. Instead, it appeared, White simply thought the Court should resolve the issue one way or another. With White's retirement at the end of the 1992-1993 term, the Court lost that voice urging it to decide more cases.

White's departure came at the end of yet another term in which the Court decided fewer cases than at any time in the 1970s or 1980s, even though the number of cases brought to the Court continued to rise sharply. The Court issued 107 signed opinions in the 1992-1993 term—the same number it handed down in the previous term and the lowest number of signed opinions since 1969. The Court also issued one *per curiam* (unsigned) opinion in a case following oral argument.

The number of signed opinions was substantially below the average of 131 opinions per term during the 1970s and 139 opinions per term in the 1980s. The Court's docket in the 1992-1993 term, however, reached a new high of 7,245 cases, a 7 percent increase from the 1991-1992 term.

Court watchers offered several reasons—more or less speculative—for the declining number of opinions. A 1988 law giving the Court almost complete freedom in selecting cases to hear contributed to the drop. With Republican-appointed judges comprising more than half of the federal judiciary, the Rehnquist Court also may have felt less need to overturn rulings from lower federal courts. In addition, at least some of the justices were thought to consider the Court's earlier workload too burdensome.

Observers also suspected tactical motives. Liberal justices, it was surmised, feared taking cases where conservatives might have the votes to establish unwelcome precedent. But conservatives too might worry about taking up issues where the votes of the centrist justices could not be predicted in advance. Most broadly, observers believed the Court was simply lowering its profile and giving greater deference to other branches of government.

With the low number of opinions, the justices also agreed more often in the 1992-1993 term. The Court was unanimous in forty-six

(43 percent) of its 107 signed opinions—a higher percentage than the previous term's thirty-nine (36 percent) unanimous rulings for the same number of opinions. In twenty-eight of the unanimous rulings, none of the justices wrote separate concurrences. That figure was also higher than the 1991-1992 number of twenty unanimous decisions with no separate concurrences.

At the same time, the number of 5-4 rulings increased in the 1992-1993 term to twenty (19 percent) from the previous term's fourteen (13 percent). The percentage of one-vote margins, however, remained below earlier levels of 33 percent in the 1989-1990 term and 20 percent for 1990-1991. In the remaining decisions for the current term, the justices divided 8-1 twelve times, 7-2 fourteen times, and 6-3 fifteen times.

Following are the case summaries for all 107 signed opinions and the one orally argued *per curiam* opinion from the 1992-1993 term:

Business Law

Antitrust

Brooke Group Ltd. v. Brown & Williamson Tobacco Corp., decided by a 6-3 vote, June 21, 1993; Kennedy wrote the opinion; Stevens, White, and Blackmun dissented.

The Court rejected a major antitrust case growing out of a cigarette industry price war in the mid-1980s. The divided ruling made it harder for a business to prevail in an antitrust suit claiming injury from a competitor's below-cost or predatory pricing scheme.

The Liggett Group—later renamed Brooke Group—won a $148.8 million jury verdict against Brown & Williamson Tobacco Corp. for an eighteen-month price war after Liggett introduced low-priced generic cigarettes. The jury agreed that Brown & Williamson had violated the Robinson-Patman Act by engaging in aggressive, below-cost pricing practices designed to injure competition. But the judge in the case overturned the verdict, and the U.S. Court of Appeals for the Fourth Circuit affirmed his ruling.

In its decision, the Supreme Court rejected the appeals court's holding that a company could not be found liable in a predatory pricing case unless it had a chance of achieving monopoly power. But the six-justice majority said that a plaintiff must prove that its price-war rival was likely to recover its losses by later raising prices above a competitive level. In this case, Kennedy wrote, Liggett's evidence was "inadequate" to show the likelihood of "recoupment through supracompetitive pricing."

The dissenting justices argued the evidence was "plainly sufficient" to support Liggett's claim. Stevens noted that once the price war had ended, the price of generic cigarettes rose to $33.75 from $19.75.

Professional Real Estate Investors, Inc. v. Columbia Pictures Industries, Inc., decided by a 9-0 vote, May 3, 1993; Thomas wrote the opinion.

The Court virtually precluded the use of antitrust laws as a defensive tactic in legal disputes between business competitors.

A defendant who claims a lawsuit brought by a competitor amounted to a violation of the antitrust law must first show that the litigation was "objectively baseless," the Court held. Then it must also show that the lawsuit was intended as "an attempt to interfere directly" with its business relationships through use of the judicial process.

The decision involved a dispute between eight major movie studios and the operators of a Palm Springs, California, resort. The studios filed a copyright infringement action to try to stop the resort owners from renting videodiscs to guests and marketing videodisc players to other hotels for a similar service. The resort responded by claiming that the lawsuit was a sham that concealed an attempt to restrain trade in violation of the Sherman Antitrust Act.

After two federal courts rejected the studios' copyright claim, the resort owners pressed their antitrust complaint. But the same courts held that the studios had "probable cause" for their suit and threw out the resort's antitrust claims. The Supreme Court unanimously upheld the ruling. Thomas's opinion for the Court tightened the protection from antitrust laws given to actions by businesses to lobby government or use the courts to strengthen their competitive position.

Thomas announced a two-part test for treating a lawsuit as a "sham" that might be subject to antitrust laws. First, he said, "the lawsuit must be objectively baseless in the sense that no reasonable litigant could realistically expect success on the merits." If that test was met, Thomas continued, a court could examine the litigant's "subjective motivation" to determine whether the suit had been intended to directly interfere with a competitor's business relationships.

Although the vote in the case was unanimous, Stevens and O'Connor did not join Thomas's opinion. Stevens said the Court should have left open the possibility that some litigation—for example, repetitive lawsuits against a business competitor—could constitute a sham even though it was not completely baseless.

Spectrum Sports, Inc. v. McQuillan DBA Sorboturf Enterprises, decided by a 9-0 vote, January 25, 1993; White wrote the opinion.

A defendant in an antitrust suit cannot be found liable for attempted monopolization unless evidence proves a dangerous probability that it would monopolize a relevant market and a specific intent to monopolize.

The decision threw out a $5.2 million award in a dispute among makers and distributors of an elastic shock-absorbing material used in medical and athletic products.

The Ninth U.S. Circuit Court of Appeals had upheld the award, saying that evidence of unfair or predatory conduct sufficed to show attempted monopolization without any proof of market power. Writing for the unanimous Court, White said the appeals court had departed from well-established interpretations of federal antitrust law.

Banking

United States National Bank of Oregon v. Independent Insurance Agents of America, Inc., decided by a 9-0 vote, June 7, 1993; Souter wrote the opinion.

The Court reinstated a 1916 federal law that federal bank regulators used to permit national banks to sell insurance from their branches in small towns on a nationwide basis.

The unanimous decision reversed a ruling by the U.S. Circuit Court of Appeals for the District of Columbia that Congress had, inadvertently, repealed the 1916 law two years later. The Supreme Court said that the apparent repeal resulted from a punctuation error and that the law "remains in force."

The ruling came in a dispute between the banking and insurance industries. The Comptroller of the Currency, one of the federal bank regulatory agencies, adopted a policy in 1986 permitting national banks to sell insurance nationally from their small-town branches. Trade groups representing insurance agents challenged the policy in court.

Even though the validity of the 1916 law had not been questioned, the federal appeals court ruled that it had been repealed by other banking amendments Congress passed in 1918. But the Supreme Court said that misplaced quotation marks were to blame. "The true meaning of the 1916 Act is clear beyond question, and so we repunctuate," Souter wrote.

The decision returned the case to the appeals court for rulings on other issues.

Bankruptcy

Rake v. Wade, Trustee, decided by a 9-0 vote, June 7, 1993; Thomas wrote the opinion.

Individuals who are granted bankruptcy court approval for plans to repay their creditors over time must pay interest on delinquent home mortgage payments.

The unanimous Court said that mortgage holders are entitled to interest even if the mortgage contract does not require interest payments.

Thomas explained that two separate provisions of the bankruptcy code entitle creditors to interest if their claim is "oversecured"—that is, if the value of the property securing the claim is greater than the amount owed. He rejected arguments by the debtors that a separate bankruptcy code section made those provisions inapplicable to home mortgages.

Nobelman v. American Savings Bank, decided by a 9-0 vote, June 1, 1993; Thomas wrote the opinion.

Homeowners given bankruptcy court approval for creditor repayment plans under Chapter 13 cannot reduce the outstanding mortgage balance to the value of the home.

The unanimous decision protected mortgage lenders' contractual rights in cases where declining property values left their loans "undersecured"—that is, secured by property worth less than the balance due. Some federal appeals courts had ruled that homeowners in such cases could "strip down" the mortgage to the home's market value.

Writing for the Court, however, Thomas said that the bankruptcy code section prohibits any modification of the "rights" of home mortgage lenders. He said that section preserved the lenders' rights to payment under the mortgage contract even though a separate section limits a secured claim to the value of the property securing the loan.

Pioneer Investment Services Co. v. Brunswick Associates Limited Partnership, decided by a 5-4 vote, March 24, 1993; White wrote the opinion; O'Connor, Scalia, Souter, and Thomas dissented.

A creditor may be allowed to file a late claim in a bankruptcy action if the delay was due to an attorney's inadvertent failure to meet the deadline.

The divided decision eased the interpretation of a bankruptcy rule permitting a tardy claim if the delay was "the result of excusable neglect." Several federal appeals courts had held that the rule could be applied only if the delay was due to circumstances beyond the creditor's control.

Writing for the majority, White said that Congress had not intended to apply such a strict standard. He said that a lower court could find that an attorney's inadvertent failure to file a claim on time constituted excusable neglect after it considered all relevant circumstances.

Other factors to be considered, White said, include prejudice to the debtor, the length of the delay and its effect on judicial economy, the reason for the delay and whether it was within the reasonable control of the creditors and their counsel, and the good faith of late filers.

Dissenting justices said the decision was inconsistent with the language of the rule and "unduly complicates the task of courts called upon to apply it."

Insurance

Hartford Fire Insurance Co. v. California, decided by votes of 9-0 and 5-4, June 28, 1993; Souter wrote the main opinion; Scalia wrote for a five-justice majority on one issue; Scalia, O'Connor, Kennedy, and Thomas dissented in part.

The Court cleared the way for the trial of a major antitrust suit by nineteen states against four big U.S. insurance companies and London-based "reinsurance" companies, including the famous Lloyds of London. But the Court threw out some of the complaint and, by a 5-4 vote, set a difficult standard for the states to prevail.

The suit claimed that the U.S. insurers and the reinsurance concerns—which insure part of a primary insurer's coverage—violated federal antitrust law by conspiring to limit general commercial liability coverage during the so-called liability crisis of the mid-1980s.

A federal district court judge dismissed the case on the ground that the McCarran-Ferguson Act exempted the insurance industry from antitrust laws. But the Ninth U.S. Circuit Court of Appeals reinstated the bulk of the complaint. It ruled that the domestic insurers forfeited their antitrust immunity by conspiring with foreign concerns. It also held that the allegations amounted to an illegal boycott not immunized by the McCarran-Ferguson Act.

In its ruling, the Supreme Court broke into two shifting majorities. The Court first held that the U.S. insurers did not forfeit their immunity from antitrust law by dealing with foreign reinsurers. The vote was 9-0. All nine justices also agreed that an illegal boycott could still be the basis of a suit. But Scalia led a five-justice majority that narrowly defined a boycott so as to exclude some counts in the states' complaint.

Scalia distinguished between what he called "a conditional boycott," which would be illegal, and "a concerted agreement to seek particular terms in particular transactions," which would not be illegal in the insurance industry because of the antitrust exemption. A boycott, Scalia explained, consists only of an absolute or conditional refusal to deal with other parties on *unrelated* transactions. The unrelated transactions, he said, "are used as leverage to achieve the terms desired."

Using that definition Scalia said the insurers and reinsurers acted legally in working together to change industry practices to limit commercial liability coverage. But he said that the London reinsurers would be guilty of an illegal boycott if the states could show that they had refused altogether to deal with U.S. insurers that did not adopt the change. Rehnquist, O'Connor, Kennedy, and Thomas joined in that part of Scalia's opinion. Souter, joined by White, Blackmun, and Stevens, argued for a broader definition that would have saved almost all of the counts in the states' complaint.

The Court also held, 5-4, that principles of international comity did not require U.S. courts to refrain from exercising jurisdiction over the foreign reinsurers. Rehnquist joined with the Souter-led justices to form a majority on the issue. Scalia, O'Connor, Kennedy, and Thomas dissented.

United States Department of the Treasury v. Fabe, Superintendent of Insurance of Ohio, decided by a 5-4 vote, June 11, 1993; Blackmun wrote the opinion; Kennedy, Scalia, Souter, and Thomas dissented.

States can adopt laws to give policyholders of insolvent insurance companies priority over the federal government in settling claims in liquidation proceedings.

The Court's narrow majority held that an Ohio law giving policyholders first crack at any remaining assets of a failed insurer was protected from federal preemption. But the Court said that states cannot rank the federal government below other creditors, including employees and general business creditors.

The Ohio law established priority for claims against a failed insurance company as follows: administrative expenses, wage claims, policyholders' claims, general creditors' claims, and claims of federal, state, or local governments. In most insurance company reorganizations, the assets cannot satisfy all creditors.

The federal government challenged the law in the liquidation of the Ohio-based American Druggists' Insurance Company. It argued that a general federal statute giving the federal government first priority in any bankruptcy proceedings preempted the state law. The Supreme Court ruled, however, that the Ohio law was partly protected by another federal law, the McCarran-Ferguson Act. It provides that no federal statute can "supersede" any state law "enacted ... for the purpose of regulating the business of insurance."

Writing for the majority, Blackmun said that the Ohio law was protected from federal preemption "to the extent that it protects policyholders." On that basis, he said Ohio could give priority to policyholders' claims and administrative expenses of the liquidation proceeding, but could not rank the federal government below other creditors. The dissenting justices argued that the state law was about bankruptcy instead of insurance and was thus preempted by the general federal priority statute.

Patents

Cardinal Chemical Co. v. Morton International, Inc., decided by a 9-0 vote, May 17, 1993; Stevens wrote the opinion.

The federal court that hears appeals in patent cases was directed to discontinue its practice of automatically refusing to rule on the validity of a patent if it first rejects a claim that the patent has been infringed.

In a unanimous decision, the Supreme Court found no legal or policy reasons for the practice adopted by the U.S. Court of Appeals for the Federal Circuit in 1987. In adopting the policy, the appeals court reasoned that the validity of a patent becomes a moot point if the holder of the disputed patent fails to prove its infringement claim.

Patent lawyers and companies involved in patent cases, however, argued that the practice caused uncertainty, confusion, and unnecessary relitigation of patent disputes. Both parties in the case before the High Court urged the policy be ended.

Writing for the Court, Stevens said the policy should be changed because of the "strong public interest in the finality of judgments in patent litigation."

Securities

Musick, Peeler & Garrett v. Employers Insurance of Wausau, decided by a 6-3 vote, June 1, 1993; Kennedy wrote the opinion; Thomas, Blackmun, and O'Connor dissented.

Defendants in federal securities fraud cases may seek to force parties not named in the suits to pay part of the damages if they have joint responsibility for the securities law violations.

The 1934 Securities Act did not explicitly authorize private antifraud suits, but the Supreme Court in 1975 upheld a so-called implied right of action under the Securities and Exchange Commission's Rule 10b-5. In this case, the Court said that it would also imply a "right of contribution" in Rule 10b-5 suits to avoid unfairness to defendants required to pay damages.

The decision sustained a suit by an insurance company representing a San Diego retail furniture chain and its officers that had paid a $13 million settlement to investors for an allegedly misleading stock offering. The insurer then sued attorneys and accountants involved in the offering to force them to pay part of the settlement. Most lower federal courts that had ruled on the issue had recognized a right of contribution in securities fraud suits. The dissenting justices argued that the Court should not further expand 10b-5 suits.

Taxation

Bufferd v. Commissioner of Internal Revenue, decided by a 9-0 vote, January 25, 1993; White wrote the opinion.

The time for the Internal Revenue Service (IRS) to challenge tax benefits of shareholders of certain types of small businesses runs from the date of the shareholder's tax return instead of the date of the business's return.

Shareholders of so-called Subchapter S corporations may claim a portion of the corporation's losses or deductions on their individual tax returns. The shareholder in this case claimed a loss deduction based on the corporation's tax return for the prior year.

When the IRS challenged the deduction, the taxpayer argued the agency had failed to act within three years of the corporation's return. The Court, however, ruled unanimously that the filing date of the shareholder's return was the relevant date.

Commissioner of Internal Revenue v. Soliman, decided by an 8-1 vote, January 12, 1993; Kennedy wrote the opinion; Stevens dissented.

The Court made it harder for a self-employed taxpayer to claim a deduction for home office expenses by tightening the rules for determining whether the home office is the taxpayer's "principal place of business." Generally, the Court said, taxpayers must spend most of their time or do the most important part of their business at home in order to qualify for the deduction.

The ruling rejected a deduction claimed by an anesthesiologist who performed medical duties at hospitals but handled paper work in a spare room in his home. The Tax Court and the Fourth U.S. Circuit Court of Appeals allowed him to claim the expenses as a deduction on the ground that he had no office space at hospitals.

Writing for the Court, Kennedy said that approach did not follow the statutory provision for deducting expenses if the home office was the taxpayer's "principal place of business." In applying that test, Kennedy said, courts should make "a comparative analysis of the [taxpayer's] various business locations." Primary consideration, he said, should be given to "the relative importance of the activities performed at each business location and the time spent at each place."

Thomas, joined by Scalia, concurred separately. Thomas said the Court's test was "unclear" and would require "full-blown evidentiary hearings" whenever a home office deduction was challenged. He said a deduction should be allowed only when the home office was the "focal point" of a taxpayer's business—"the place where the taxpayer renders the services for which he is paid or sells his goods."

In a dissent, Stevens said the decision would "unfairly penalize deserving taxpayers."

Newark Morning Ledger Co., as Successor to The Herald Company v. United States, decided by a 5-4 vote, April 20, 1993; Blackmun wrote the opinion; Souter, Rehnquist, White, and Scalia dissented.

A business taxpayer is entitled to take a depreciation deduction for the value of a customer list if it can show that the customers' continued patronage has a value that diminishes over time.

The closely divided ruling—a multibillion-dollar victory for businesses—rejected the argument by the Internal Revenue Service (IRS) that customer lists are part of a company's "goodwill." Under the IRS's position, the value of the lists was a capital asset that could not be depreciated but could be offset against any capital gains if the business was later sold.

The decision allowed a deduction for newspaper subscriber lists valued at $67.8 million that a New Jersey-based company acquired when it purchased a chain of eight Michigan newspapers. The Court wrote the ruling broadly to apply to all types of "customer-based intangibles," ranging from insurance policies and bank deposits to cleaning-service accounts and prescription drug files.

Writing for the five-justice majority, Blackmun said that a taxpayer may depreciate the value of a customer list if it shows that the list has "an ascertainable value and a limited useful life, the duration of which can be ascertained with reasonable accuracy." Blackmun said the burden of proof to separate the value of the list from a business's goodwill would often be "too difficult" for the taxpayer, but the business was entitled to try. The ruling would turn on the facts of each case, he said.

Souter, writing for the four dissenters, said the newspaper subscriber list was "unmistakably a direct measurement of goodwill." He said the decision went against well-established tax regulations and federal court rulings that set a per se rule against depreciation of goodwill.

United States v. Hill, decided by a 9-0 vote, January 25, 1993; Souter wrote the opinion.

The Court limited a tax break used by investors in exploration for oil, gas, coal, or other minerals.

The unanimous decision prevented taxpayers from using the cost of tools and equipment to increase the income sheltered under the percentage depletion allowance. This controversial tax provision is intended to take account of the "depletion" of mineral deposits as they are extracted. But it can be calculated to allow tax deductions in excess of the taxpayer's actual investment.

In a densely written opinion, the Court held that the cost of tangible items such as tools and equipment could not be included in the taxpayer's investment—his "adjusted basis"—in the mineral deposit. Instead, the Court said, those costs can be deducted only according to normal, less generous depreciation rules.

The government had warned that a broader interpretation could have cost $1 billion a year in tax revenue.

United States by and through Internal Revenue Service v. McDermott, decided by a 6-3 vote, March 24, 1993; Scalia wrote the opinion; Thomas, Stevens, and O'Connor dissented.

The Court gave the Internal Revenue Service preference in seeking to collect unpaid taxes from people who also owe money to private creditors.

The case involved how to determine the priority of creditors' competing "liens" on property owned by the debtor. Ordinarily, the creditor who "perfects" a lien first has first claim on the property.

Applying that principle, the Court held that a federal tax lien filed before a delinquent taxpayer acquires real property must generally be given priority over a private creditor's lien in the same property. The Court said that under federal law, a federal tax lien is dated from the filing of the lien, while the creditor's lien cannot attach until after the debtor acquires the property.

Courts and Procedure

Evidence

Daubert v. Merrell Dow Pharmaceuticals, Inc., decided by votes of 9-0 and 7-2, June 28, 1993; Blackmun wrote the opinion; Rehnquist and Stevens dissented in part.

The Court threw out a strict rule for limiting the use of scientific evidence in federal courts, but told federal judges they should act as "gatekeepers" to make sure such evidence is "not only relevant, but reliable."

The Court unanimously held that the liberal Federal Rules of Evidence governed the use of scientific testimony in federal courts. The ruling scrapped a seventy-year-old case, *Frye v. United States* (1923), that required "general acceptance" of a scientific method or theory before it could be used in trials.

Writing for seven of the justices, however, Blackmun went on to say that federal judges were required under the rules to screen scientific evidence. "[T]he Rules of Evidence . . . assign to the trial judge the task of ensuring that an expert's testimony both rests on a reliable foundation and is relevant to the task at hand," Blackmun wrote.

Rehnquist, joined by Stevens, agreed with the Court's initial ruling, but dissented from the additional directions to federal judges. Rehnquist said federal judges were not required to become "amateur scientists" to rule on scientific evidence. *(See entry, p. 40; excerpts, p. 205.)*

Federal Courts

Church of Scientology of California v. United States, decided by a 9-0 vote, November 16, 1992; Stevens wrote the opinion.

A taxpayer may go to court to challenge the Internal Revenue Service's efforts to obtain confidential records even if the records have already been turned over to the IRS.

The issue arose in a protracted dispute between the IRS and the Church of Scientology. The IRS obtained under court order tape recordings of conversations between church officials and their attorneys. The church claimed the conversations were privileged, but the tapes were turned over while the issue was being appealed. At that point, a federal appeals court dismissed the church's case as moot because the tapes had already been turned over.

The Supreme Court unanimously disagreed, saying that a court could still grant the church some legal relief. Stevens explained that even though the government had already received the tapes, a court could order the IRS to destroy or return any copies. "The availability of this possible remedy," he wrote, "is sufficient to prevent this case from being moot."

Keene Corp. v. United States, decided by an 8-1 vote, May 24, 1993; Souter wrote the opinion; Stevens dissented.

The Court upheld the dismissal of claims filed by a manufacturer of asbestos products against the United States in the Court of Federal Claims because the company had filed similar claims in federal district courts.

In a significant but highly technical ruling, the Court declined to create an exception to a federal law that bars the Court of Federal Claims from exercising jurisdiction over a claim if the plaintiff has a similar suit "pending in any other court." Keene Corporation had filed actions in two federal district courts and in the Court of Federal Claims seeking reimbursement from the United States for costs and damages it had paid in asbestos litigation. The company dropped the district court suits before the claims court ruled. But the Supreme Court said the provision barring jurisdiction still applied.

In a dissent, Stevens said the statutory langauge did not require the "harsh result" in the case.

Indigents

Rowland, Former Director, California Department of Corrections v. California Men's Colony, Unit II Men's Advisory Council, decided by a 5-4 vote, January 12, 1993; Souter wrote the opinion; Thomas, Blackmun, Stevens, and Kennedy dissented.

Only individuals—not groups, associations, or corporations—qualify as "persons" who may be entitled to bring a federal court suit without paying filing fees and other court costs.

A group of California inmates challenging a decision to discontinue free tobacco for prisoners tried to bring their suit under a federal law that spares poor litigants the need to prepay fees, costs, or appeal bonds. A federal district court judge rejected the request, but the Ninth U.S. Circuit Court of Appeals ruled that an "association" could be treated as a "person" under the law.

In a 5-4 decision, the Court disagreed. Writing for the majority, Souter listed four contextual features that he said showed Congress intended "person" in this law to refer only to natural persons. Associations or corporations are not ordinarily described as poor, Souter said, and it would be difficult to adopt standards for determining when they were unable to pay court fees.

In a dissent, Thomas argued that the decision ignored another federal law generally requiring "person" to be interpreted to include associations or corporations. He also said the ruling was based on policy considerations that were for Congress rather than the Court to decide.

Criminal Law

Appeals

Ortega-Rodriguez v. United States, decided by a 5-4 vote, March 8, 1993; Stevens wrote the opinion; Rehnquist, White, O'Connor, and Thomas dissented.

The Court struck down a federal appeals court rule prescribing automatic dismissal of an appeal by a defendant who becomes a fugitive while awaiting sentencing but is recaptured before filing an appeal.

Since 1876 the Court had recognized that an appellate court may dismiss an appeal by a defendant who is at large while the appeal is pending. In 1975 the Court also upheld a Texas law mandating dismissal of a fugitive's appeal. In this case, however, the Court said that the automatic fugitive appeal dismissal rule adopted by the Eleventh U.S. Circuit Court of Appeals went too far. Writing for the five-justice majority, Stevens said the appeals court did not have sufficient interest in the defendant's escape while the defendant was still awaiting sentencing by the district court. "Absent some connection between a defendant's fugitive status and his appeal . . . the justifications advanced for dismissal of fugitives' pending appeals generally will not apply," Stevens wrote.

Rehnquist, writing for the dissenters, argued that a defendant's escape imposed a burden on the appellate courts whether or not the defendant had already started the appeal.

Capital Punishment

Arave, Warden v. Creech, decided by a 7-2 vote, March 30, 1993; O'Connor wrote the opinion; Blackmun and Stevens dissented.

The Court upheld a provision of Idaho's capital punishment statute allowing the death penalty for murderers who show "utter disregard for human life." The ruling came in the case of an Idaho prisoner who had pleaded guilty to fatally beating another inmate.

The justices, overturning a federal appeals court decision that the law was too vague, said that the Idaho Supreme Court had adequately narrowed the aggravating circumstance to refer to a "cold-blooded, pitiless slayer." O'Connor said the Idaho court's interpretation "defines a state of mind that is ascertainable from surrounding facts." She also said the provision satisfied a second rule that a capital sentencing scheme must "genuinely narrow the class of defendants eligible for the death penalty."

Blackmun, in a dissent joined by Stevens, called the Idaho court's construction of the law "vague and unenlightening." The case was remanded for resentencing on other issues.

Herrera v. Collins, Director, Texas Department of Criminal Justice, Institutional Division, decided by a 6-3 vote, January 25, 1993; Rehnquist wrote the opinion; Blackmun, Stevens, and Souter dissented.

A death row inmate ordinarily is not entitled to federal habeas corpus relief based solely on a claim that he is actually innocent. The inmate must also have an independent claim of constitutional error in his state court trial or other proceedings.

The ruling came in the case of a Texas prisoner, Leonel Herrera, sentenced to death for the killing of a police officer in 1981. Ten years after his conviction, Herrera filed a federal habeas corpus petition—his second—claiming that newly discovered evidence showed someone else committed the crime. On that basis, he argued that his execution would violate the Eighth Amendment's ban on cruel and unusual punishment and the Fourteenth Amendment's Due Process Clause.

The Court, however, said federal courts should not consider Herrera's "actual innocence" claim. "[F]ederal habeas courts sit to ensure that individuals are not imprisoned in violation of the Constitution—not to correct errors of fact," Rehnquist wrote.

On the due process issue, Rehnquist said the refusal of Texas courts to consider Herrera's new evidence so long after his conviction did not violate "principles of fundamental fairness." He also said Herrera could still seek executive clemency, which Rehnquist called the "historic remedy for preventing miscarriages of justice." Rehnquist concluded by saying that even if a "truly persuasive demonstration of 'actual innocence' made after trial would render an execution unconstitutional," Herrera's evidence "falls far short of any such threshold."

Dissenting justices argued that a death row inmate should be granted a federal habeas hearing if he can show that he is "probably innocent." *(See entry, p. 35; excerpts, p. 118.)*

Johnson v. Texas, decided by a 5-4 vote, June 24, 1993; Kennedy wrote the opinion; O'Connor, Blackmun, Stevens, and Souter dissented.

Texas's former capital punishment law adequately allowed juries to consider a defendant's youth as a mitigating factor in deciding whether to impose the death penalty.

The closely divided Court rejected for a second time this term a challenge to sentences imposed under the law, which was in effect from 1976 to 1991. The law provided the death penalty in first-degree murder cases if a jury found the murder was committed deliberately and the defendant would probably commit violent crimes in the future. Dorsie Johnson, convicted of killing a convenience store clerk when he was nineteen years old, challenged his death sentence on the ground that this so-called "special issues" procedure did not allow the jury to consider his youth as a mitigating factor.

Rejecting the argument, Kennedy said that the jury was not prevented from considering "the relevant aspects" of the defendant's youth. "We believe that there is ample room in the assessment of future dangerousness for a juror to take account of the difficulties of youth as a mitigating force in the sentencing determination," Kennedy wrote.

The dissenting justices countered that the procedure did not allow the jury to give "full effect" to the defendant's youth. "[N]ot one of the special issues under the former Texas scheme allows a jury to give effect to the most relevant mitigating aspect of youth: its relation to a defendant's culpability for the crime he committed," O'Connor wrote.

Johnson's case reached the Court directly from the Texas Supreme Court. Earlier in the term, the justices rejected a similar challenge to the Texas procedure in a federal habeas corpus case, *Graham v. Collins. (See p. 64.)*

Richmond v. Lewis, Director, Arizona Department of Corrections, decided by an 8-1 vote, December 1, 1992; O'Connor wrote the opinion; Scalia dissented.

An Arizona murderer twice sentenced to death won a reprieve because a lower court judge used an unconstitutionally vague sentencing factor and the state's supreme court failed to correct the error.

The Court's rare ruling for a death row inmate came in the case of a man sentenced for a 1973 robbery-murder. His original death sentence was thrown out in 1978, but he was given a second capital sentence in 1980. The Arizona Supreme Court upheld the sentence in 1983, and federal courts rejected the inmate's petition for habeas corpus relief.

The Supreme Court, however, ruled that a state law provision permitting the death penalty for an "especially heinous, cruel or depraved" murder tainted the defendant's second sentence. The factor was one of three the judge cited in imposing the death sentence. O'Connor said that the provision was "facially vague." In affirming the sentence, she said, the Arizona Supreme Court had not adequately reweighed aggravating and mitigating circumstances to correct the error.

Scalia, in a lone dissent, said the death penalty should be upheld because of the two other valid aggravating circumstances.

Criminal Procedure

Crosby v. United States, decided by a 9-0 vote, January 13, 1993; Blackmun wrote the opinion.

A court cannot try a defendant in his absence if the defendant is not present at the beginning of the trial.

The ruling limited the use of a federal rule of criminal procedure that permits a trial to proceed in the defendant's absence if he "is voluntarily absent after the trial has commenced." On the basis of that rule, a federal district court had conducted a trial in a complex mail fraud case even though one of the defendants had absconded and was not present for the start of the trial.

In a brief, unanimous opinion, Blackmun said that "the language and structure of the rule" strictly limited the circumstances for permitting an *in absentia* trial. By basing its decision on the federal rule, the Court put off the question of whether the Constitution itself prohibits a court from beginning a trial with the defendant absent.

Fex v. Michigan, decided by a 7-2 vote, February 23, 1993; Scalia wrote the opinion; Blackmun and Stevens dissented.

The 180-day limit for bringing a prisoner to trial on a charge lodged by another state begins when prosecutors receive the prisoner's request to dispose of the charge, not when the prisoner makes the request.

The ruling backed states and the federal government in interpreting a provision of the Interstate Agreement on Detainers that gives prisoners the right to demand resolution of charges pending against them in another state. A detainer is a legal notice sent by one state to another asking that a prisoner be held on charges pending in the first state. The case arose after an Indiana inmate was brought to trial in Michigan 177 days after

Michigan authorities received his request to settle the case but 196 days after the inmate gave his request to the Indiana prison warden for delivery.

Writing for the Court, Scalia said the language of the deadline provision was ambiguous, but appeared to envision delivery of the request as the trigger for the deadline. Dissenting justices argued that interpretation would defeat the purpose of providing "a swift and certain means for resolving the uncertainties and alleviating the disabilities created by outstanding detainers."

Godinez, Warden v. Moran, decided by a 7-2 vote, June 24, 1993; Thomas wrote the opinion; Blackmun and Stevens dissented.

A defendant who is found mentally competent to stand trial is not entitled to a stricter evaluation of his mental competence to plead guilty or waive the right to counsel.

The Court refused to tighten the standard it adopted in 1960, which requires a defendant be able to understand the charges against him and to consult with a lawyer to be found competent to stand trial. "[W]e can conceive of no basis for demanding a higher level of competence for those defendants who choose to plead guilty," Thomas wrote. The decision overturned a ruling by the Ninth U.S. Circuit Court of Appeals that had ordered a new competency hearing for a Nevada man sentenced to death for two barroom killings and to life imprisonment for the murder of his wife. After psychiatrists found him mentally competent, the man fired his public defender and pleaded guilty to the charges.

Blackmun, in a dissent joined by Stevens, agreed with the appeals court that a higher standard of competence should be required before permitting a defendant to waive his rights to trial and counsel. He also said the guilty plea may have resulted from mental illness or medication.

Zafiro v. United States, decided by a 9-0 vote, January 25, 1993; O'Connor wrote the opinion.

Codefendants are not entitled to separate trials under federal rules of criminal procedure merely because they plan to present "mutually antagonistic" defenses.

Instead, O'Connor wrote, a defendant has a right to a "severance" of his case "only if there is serious risk that a joint trial would compromise a specific trial right . . . or prevent the jury from making a reliable judgment about guilt or innocence."

The decision unanimously upheld rulings by lower federal courts that permitted a joint trial of four defendants in a cocaine conspiracy case. Stevens did not join O'Connor's opinion, however. He said that the defendants' defenses were not inconsistent and that the broader legal question did not need to be decided.

Double Jeopardy

United States v. Dixon and Foster, decided by votes of 5-4 and 6-3, June 28, 1993; Scalia wrote the opinion; White, Blackmun, Stevens, and Souter dissented on the main legal issue; Rehnquist, Blackmun, O'Connor, and Thomas dissented from the result in *Dixon;* White, Stevens, and Souter dissented from the result in *Foster.*

The Court eased the constitutional bar against double jeopardy by scrapping a three-year-old precedent and holding that multiple prosecutions are permitted if the two offenses contain different elements.

The justices voted 5-4 to overturn the earlier ruling, *Grady v. Corbin* (1990). In that decision, the Court had broadened the double jeopardy provision to bar multiple prosecutions whenever the two offenses involved the same conduct. Scalia, who had led four dissenters in the 1990 case, said the ruling contradicted earlier cases, contained inaccurate historical analysis, and had produced confusion in lower court rulings. Thomas, who joined the Court in 1991, voted to overturn the ruling, along with the other previous dissenters: Rehnquist, O'Connor, and Kennedy.

The four justices who voted to retain the stricter "same-conduct" test said that the new ruling weakened the constitutional safeguard against successive prosecutions.

The justices broke into different majorities in applying the double jeopardy rule to the two cases before them. Both involved criminal contempt convictions that were followed by prosecutions for substantive offenses. In one, the Court voted 5-4 to bar the drug prosecution of a defendant, Alvin Dixon, earlier convicted of contempt for violating a court order not to commit any crimes while on probation for a previous offense. Scalia and Kennedy said Dixon's later prosecution was barred even under the eased double jeopardy rule. White, Stevens, and Souter joined in voting to block the second prosecution.

In the other case, however, the Court voted 6-3 to uphold most of an assault indictment against a domestic violence defendant. Michael Foster had already been convicted of criminal contempt for violating a court order not to "assault or threaten" his estranged wife. Scalia and Kennedy found that four of the five counts in Foster's new indictment required proof of elements different from the contempt prosecution and were therefore permissible under the "same elements" test.

Rehnquist, O'Connor, and Thomas voted in both cases to permit the subsequent prosecutions. Blackmun voted separately to permit the subsequent prosecutions in both cases. He argued that double jeopardy does not apply to criminal contempt proceedings.

Forfeiture

Alexander v. United States, decided by a 5-4 vote, June 28, 1993; Rehnquist wrote the opinion; Kennedy, Blackmun, Stevens, and Souter dissented.

The seizure of a chain of adult bookstores and destruction of their entire inventory under the forfeiture provisions of the federal antiracketeering law did not violate the First Amendment.

The government had seized the stores and inventory following Ferris Alexander's conviction on seventeen obscenity counts and three counts of violating the Racketeer Influenced and Corrupt Organizations Act (RICO). Alexander, who operated thirteen adult bookstores and theaters in Minnesota valued at about $25 million, was also given a six-year prison sentence and $100,000 fine.

In a 5-4 decision, the Court rejected arguments that the forfeiture was an impermissible prior restraint; rather, it was aimed at punishing past conduct instead of suppressing speech. "[T]he assets in question were not ordered forfeited because they were believed to be obscene," Rehnquist wrote, "but because they were directly related to [Alexander's] past racketeering violations." Rehnquist also said the forfeiture had "no more of a chilling effect on free expression than threat of a prison term or large fine."

The Court remanded the case to a federal appeals court, however, to reconsider Alexander's claim that the forfeiture violated the Eighth Amendment's prohibitions against "excessive fines." Rehnquist said that the amendment does limit criminal forfeitures—citing the Court's companion decision the same day in *Austin v. United States.* But he said the appeals court should weigh Alexander's claim "in the light of the extensive criminal activities which [Alexander] apparently conducted through this racketeering enterprise over a substantial period of time."

In a dissenting opinion, Kennedy called the ruling "a grave repudiation of First Amendment principles."

Austin v. United States, decided by a 9-0 vote, June 28, 1993; Blackmun wrote the opinion.

The Eighth Amendment's prohibition against excessive fines limits the government's power in civil forfeiture proceedings to seize the property of criminals or suspects.

The Court's unanimous decision—along with its ruling the same day in a criminal forfeiture case, *Alexander v. United States*—marked the first broad constitutional limit on the government's increasing use of forfeiture in drug trafficking, racketeering, money-laundering, and other offenses. The ruling came in the case of a South Dakota man whose mobile home and auto body shop were seized by the government in a civil forfeiture proceeding after he had pleaded guilty in a state drug case.

The Court rejected the government's argument that the Eighth Amendment did not apply to the civil proceeding or that the amendment's Excessive Fines Clause did not apply to forfeiture. "The purpose of the Eighth Amendment . . . was to limit the government's power to punish," Blackmun wrote for five of the justices.

Scalia and Kennedy wrote separate concurrences agreeing with the result but differing with Blackmun's interpretation of the history of forfeitures. Rehnquist and Thomas joined Kennedy's opinion. *(See entry, p. 33; excerpts, p. 196.)*

Republic National Bank of Miami v. United States, decided by a 9-0 vote, December 14, 1992; Blackmun and Rehnquist wrote opinions.

A federal appeals court can rule on the government's seizure of a house under the drug forfeiture law even if the house has been sold and the proceeds deposited to the federal Treasury.

The unanimous ruling reinstated an appeal by a Miami bank, which had contested the forfeiture under the "innocent owner" defense. The lower court had rejected the bank's argument, and the government sold the house while the appeal was pending.

Blackmun wrote the Court's main opinion, easily rejecting the government's claim that the appeals court no longer had jurisdiction. The justices divided, however, on a second issue: whether the Constitution's Appropriations Clause would prevent a lower court from ordering the government to pay the money to the bank. Rehnquist—writing for six justices—said that a general appropriations law authorizing payment of money judgments would cover the situation. Blackmun, joined by Stevens and O'Connor, argued instead that no congressional appropriation was needed because the proceeds were not "public money" if the forfeiture was invalid.

United States v. A Parcel of Land, Buildings, Appurtenances and Improvements, known as 92 Buena Vista Avenue, Rumson, New Jersey, decided by a 6-3 vote, February 24, 1993; Stevens wrote the main opinion; Kennedy, Rehnquist, and White dissented.

The government cannot seize property bought with drug money after it has been given to or purchased by someone who can show she had no knowledge of the source of the funds.

The decision said the "innocent owner" defense included in a 1978 drug forfeiture law was not limited to "bona fide purchasers" but could also be used by someone who was given property. The Court also rejected the government's argument that it could claim ownership of property from the time it was purchased with proceeds of illegal transactions.

Stevens' plurality opinion was joined by Blackmun, O'Connor, and Souter. Scalia, joined by Thomas, reached the same result by different reasoning.

In a dissent, Kennedy argued that the decision "rips out the most effective enforcement provisions in all of the drug forfeiture laws."

Habeas Corpus

Brecht v. Abrahamson, Superintendent, Dodge Correctional Institution, decided by a 5-4 vote, April 21, 1993; Rehnquist wrote the opinion; White, Blackmun, O'Connor, and Souter dissented.

Improper use at trial of a defendant's silence after being given *Miranda* warnings is not ground for federal habeas corpus relief unless the evidence had a substantial effect on the verdict.

Writing for a five-justice majority, Rehnquist announced a relaxed rule for reviewing trial-related errors in habeas corpus cases. Previously, the Court had required that errors be proved harmless beyond a reasonable doubt. Under the new standard, habeas corpus relief is available only if an error had "substantial and injurious effect or influence in determining the jury's verdict."

The decision upheld the first-degree murder conviction of a man who claimed at trial that the fatal shooting of his brother-in-law was an accident. The prosecutor tried to discredit the testimony by pointing out that the defendant had not told that story before trial. Rehnquist said the prosecutor's remarks violated the Supreme Court's rule in an earlier case, *Doyle v. Ohio* (1976), prohibiting mention of a suspect's post-*Miranda* silence. But Rehnquist said the references were "infrequent" and did not influence the verdict.

Dissenting justices objected to adopting a different harmless error standard for habeas corpus cases from that used in direct appeals.

Gilmore v. Taylor, decided by a 7-2 vote, June 7, 1993; Rehnquist wrote the opinion; Blackmun and Stevens dissented.

The Court refused to grant federal habeas relief based on a decision finding a constitutional defect in part of the standard jury instructions used in Illinois murder cases.

The Court said the federal appeals court decision amounted to a "new" rule that a prisoner could not use to upset a state court conviction that had already been upheld on direct appeal. The ruling barred relief for a defendant whose murder conviction had been upheld by Illinois appellate courts in 1989. In his habeas corpus petition, he invoked a ruling by the Seventh U.S. Circuit Court of Appeals in 1990 that the Illinois jury instructions violated due process by failing to direct jurors on voluntary manslaughter. Applying the Court's ruling in *Teague v. Lane*

(1989), however, Rehnquist said the appeals court decision was not "dictated" by precedent and therefore could not be applied retroactively in habeas cases.

Dissenting justices argued that the appeals court ruling fell within an exception that permits new rulings involving issues of "fundamental fairness" to be applied in habeas cases.

Graham v. Collins, Director, Texas Department of Criminal Justice, Institutional Division, decided by a 5-4 vote, January 25, 1993; White wrote the opinion; Souter, Blackmun, Stevens, and O'Connor dissented.

The Court turned aside a Texas death row inmate's argument that the state's former capital punishment law improperly limited a jury's role in considering evidence favorable to defendants.

The Court rejected the inmate's federal habeas corpus petition on the ground that he was asking for a new rule of constitutional law. In a 1989 decision, *Teague v. Lane,* the Court said that it will not announce new constitutional rulings in habeas corpus cases except in two limited circumstances. The justices extensively debated the former Texas law, which was changed in 1991, even though they technically did not rule on it. Later in the term, the Court voted in another case, *Johnson v. Texas,* to uphold the procedure. *(See p. 57.)*

Under the so-called "special issues" procedure, a defendant was given a death sentence if a jury gave affirmative answers to two questions: whether the murder was deliberate and whether the defendant would commit violent crimes again. Gary Graham, convicted of killing a grocery store customer when he was seventeen years old, argued in his habeas corpus petition that the law prevented the jury from considering mitigating evidence about his youth, family background, and character.

Writing for the five-justice majority, White said the Texas law would not have been found invalid in 1984 when Graham exhausted his first round of appeals. White said the procedure "permitted [Graham] to place before the jury whatever mitigating evidence he could show ... while focusing the jury's attention upon what that evidence revealed about the defendant's capacity for deliberation and prospects for rehabilitation."

Dissenting justices argued that the Texas procedure violated the Court's precedents requiring that a jury be able to give "full weight" to mitigating evidence.

Withrow v. Williams, decided by a 5-4 vote, April 21, 1993; Souter wrote the opinion; O'Connor, Rehnquist, Scalia, and Thomas dissented.

Federal courts in habeas corpus cases may throw out state court convictions when police fail to advise a suspect of his *Miranda* rights before interrogating him.

The decision ordered a new trial for a defendant in a double murder case who had confessed without having been advised of his right to remain silent. State courts had found no *Miranda* violation. In granting the inmate's bid for a new trial, the Court narrowly refused to extend an earlier decision, *Stone v. Powell* (1976), that generally bars federal habeas corpus relief based on illegal searches or seizures. Souter explained that the *Miranda* guidelines "safeguard a fundamental trial right" and help prevent the use of "unreliable statements" at trial. In addition, he said, excluding *Miranda* claims from habeas proceedings would not reduce the federal courts' caseloads because prisoners could still challenge confessions as involuntary.

O'Connor, in a dissent joined by Rehnquist, said, "[T]he interests of federalism, finality, and fairness compel *Miranda's* exclusion from habeas." Scalia, in a separate dissent joined by Thomas, went further. He argued that most legal claims should be barred from federal habeas proceedings if the defendant had a "full and fair opportunity" to raise the issue in state courts.

Juries

Sullivan v. Louisiana, decided by a 9-0 vote, June 1, 1993; Scalia wrote the opinion.

A criminal conviction must be thrown out if a jury is not properly instructed on the need for proof beyond a reasonable doubt before returning a guilty verdict.

The Court unanimously said that an improper instruction on the reasonable doubt standard can never be deemed a harmless error that does not require reversal. In a brief opinion, Scalia said that an erroneous instruction on the issue "vitiates *all* the jury's findings" in a case.

The decision ordered a new trial for a Louisiana man originally sentenced to death for a 1980 barroom shooting. His death sentence previously had been reduced to life imprisonment because of ineffective assistance of counsel during the sentencing hearing.

United States v. Olano, decided by a 6-3 vote, April 26, 1993; O'Connor wrote the opinion; Stevens, White, and Blackmun dissented.

A federal appeals court may not reverse a criminal conviction on its own because a trial judge wrongly allowed alternate jurors to be present during jury deliberations.

The ruling upheld the conviction of two savings and loan executives in a loan kickback case. The defendants failed to object when the trial judge suggested that two alternates be allowed to watch—but not take part in—the jury's deliberations.

Writing for the Court, O'Connor acknowledged the mistake was a "plain error," but said it did not affect "substantial rights" because there was no evidence the alternate jurors had participated in or chilled the jurors' deliberations.

Stevens, in a dissent joined by White and Blackmun, argued that the appeals court had discretion to reverse the convictions "to protect the integrity of jury deliberations."

Prisons and Jails

Helling v. McKinney, decided by a 7-2 vote, June 18, 1993; White wrote the opinion; Thomas and Scalia dissented.

The Court opened the door to prison inmate suits claiming that involuntary exposure to second-hand tobacco smoke poses an unreasonable risk to health in violation of the Eighth Amendment's ban on cruel and unusual punishment.

The 7-2 ruling, however, laid out a number of conditions an inmate must meet to prevail in a suit over so-called environmental tobacco smoke (ETS). The decision returned to lower federal courts a suit brought by a Nevada state prisoner who had been housed in a cell with another inmate who smoked five packs of cigarettes a day.

Writing for the majority, White rejected an argument by Nevada officials that the Eighth Amendment protects inmates only against current and not future harm. He also rejected as premature an argument by the federal government urging dismissal of the suit on the ground that the harm from second-hand smoke was too speculative. On remand, White said the inmate would have to prove that he was being exposed to "unreasonably high levels" of ETS and that the risk "is not one that today's society chooses to tolerate." In addition, White said, the inmate must show that Nevada officials had been guilty of "deliberate indifference" in exposing him to ETS.

By the time of the decision, the inmate had been moved to a new prison and was no longer a cellmate of the five-pack-a-day smoker. Moreover, Nevada officials had adopted a policy separating smoking and nonsmoking prisoners where possible and prohibiting smoking in most common areas. White said the new policy might make it "impossible" for the inmate to prove his case.

Thomas, in a dissent joined by Scalia, repeated arguments they made unsuccessfully in a 1992 decision, *Hudson v. McMillian,* that the Eighth Amendment should not apply to prison conditions. In any event, Thomas said, the amendment should not be extended to cover "the risk of injury" to a prison inmate.

Right to Counsel

Lockhart, Director, Arkansas Department of Correction v. Fretwell, decided by a 7-2 vote, January 25, 1993; Rehnquist wrote the opinion; Stevens and Blackmun dissented.

A death row inmate lost a bid for a new trial based on his attorney's failure to raise an objection at trial under a court decision on the books at the time but later overturned.

The Court rejected the inmate's argument that the lawyer's "deficient performance" amounted to ineffective assistance of counsel in violation of the Sixth Amendment. Instead, the seven-justice majority said, the inmate had not suffered any "prejudice" as defined in earlier cases dealing with the effective assistance of counsel.

An Arkansas jury had sentenced the inmate to death in 1985 for a robbery-murder. The judge used a jury instruction that was invalid under a case on the books at the time, but the defense attorney did not object. Although the legal rule was thrown out in 1989, a federal appeals court in 1991 granted the inmate a new trial. Writing for the Supreme Court, Rehnquist said that to win a new trial a defendant must show that a lawyer's errors made a proceeding "unreliable [or] fundamentally unfair."

Stevens, in a dissent joined by Blackmun, complained that the ruling gave the state a "windfall" by allowing it to "carry out a death sentence that was invalid when imposed."

Search and Seizure

Minnesota v. Dickerson, decided by a 6-3 vote, June 7, 1993; White wrote the opinion; Rehnquist, Blackmun, and Thomas dissented in part.

Police may seize drugs or other contraband from a suspect if they can feel the material during a limited "stop-and-frisk" search for weapons.

The Court unanimously adopted a "plain feel" exception to the general rule requiring police to have either a warrant or probable cause to believe a crime has been committed before searching a suspect. White said that the "plain feel" exception would not interfere with a suspect's privacy rights any more than already allowed under Court rulings permitting a limited patdown for weapons. But White said police could seize material only if they felt it through the suspect's outer clothing and if its identity as contraband was "immediately apparent."

The justices split 6-3 in applying the new exception to the Minnesota drug case that raised the issue. White said the officer who found a package of cocaine in a suspect's jacket should have stopped once he determined the material was not a weapon. Rehnquist, Blackmun, and Thomas said they would have returned the case to Minnesota courts for a new hearing on the officer's search.

United States v. Padilla, decided by a 9-0 vote, May 3, 1993; *per curiam* opinion.

Criminal co-conspirators have no legal right to contest police searches of one another's cars, homes, or other possessions.

The Court unanimously threw out a rule adopted by a single federal appeals court—the Ninth U.S. Circuit Court of Appeals—that granted co-conspirators legal "standing" to challenge searches of each other's belongings. In a brief, unsigned decision, the Supreme Court said the rule "squarely contradicts" a 1969 precedent. A co-conspirator must prove an individual property or privacy right to block a police search, the Court said.

The ruling overturned a decision in favor of an accused drug trafficker who had challenged a police search of a car being driven by an alleged courier. Lower courts had ruled police had no legal grounds for the search, which uncovered 560 pounds of cocaine.

Sentencing

Deal v. United States, decided by a 6-3 vote, May 17, 1993; Scalia wrote the opinion; Stevens, Blackmun, and O'Connor dissented.

A federal law providing a mandatory twenty-year sentence for a "second or subsequent conviction" of a crime committed with the use of a firearm can be applied to a defendant convicted of multiple counts in a single trial.

The decision upheld use of the provision against a defendant convicted of six bank robberies. In a brief opinion, Scalia said Congress's use of "convictions" instead of "offenses" in the law allowed the repeat offender penalty to be imposed in a single trial.

Dissenting justices called the decision "unwarranted and unnecessarily harsh."

Parke, Warden v. Raley, decided by a 9-0 vote, December 1, 1992; O'Connor wrote the opinion.

A state may count convictions based on guilty pleas to increase a repeat offender's sentence even if there is no transcript of the earlier proceedings.

The unanimous Court rejected a Kentucky prisoner's claim that the state had to present independent proof that he had pleaded guilty knowingly and voluntarily in the earlier cases. O'Connor said that the state was entitled to a "presumption of regularity" in the earlier judgments and that placing the burden of proving otherwise on the prisoner did not violate due process.

Smith v. United States, decided by a 6-3 vote, June 1, 1993; O'Connor wrote the opinion; Scalia, Stevens, and Souter dissented.

A defendant who offered to swap a machine gun for drugs was properly sentenced under a provision imposing a mandatory thirty-year sentence for using a firearm during a drug-related crime.

The decision settled an issue that had divided federal appeals courts. Writing for the Court, O'Connor said the defendant's attempted trade "falls squarely within" the everyday meaning and dictionary definitions of the word "use."

Dissenting justices argued the ruling ignored the context. "The Court does not appear to grasp the distinction between how a word *can be* used and how it *ordinarily is* used," Scalia wrote.

Stinson v. United States, decided by a 9-0 vote, May 3, 1993; Kennedy wrote the opinion.

The Court strengthened the power of the U.S. Sentencing Commission by ruling that federal courts generally must follow the commentary as well as the main provisions of the commission's guidelines manual.

The manual includes detailed sentencing guidelines, which are subject to review by Congress, and commentary written by the commission to explain the guidelines or deal with issues not specifically covered. In 1991 the commission revised one section of commentary to provide that unlawful possession of a firearm by a convicted felon may not be treated as a "crime of violence" for purposes of sentencing the defendant as a career offender.

The effect of the revision was disputed in a bank robbery case from Florida tried before the commission's revised commentary was issued. The federal district court judge used the felon-in-possession offense to sentence the defendant as a career offender. After the commentary went into effect, the Eleventh U.S. Circuit Court of Appeals upheld the sentence. It ruled that commentary to the guidelines is not binding on federal courts.

The Supreme Court unanimously disagreed. "[C]ommentary in the Guidelines Manual that interprets or explains a guideline is authoritative unless it violates the Constitution or a federal statute or is inconsistent with, or a plainly erroneous reading of, that guideline," Kennedy wrote.

The Court declined to rule, however, on whether the revised commentary could be applied retroactively. The case was remanded to resolve that issue.

United States v. Dunnigan, decided by a 9-0 vote, February 23, 1993; Kennedy wrote the opinion.

A federal sentencing guideline that permits a judge to give a stiffer sentence to a defendant who lies on the witness stand does not violate the defendant's right to testify.

The guidelines provide for increasing a defendant's sentence if the defendant "willfully impeded or obstructed, or attempted to impede or obstruct the administration of justice during the investigation or prosecution" of the case.

The unanimous Court overturned a ruling by the Fourth U.S. Circuit Court of Appeals that a sentence enhancement for perjury during a trial would be unconstitutional. "A defendant's right to testify does not include the right to commit perjury," Kennedy wrote. But Kennedy said judges should make specific findings to support all the elements of a perjury violation before increasing a defendant's sentence.

Wisconsin v. Mitchell, decided by a 9-0 vote, June 11, 1993; Rehnquist wrote the opinion.

States may impose increased penalties on criminals who select their victims on the basis of race, religion, ethnic origin, or other protected status.

The unanimous Court held that so-called hate crime penalty enhancement laws do not violate the First Amendment's guarantee of freedom of speech. Rehnquist rejected arguments that the law amounted to punishment of speech or would impermissibly chill freedom of expression. *(See entry, p. 38; excerpts, p. 140.)*

Miscellaneous Criminal Case

Negonsott v. Samuels, Warden, decided by a 9-0 vote, February 24, 1993; Rehnquist wrote the opinion.

Kansas state courts have jurisdiction, under a 1940 federal law, to prosecute violations of state criminal law committed by or against Indians on reservations.

The decision upheld a state court conviction of a member of the Kickapoo tribe for aggravated battery. He had argued that the 1885 Indian Major Crimes Act gave federal courts exclusive jurisdiction of major crimes committed on Indian reservations.

In a unanimous ruling, the Supreme Court said that the Kansas Act of 1940 "unambiguously" gave Kansas courts jurisdiction over offenses as defined by state law but without depriving federal courts of their power to try cases covered by the earlier law. Congress in 1946 and 1948 passed similar acts for the states of North Dakota and Iowa.

Election Law

Reapportionment and Redistricting

Growe, Secretary of State of Minnesota v. Emison, decided by a 9-0 vote, February 23, 1993; Scalia wrote the opinion.

Federal courts generally should defer to state courts if both are hearing legal challenges to state redistricting plans.

The unanimous decision threw out a federal court ruling that had blocked a legislative redistricting plan devised by a state court and instead adopted its own plan. The federal court's plan included a "super-majority-minority" legislative district in the city of Minneapolis. Writing for the Court, Scalia said the federal panel erred by not deferring to the state court's "timely efforts" to redraw the districts. "Absent evidence that [the state legislature and courts] cannot timely perform their duty, a federal court cannot affirmatively obstruct, or permit federal litigation to impede, state reapportionment," Scalia wrote.

Scalia also said the federal court erred in finding that the state districting plans diluted minority voting strength in violation of the federal Voting Rights Act. Scalia said plaintiffs had failed to present either "statistical evidence" or "even anecdotal evidence" of minority political cohesion or majority bloc voting.

Shaw v. Reno, Attorney General, decided by a 5-4 votes, June 28, 1993; O'Connor wrote the opinion; White, Blackmun, Stevens, and Souter dissented.

White voters can use the Equal Protection Clause to challenge a congressional redistricting plan creating a highly irregular district that can be understood only as an effort to separate voters by race. Federal courts can order the district redrawn if the plan lacks sufficient justification.

The Court's 5-4 decision opened the door to new legal contests over "majority-minority" districts for congressional or state legislative seats. The ruling reinstated a challenge by white voters in North Carolina to the state's new Twelfth Congressional District. The serpentine 160-mile-long district was drawn to include a majority black population and elected a black representative to Congress in 1992.

Writing for the majority, O'Connor said, "[A] racial gerrymander may exacerbate the very patterns of racial bloc voting that majority-minority districting is sometimes said to counteract." To justify such a plan, O'Connor said, the government must show that it is narrowly tailored to serve a compelling government interest. The case was remanded for further hearings before a three-judge federal district court that earlier had voted 2-1 to uphold the plan.

White, in a dissent joined by Blackmun and Stevens, said that it was "unrealistic" to try to eliminate consideration of race from the redistricting process. He said the Court's previous decisions recognized an equal protection violation only when a redistricting plan had the purpose and effect of excluding an identifiable group from the political process. In a separate dissent, Souter criticized the decision to apply the strict-scrutiny standard to racial gerrymandering. *(See entry, p. 20; excerpts, p. 174.)*

Voinovich, Governor of Ohio v. Quilter, Speaker Pro Tempore of Ohio House of Representatives, decided by a 9-0 vote, March 2, 1993; O'Connor wrote the opinion.

The federal Voting Rights Act does not prevent states from deliberately creating legislative districts dominated by minority voters unless the plan dilutes the minority bloc's voting strength.

The unanimous decision overturned a lower court's ruling that blocked an Ohio legislative redistricting plan. The three-judge panel said states cannot create so-called "majority-minority" districts except to remedy a previous Voting Rights Act violation. In her opinion for the Court, however, O'Connor said federal courts "are bound to respect the States' apportionment choices unless those choices contravene federal requirements." She said that a plan devised to create majority black districts would violate the Voting Rights Act only if "has the effect of diminishing or abridging the voting strength" of black voters.

The Court also reversed a finding that the plan violated the Fifteenth Amendment, saying there was no evidence of intentional discrimination against blacks. But the case was remanded for further hearings on whether the population disparities between legislative districts under the plan violated the Fourteenth Amendment.

Federal Government

Federal Regulation

Cisneros, Secretary of Housing and Urban Development v. Alpine Ridge Group, decided by a 9-0 vote, May 3, 1993; White wrote the opinion.

The federal government may use market studies to limit annual adjustments in rental subsidies paid to developers of low-income housing.

The decision favored the Department of Housing and Urban Development (HUD) in a dispute with landlords who participate in the so-called Section 8 housing program. The program, created in 1974, subsidizes private landlords who rent housing to low-income tenants.

The assistance contracts between HUD and landlords provided for "automatic" annual adjustments in the subsidy. But beginning in the 1980s, HUD sought to limit the increases by using "comparability studies" to show that the subsidized rents exceeded market levels. After a group of landlords won a legal ruling against the practice in 1988, Congress revised the law to permit HUD to use market studies to determine the subsidy payments. A group of landlords then brought a new legal action, claiming the use of such studies violated their contract rights under the Fifth Amendment's Due Process Clause.

Writing for the unanimous Court, White said that HUD had the authority under its contracts to use market studies to limit the "formula-based rent adjustments." On that basis, White said it was unnecessary to consider the landlords' constitutional claim since they had no contractual right to the automatic increases. White added that if the landlords believed the market studies were "shoddy," they should challenge the studies rather than deny HUD's authority to make the comparisons.

CSX Transportation, Inc. v. Easterwood, decided by a 7-2 vote, April 21, 1993; White wrote the opinion; Thomas and Souter dissented in part.

Federal railroad safety regulations preempt a state law wrongful death action based on a claim that a railroad train was traveling at excessive speed. But the regulations do not preempt a claim based on the alleged absence of proper warning devices at a street crossing.

The Federal Railroad Safety Act of 1970 permitted states to enforce rail safety regulations until the secretary of transportation adopted regulations "covering" the same subject. When a Georgia woman filed a suit in state court for the death of her husband in a car-train collision, CSX Transportation argued that the action was preempted by federal speed limit and street-crossing regulations.

In a mixed ruling, the Supreme Court held that federal railroad speed limits "cover" the same subject as state common-law restrictions on train speeds. But the Court held that the plaintiff's claim involving alleged lack of warning devices could proceed because the limited federal actions concerning grade-crossing safety did not "cover" that subject.

Thomas, joined by Souter, argued that neither of the plaintiff's state law claims was preempted.

Darby v. Cisneros, Secretary of Housing and Urban Development, decided by a 9-0 vote, June 21, 1993; Blackmun wrote the opinion.

A party challenging a federal agency's action in court under the Administrative Procedure Act (APA) does not have to exhaust administrative remedies unless a separate law or agency rule specifically imposes such a requirement.

The decision reinstated a real estate developer's challenge to an administrative law judge's ruling to bar him from contracts with the Department of Housing and Urban Development (HUD) for eighteen months. A federal appeals court had ordered the case dismissed because the developer did not ask the HUD secretary to review the judge's decision.

In a unanimous opinion, Blackmun said that federal courts may not impose such a requirement under the APA "where neither the statute nor agency rules specifically mandate exhaustion as a prerequisite to judicial review."

Federal Communications Commission v. Beach Communications, Inc., decided by a 9-0 vote, June 1, 1993; Thomas wrote the opinion.

The Court upheld a provision of the 1984 cable television act that exempted some "private cable systems" serving big apartment buildings from local franchising requirements.

Private cable systems—also called satellite master antenna television systems (SMATVs)—provide cable service to one or more buildings by means of a master antenna constructed by a building owner. The Cable Communications Policy Act exempted such systems from local franchising requirements if they served buildings under common ownership, but not if they served buildings owned by different owners. A federal appeals court ruled the provision unconstitutional on equal protection grounds because the distinction had no rational basis.

Writing for the Supreme Court, Thomas said that distinctions established by social or economic legislation must be upheld against equal protection challenge if any conceivable justification can be found. In this case, Thomas said, the exemption for cable systems serving commonly owned buildings could be justified on two grounds. First, he said, the cost of regulation could have been deemed to exceed the benefits. Second, he said, Congress might have thought regulation of systems serving buildings with different owners was needed to prevent one owner from exercising monopoly power against others.

Good Samaritan Hospital v. Shalala, Secretary of Health and Human Services, decided by a 6-3 vote, June 7, 1993; White wrote the opinion; Souter, Stevens, and Scalia dissented.

The federal government does not have to reimburse hospitals or other health care providers under the Medicare program for costs beyond the "reasonable costs" set by the Department of Health and Human Services (HHS).

The decision involved a section of the Medicare law requiring that the government "provide for the making of suitable retroactive cost adjustments" for health care providers. Six nursing home operators argued the law required reimbursements whenever actual costs exceeded the costs allowed by the government. The government said the law required only a "year-end book balancing" of monthly advance payments already received by the homes. Writing for the Court, White acknowledged the law was ambiguous, but said the department's position was entitled to deference.

Reiter v. Cooper, Trustee for Carolina Motor Express, Inc., decided by an 8-1 vote, March 8, 1993; Scalia wrote the opinion; Blackmun dissented.

A shipper may seek to recover money paid under an "unreasonable rate" charged by a motor carrier through a counterclaim in a legal action initiated by the carrier. The shipper does not have to present the "unreasonable rate" claim first to the Interstate Commerce Commission (ICC), but a federal court may refer the issue to the agency after balancing the equities in an individual case.

The Court said that the case involved a common pattern under the Motor Carrier Act of 1980, which allowed shippers and carriers to negotiate rates lower than the shipper's rates filed with the ICC. Under this deregulation, many shippers went bankrupt. Trustees for the bankrupt carriers then sought to recover the difference between the negotiated rates and the tariff rates. Shippers defended by claiming the rates were unreasonably high.

In a limited procedural ruling, the Court held that the shippers' defense in this case could be treated as a counterclaim to the suit initiated by the bankrupt carrier's trustee and could be ruled on without a prior referral to the ICC. The case was remanded for further proceedings.

Freedom of Information

United States Department of Justice v. Landano, decided by a 9-0 vote, May 24, 1993; O'Connor wrote the opinion.

The FBI may not rely on a blanket presumption that all sources providing information in connection with criminal investigations are confidential to protect the information from disclosure under the Freedom of Information Act (FOIA).

The unanimous decision rejected a sweeping assertion of confidentiality made by the FBI in opposing an FOIA request filed by a man seeking information to challenge his conviction for the slaying of a Newark, New Jersey, police officer. Writing for the Court, O'Connor said that even though "many, or even most, individual sources will expect confidentiality," the government had offered "no explanation, other than ease of administration, why that expectation always should be presumed." O'Connor said, however, that the government in some cases could support an inference of confidentiality in certain "narrowly defined circumstances," such as a paid informant or a witness to a gang-related murder.

Impeachment

Nixon v. United States, decided by a 9-0 vote, January 13, 1993; Rehnquist wrote the opinion.

A Senate rule permitting evidence in impeachment proceedings to be heard by a fact-finding committee instead of the full Senate cannot be challenged in federal court.

The unanimous decision upheld a procedural shortcut that the Senate had used in removing three federal judges since 1986. The judges argued that the procedure violated the Constitution's provision that the "Senate shall have the sole Power to try all Impeachments."

Writing for six members of the Court, Rehnquist said the claim was "nonjusticiable"—that is, one that cannot be considered by the courts. Emphasizing the Senate's "sole power" to try impeachments, Rehnquist said, "The common sense meaning of the word 'sole' is that the Senate alone shall have authority to determine whether an individual should be acquitted or convicted." Rehnquist added that there was no evidence that the Framers thought the courts should play any role in the impeachment process. And he said the courts would not be able to find "any judicially manageable standard of review" if they tried to define the specific procedural requirements for the Senate to follow in impeachment trials.

The decision upheld the 1989 removal of Walter L. Nixon, formerly the chief federal district court judge in Mississippi, who was impeached and convicted following a criminal conviction for perjury. The same procedure had been used in removing Judge Harry T. Claiborne of Nevada in 1986 and Judge Alcee Hastings of Florida in 1989.

In a separate concurrence, Souter agreed with the majority that impeachment was generally not subject to judicial review. But he left open the possibility of judicial scrutiny if the Senate "were to act in a manner seriously threatening the integrity of its results"—for example, by a coin toss.

White, joined by Blackmun, also voted to reject Nixon's claim, but said courts did have the power to review the Senate's procedures. White said the Senate's committee procedure was "entirely compatible with" the impeachment trial clause, which he said "was not meant to bind the hands of the Senate beyond establishing a set of minimal procedures."

Military

Conroy v. Aniskoff, decided by a 9-0 vote, March 31, 1993; Stevens wrote the opinion.

A member of the armed services does not have to show prejudice or hardship to take advantage of a federal law that delays forfeiture proceedings for failure to pay real estate property taxes during a period of military service.

The 1940 Soldiers' and Sailors' Civil Relief Act provides that the period of military service "shall not be included in computing any period ... provided by any law for the redemption of real property sold or forfeited to enforce any obligation, tax, or assessment." In a unanimous ruling, the Court said the provision was "unambiguous, unequivocal, and unlimited." The Court rejected a ruling by Maine state courts that a member of the armed forces must first demonstrate some hardship or prejudice resulting from military service.

The decision favored a career Army officer whose property was sold after he failed to pay real estate taxes on a vacant lot for 1984, 1985, and 1986. He claimed that he had not received tax bills for those years and that his letters asking for bills had gone unanswered.

Native Americans

Lincoln, Acting Director, Indian Health Service v. Vigil, decided by a 9-0 vote, May 24, 1993; Souter wrote the opinion.

The Court rejected a challenge to a decision by the Indian Health Service to terminate a program providing services to handicapped children in the Southwest and use the funds to establish a nationwide treatment program.

The program, in operation from 1979 to 1985, had been funded from a general appropriations measure. A group of children eligible to receive services from the program challenged the agency's decision to shift the funds to a nationwide program. In a unanimous ruling, the Court said that the allocation of funds from a lump-sum appropriation was protected from judicial review because it was "traditionally regarded as committed to agency discretion." The Court also rejected a second argument that the agency had to provide notice and a public hearing before shifting the funds.

South Dakota v. Bourland, decided by a 7-2 vote, June 14, 1993; Thomas wrote the opinion; Blackmun and Souter dissented.

The Cheyenne River Sioux Tribe has no power to regulate hunting or fishing by non-Indians on lands and waters located along the Oahe Dam and Reservoir in north-central South Dakota.

The federal government acquired the lands, located within the tribe's reservation, under a 1944 act that authorized construction of a series of dams on the Missouri River to control flooding. Under a 1954 act, the government paid the tribe $10.6 million for the lands.

In a 7-2 decision, the Court ruled that the two acts abrogated the tribe's authority under nineteenth century treaties to regulate the activities of non-Indians on the lands. Thomas noted that Congress had given the Army Corps of Engineers authority to regulate "recreational" activities in the area and had not reserved any regulatory authority for the tribe. The decision came in a suit brought by the state of South Dakota after the tribe announced that it would no longer honor state-issued hunting or fishing licenses. The Court did not address the issue of the state's jurisdiction to regulate hunting or fishing in the area.

Miscellaneous Federal Case

United States v. Texas, decided by an 8-1 vote, April 5, 1993; Rehnquist wrote the opinion; Stevens dissented.

States may be required, under federal common law, to pay prejudgment interest—interest calculated from some date prior to a court judgment—on debts owed to the federal government.

The Court rejected an argument by the state of Texas that the Debt Collection Act of 1982 exempted states from paying prejudgment interest on debts to the federal government. The 1982 act requires federal agencies to collect prejudgment interest at preestablished rates from private debtors, but exempted states from its provisions. The Court, however, held that the act "left in place" federal courts' "more flexible" power under federal common law to impose prejudgment interest against state and local governments.

The decision upheld an interest award on a $412,385 debt that Texas owed for losses from administering the federally funded food stamps program.

First Amendment

Church and State

Church of the Lukumi Babalu Aye, Inc. v. City of Hialeah, decided by a 9-0 vote, June 11, 1993; Kennedy wrote the opinion.

The Court unanimously struck down a Florida city's ban on ritual animal sacrifices, saying that the ordinances unconstitutionally interfered with the practices of an Afro-Cuban religion.

The Court said that the city of Hialeah, Florida, had improperly targeted followers of the Santeria religion in 1987 when it adopted four ordinances prohibiting ritual sacrifice of animals. Enactment of the ordinances followed a public clamor in Hialeah touched off by the establishment of a Santerian church. Animal sacrifice plays a central part in Santerians' religious ceremonies.

All nine justices agreed that the ordinances infringed on the Santerians' freedom to exercise religion under the First Amendment. The justices were less unified in their reasoning, however. Writing for the Court, Kennedy said the evidence showed that "suppression of the Santeria worship service was the object of the ordinances." He noted that even though the ordinances ostensibly sought to protect public health or prevent cruelty to animals, they applied only to "ritual sacrifice" and not to other killings.

Kennedy's opinion distinguished the case from a 1990 decision, *Employment Div., Dept. of Human Resources of Oregon v. Smith,* that had allowed the enforcement of a law banning use of peyote against Native Americans who used it in religious ceremonies. Stevens joined Kennedy's opinion in full; five other justices—Rehnquist, White, Scalia, Souter, and Thomas—joined most of it.

In a separate concurrence, Blackmun and O'Connor repeated their disagreement with the *Smith* case, saying it "ignored the value of religious freedom." Souter, who joined the Court after *Smith,* also criticized the ruling in a lengthy concurring opinion and called for it to be reexamined.

Lamb's Chapel v. Center Moriches Union Free School District, decided by a 9-0 vote, June 7, 1993; White wrote the opinion.

A school district policy that permits the use of school buildings after hours by community groups but bars similar use by religious groups violates the First Amendment's Freedom of Speech Clause.

The unanimous ruling upset a decision by a local school board in New York to prevent an evangelical group from using school buildings to show a series of religious-oriented films on family and child-rearing issues. Writing for the Court, White said that the policy was unconstitutional because it denied a speaker the use of government facilities based solely on the speaker's point of view. White also said that the exhibition of the films would not amount to "endorsing religion" or violate the test adopted in *Lemon v. Kurtzman* (1971) for determining when government actions operate as an impermissible establishment of religion.

Kennedy and Scalia wrote separate concurrences, agreeing with the free speech ruling but complaining of the Court's use of the *Lemon* standard. Kennedy called the reference "unnecessary and unsettling." Scalia, joined by Thomas, noted that the strict test had been repeatedly criticized by six of the Court's current members. *(See entry, p. 31; excerpts, p. 133.)*

Zobrest v. Catalina Foothills School District, decided by a 5-4 vote, June 18, 1993; Rehnquist wrote the opinion; Blackmun, Stevens, O'Connor, and Souter dissented.

The government can pay for a sign-language interpreter to accompany a deaf student in a parochial school without violating the separation of church and state.

The decision reversed lower court rulings that found the practice would violate the First Amendment's Establishment Clause. The case arose when Arizona officials refused to pay for an interpreter to accompany a deaf ninth-grade student at a Roman Catholic school in Tucson. Writing for the Court, Rehnquist said the service was "part of a general government program that distributes benefits neutrally to any child qualifying as 'handicapped'" under a federal law guaranteeing educational opportunities for the disabled.

Dissenting justices objected on procedural and substantive grounds. All four dissenters said the Court should have returned the case to lower courts to consider the nonconstitutional issues of whether furnishing an interpreter was either required by federal law or, alternatively, prohibited by the federal regulation implementing the law. Blackmun, joined by Souter, also disagreed with the majority on the constitutional issue. He said the ruling "authorized a public employee to participate directly in religious indoctrination." *(See entry, p. 29; excerpts, p. 144.)*

Commercial Speech

City of Cincinnati v. Discovery Network, Inc., decided by a 6-3 vote, March 24, 1993; Stevens wrote the opinion; Rehnquist, White, and Thomas dissented.

The Court struck down a Cincinnati ordinance that prohibited the use of newsracks on public property to distribute "commercial handbills" but permitted sidewalk vending machines for newspapers.

Writing for a six-justice majority, Stevens said the city had failed to show a "reasonable fit" between the ordinance and its interest in "the safety and attractive appearance of its streets and sidewalks." He noted lower court findings in the case that the aesthetic or safety benefits of removing just 62 newsracks out of a total of 1,500 to 2,000 was "minimal" or "paltry." The Court left open the possibility, however, that a city "might be able to justify differential treatment for commercial and noncommercial newsracks" with different evidence.

Dissenting justices argued that the city's selective ban on commercial newsracks was permitted by the lower degree of constitutional protection for commercial speech.

Edenfield v. Fane, decided by an 8-1 vote, April 26, 1993; Kennedy wrote the opinion; O'Connor dissented.

A state may not prohibit accountants from personally soliciting new clients.

The decision struck down a rule by the Florida Board of Accountancy that prohibited certified public accountants from engaging in "direct, in-person, uninvited solicitation" to obtain new clients. Three other states—Louisiana, Minnesota, and Texas—had similar rules.

The Court in 1978 had upheld a ban on in-person solicitation of clients by lawyers (*Ohralik v. Ohio State Bar Assn.*). But in a nearly unanimous opinion, Kennedy said that the rule for accountants did not meet the tests for regulating commercial speech. Kennedy said that the state's asserted reasons for the rule—protecting consumers from fraud or overreaching and maintaining accountants' independence—were legitimate. But he said the state failed to prove that in-person solicitation by accountants posed any of those dangers. Kennedy distinguished the ban on solicitation by lawyers. Unlike lawyers, he said, accountants are not trained in advocacy and persuasion, and their prospective clients are sophisticated business executives who are not "susceptible to manipulation."

In a lone dissent, O'Connor said she saw "no constitutional difference" between the ban on solicitation by lawyers and the rule against solicitation by accountants.

United States v. Edge Broadcasting Co., decided by a 7-2 vote, June 25, 1993; White wrote the opinion; Stevens and Blackmun dissented.

The Court upheld a federal law that banned the broadcast of lottery advertising by radio and television stations licensed to a state that prohibits lotteries but permitted such advertising on stations in states where lotteries are legal.

The decision rejected a First Amendment challenge brought by a radio station located in North Carolina, a nonlottery state, near the Virginia border. The station said that 90 percent of its listeners live in Virginia, which permits state lotteries. Writing for a somewhat splintered seven-justice majority, White said that the law furthered a substantial government interest in supporting the policy of nonlottery states while not interfering with the policy of lottery states.

Stevens, in a dissent joined by Blackmun, argued that nonlottery states do not have a substantial interest in discouraging their citizens from participating in legal lotteries in other states. He noted that thirty-four states and the District of Columbia permitted lotteries and that others, including North Carolina, were considering establishing lotteries.

Immigration Law

Reno, Attorney General v. Catholic Social Services, Inc., decided by a 6-3 vote, June 18, 1993; Souter wrote the opinion; Stevens, White, and Blackmun dissented.

The Court threw out the bulk of two lawsuits challenging regulations that had restricted access to the government's amnesty program for undocumented aliens. The ruling had the effect of overturning lower court decisions extending the congressional deadline for aliens to apply for the amnesty.

In a significant procedural ruling, the Court held that the aliens' claims were not "ripe" because they had not been concretely affected by the regulations. Souter said that the regulations "impose no penalties . . . , but limit access to a benefit created by [the 1986 immigration reform act] but not automatically bestowed on eligible aliens." The Court said, however, that some aliens who had been barred from filing for amnesty might have valid claims. It remanded the suits for further hearings on that issue.

O'Connor disagreed with the Court's ruling on the ripeness issue, but said the lower courts had no authority to extend the amnesty deadline.

Dissenting justices argued that the aliens' claims "were ripe as soon as the concededly invalid regulations were promulgated."

Reno, Attorney General v. Flores, decided by a 7-2 vote, March 23, 1993; Scalia wrote the opinion; Stevens and Blackmun dissented.

The Court upheld an Immigration and Naturalization Service (INS) policy of detaining alien juveniles while awaiting deportation hearings unless they can be released to a parent, close relative, or legal guardian.

The 7-2 ruling overturned lower court decisions striking down the INS policy of refusing to release the juveniles to other responsible adults or a social service agency. The Court said the policy did not violate due process or exceed the agency's discretion for dealing with arrested aliens. "Where a juvenile has no available parent, close relative, or legal guardian, where the government does not intend to punish the child, and where the conditions of custody are decent and humane, such custody surely does not violate the Constitution," Scalia wrote.

Dissenting justices argued the government should be required to conduct individual hearings to determine whether detention is in the juvenile's best interest.

Sale, Acting Commissioner, Immigration and Naturalization Service v. Haitian Centers Council, Inc., decided by an 8-1 vote, June 21, 1993; Stevens wrote the opinion; Blackmun dissented.

The president has the power to order the Coast Guard to intercept undocumented aliens on the high seas and return them to their home country without conducting hearings to determine whether they are refugees who qualify for asylum.

The nearly unanimous decision upheld a policy adopted by the Bush administration and defended by the Clinton administration of stopping Haitians seeking to sail to the United States and summarily returning them to Haiti. Writing for the Court, Stevens said the policy did not violate the 1980 Refugee Act or the United Nations Convention Relating to the Status of Refugees. Stevens said that provisions in the law and treaty that barred the "return" of aliens to countries where they faced persecution did not apply beyond U.S. borders.

In a lone dissent, Blackmun interpreted the legal provisions differently. "The terms are unambiguous," Blackmun wrote. "Vulnerable refugees shall not be returned." *(See entry, p. 27; excerpts, p. 153.)*

Individual Rights

Abortion

Bray v. Alexandria Women's Health Clinic, decided by votes of 6-3 and 5-4, January 13, 1993; Scalia wrote the opinion; Souter dissented in part; Stevens, Blackmun, and O'Connor dissented.

A Reconstruction-era civil rights law that prohibits conspiracies to deprive any person or class of equal protection of the laws cannot be used to prevent blockades of abortion clinics by antiabortion demonstrators.

The Court held that the blockades did not involve "invidious discrimination" against women by reason of their sex. On that basis, Scalia said, the demonstrations did not fall under the 1871 civil rights law as interpreted by the Court in a decision a century later, *Griffin v. Breckenridge* (1971). The ruling, in a case first argued in the 1991-1992 term, overturned a lower federal court order prohibiting blockades by the antiabortion group Operation Rescue at several Northern Virginia clinics where abortions were performed.

The majority declined to rule on whether plaintiffs could rely on a second clause in the law that prohibits conspiracies aimed at hindering or preventing state authorities from protecting equal rights. But Scalia said in dictum that the hindrance clause would also require proof of invidious discrimination.

Souter concurred with the ruling on the act's "deprivation clause," but said the "hindrance clause" could be applied to the demonstrations if they were aimed at preventing local authorities from safeguarding the rights of women seeking to use the clinics. He voted to remand the case on that issue.

In separate dissents, Stevens and O'Connor both said that either of the statute's two clauses applied to the demonstrators' activities. Blackmun joined both dissents. *(See entry, p. 23; excerpts, p. 101.)*

Affirmative Action

Northeastern Florida Chapter of the Associated General Contractors of America v. City of Jacksonville, Florida, decided by a 7-2 vote, June 14, 1993; Thomas wrote the opinion; O'Connor and Blackmun dissented.

A nonminority contractor may challenge a minority set-aside ordinance without demonstrating that it would have been awarded a contract but for the law.

The ruling reinstated a challenge by a group of contractors to a 1984 Jacksonville, Florida, ordinance—later amended—that set aside 10 percent of the amount spent on city contracts for "minority business enterprises." Writing for the Court, Thomas said the contractors had alleged an "injury in fact" necessary to establish legal standing to challenge the ordinance. "[I]n the context of a challenge to a set-aside program, the 'injury in fact' is the inability to compete on an equal footing in the bidding process, not the loss of a contract," Thomas said. Several civil rights groups filed briefs supporting the contractors' position on legal standing even though they also supported the city's ordinance.

The dissenting justices argued that the case was moot because the city had changed the law.

Age Discrimination

Hazen Paper Co. v. Biggins, decided by a 9-0 vote, April 20, 1993; O'Connor wrote the opinion.

The Court limited the use of the Age Discrimination in Employment Act (ADEA) in cases that allege interference with employees' pension rights. But the Court also eased the requirements for plaintiffs to prove a "willful" violation of the act to recover double damages in an age discrimination suit.

The unanimous Court held that an employer's decision to dismiss an employee to deprive him of his pension rights does not necessarily amount to age discrimination. O'Connor noted, however, that the dismissal might violate a separate federal law, the Employee Retirement Income Security Act (ERISA). The ruling sent back for further consideration a case in which a sixty-two-year-old employee was fired in 1986 just months short of his ten-year anniversary when his pension rights would have been vested. Because of the remand, the Court also set out the standard of proof the lower courts should apply in weighing the plaintiff's age-discrimination claim.

The ADEA allows a judge or jury to double a plaintiff's back-pay award if the employer's action was a "willful" violation of the law. Some lower courts had interpreted that standard to require plaintiffs to show that an employer's conduct was outrageous, to produce direct evidence of the employer's discriminatory motivation, or to show that age was the predominant factor in the employment decision. O'Connor said that none of those elements was required by the statute or by the Court's previous decisions. Instead, she explained, a plaintiff could prove a willful violation merely by showing that the employer "either knew or showed reckless disregard for the matter of whether its conduct was prohibited by the statute."

Attorneys' Fees

Farrar and Smith, Co-Administrators of Estate of Joseph D. Farrar v. Hobby, decided by a 5-4 vote, December 14, 1992; Thomas wrote the opinion; White, Blackmun, Stevens, and Souter dissented.

A plaintiff in a federal civil rights suit who wins only nominal damages and no other significant legal relief is ordinarily not entitled to an award of attorneys' fees.

The decision threw out a $280,000 award for attorneys' fees for a plaintiff who won a nominal $1 damage award in a malicious prosecution suit. Federal civil rights law provides that a court may award attorneys' fees to the "prevailing party" in certain civil rights suits. Writing for the majority, Thomas said that the plaintiff qualified as the prevailing parties for purposes of the law, but was not entitled to a fee award because of the failure to prove actual, compensable injury. "When a plaintiff recovers only nominal damages because of his failure to prove an essential element of his claim for monetary relief . . . ," Thomas wrote, "the only reasonable fee is usually no fee at all."

The dissenting justices said the case should have been remanded to decide whether the fee was excessive.

Shalala, Secretary of Health and Human Services v. Schaefer, decided by 7-2 and 9-0 votes, June 24, 1993; Scalia wrote the opinion; Stevens and Blackmun concurred in the judgment.

The Court set an earlier deadline for Social Security claimants to apply for attorneys' fees in suits challenging administrative decisions to deny benefits.

The ruling came in a case where a man successfully challenged the Social Security Administration's decision to deny him disability benefits. After the agency's new decision in the case, the man sought and was awarded attorneys' fees under the Equal Access to Justice Act. Writing for the majority, Scalia said that ordinarily the time for seeking attorneys' fees in such a case begins after a federal judge remands the proceeding to the agency instead of after the agency's final action. In this case, however, Scalia said the judge failed to issue a "final judgment" and the time limit for seeking attorneys' fees had not expired.

Stevens, joined by Blackmun, disagreed with the legal ruling but agreed with the result.

Damage Suits

Antoine v. Byers & Anderson, Inc., decided by a 9-0 vote, June 7, 1993; Stevens wrote the opinion.

A court reporter is not absolutely immune from damages liability for failing to produce a transcript of a federal criminal trial.

In a brief opinion, the Court said that court reporters do not exercise the kind of discretionary judgment that is protected by the doctrine of judicial immunity. The decision remanded a suit brought by a defendant whose appeal had been delayed for four years because of a court reporter's failure to produce a transcript.

Buckley v. Fitzsimmons, decided by 9-0 and 5-4 votes, June 24, 1993; Stevens wrote the opinion; Kennedy, Rehnquist, White, and Souter dissented in part.

Prosecutors do not enjoy absolute immunity from damage suits for conducting investigative actions normally performed by police officers or for making statements to the news media.

The decision reinstated a federal civil rights suit by a defendant in a publicized murder case who charged state prosecutors in Illinois with fabricating evidence and making false statements against him. Charges against the man were dropped after a jury failed to reach a verdict in the case.

In previous cases, the Court had ruled that prosecutors have absolute immunity from damage suits for actions in connection with the traditional role of courtroom advocacy. But prosecutors enjoy only "qualified immunity" for other actions and can be liable for damages if they violate an individual's clearly established legal rights. Applying those principles, the Court unanimously held that statements made in a news conference were not protected by absolute immunity. Stevens said that the statements had "no functional tie to the judicial process."

The justices split 5-4, however, on whether investigative actions by prosecutors were subject to suit. For the majority, Stevens said, "There is a difference between the advocate's role in evaluating evidence and interviewing witnesses as he prepares for trial . . . and the detective's role in searching for the clues and corroboration that might give him probable cause to recommend that a suspect be arrested."

In his dissenting opinion, Kennedy said that permitting damage suits against prosecutors for consulting with witnesses before indictment or trial "would frustrate and impede the judicial process." Rehnquist, White, and Souter joined the opinion.

Leatherman v. Tarrant County Narcotics Intelligence and Coordination Unit, decided by a 9-0 vote, March 3, 1993; Rehnquist wrote the opinion.

Plaintiffs in federal civil rights suits against local governments do not have to provide more detail in their complaints than plaintiffs in other types of suits.

The Federal Rules of Civil Procedure generally provide that a complaint must include only "a short and plain statement of the claim" for legal relief. In a number of cases, however, the Fifth U.S. Circuit Court of Appeals had imposed a "heightened pleading standard" in civil rights suits brought against local governments.

In a brief, unanimous opinion, the Supreme Court said the federal rules did not permit a more stringent standard for suits against local governments. The decision returned for trial two suits brought by homeowners who claimed that poorly trained police officers had violated their rights in drug raids.

Soldal v. Cook County, Illinois, decided by a 9-0 vote, December 8, 1992; White wrote the opinion.

A federal civil rights plaintiff may use the Fourth Amendment to recover damages for violation of his property rights even if his privacy or liberty was not harmed.

The decision allowed an Illinois man to proceed with a suit claiming that Cook County sheriff's deputies violated his civil rights by assisting the owners of a trailer park in an unlawful eviction. The Seventh U.S. Circuit Court of Appeals dismissed the suit because the action affected only property rights. The unanimous Court rejected what it called the appeals court's "novel" interpretation. "[T]he [Fourth] Amendment protects property as well as privacy," White wrote. "We fail to see how being unceremoniously dispossessed of one's home in the manner alleged to have occurred here can be viewed as anything but a seizure involving the protection of the Fourth Amendment," White added.

Mental Health

Heller, Secretary, Kentucky Cabinet for Human Resources v. Doe, decided by a 5-4 vote, June 24, 1993; Kennedy wrote the opinion; Souter, Blackmun, Stevens, and O'Connor dissented.

A state law that makes it easier to commit the mentally retarded involuntarily than to commit the mentally ill does not violate the Equal Protection or Due Process clauses of the Fourteenth Amendment.

The decision upheld a Kentucky law that allowed mentally retarded individuals to be committed based on "clear and convincing evidence," but required proof "beyond a reasonable doubt" to commit mentally ill individuals. The law was challenged by a group of mentally retarded persons who had been involuntarily committed.

Writing for the majority, Kennedy said the law satisfied the Equal Protection Clause because it had a "rational basis." First, he said, mental illness is more difficult to diagnose than mental retardation. Second, treatment for the mentally ill is typically "more invasive" than treatment for the mentally retarded. The Court followed earlier rulings in refusing to apply the heightened "strict scrutiny" test used in some equal protection cases to laws affecting the mentally retarded.

The dissenting justices argued that the law did not have a rational justification.

The Court also ruled, 6-3, that a provision allowing relatives and legal guardians of mentally retarded individuals to participate as parties in commitment proceedings did not violate equal protection or due process. O'Connor joined the majority on this point.

Job Discrimination

St. Mary's Honor Center v. Hicks, decided by a 5-4 vote, June 25, 1993; Scalia wrote the opinion; Souter, White, Blackmun, and Stevens dissented.

A plaintiff in a job discrimination suit is not automatically entitled to a judgment when a judge or jury rejects the employer's nondiscriminatory explanations for an adverse employment action. Instead, the Court held, the plaintiff must prove a discriminatory motive for the action.

The decision overturned a federal appeals court ruling in favor of a black man who had been fired from his job as a correctional officer at a Missouri state prison. The lower court judge in the case did not believe the prison officials' reasons for the dismissal, but ruled that the plaintiff had still failed to show evidence of a racial motive for his discharge. The appeals court said, however, that a plaintiff should win once an employer's explanation is rejected.

Writing for a five-justice majority, Scalia said that ruling went beyond the Court's precedents dealing with burdens of proof in job discrimination suits. "We have no authority to impose liability upon an employer for alleged discriminatory employment practices unless an appropriate factfinder determines, according to proper procedures, *that the employer has actually discriminated,*" Scalia wrote.

The dissenting justices argued that the ruling "departs from settled precedent" and would be "unfair and unworkable" for Title VII plaintiffs. *(See entry, p. 25; excerpts, p. 167.)*

International Law

Saudi Arabia v. Nelson, decided by votes of 8-1 and 6-3, March 23, 1993; Souter wrote the opinion; Kennedy and Blackmun dissented in part; Stevens dissented.

Americans who are mistreated by foreign law-enforcement officials while working abroad generally cannot sue the foreign government in United States courts.

The decision barred a suit by an American who claimed he was beaten and tortured while in a Saudi jail after having been recruited in the United States to work as a safety engineer for a Saudi-owned hospital. Scott Nelson claimed that the mistreatment came after he warned hospital and government officials about safety problems at the facility. When Nelson returned to the United States, he filed a federal court suit against the Saudi government, the hospital, and the Saudi-owned company that recruited him.

A federal district court judge dismissed the suit on the basis of the Foreign Sovereign Immunities Act, which bars most suits against foreign governments in U.S. courts. But the Eleventh U.S. Circuit Court of Appeals reinstated the suit. It found that the alleged abuse fell within a provision of the act permitting suits "based on commercial activity carried on in the United States by a foreign state."

In a splintered opinion, the Supreme Court barred the suit. Writing for a six-justice majority, Souter said that abuse of police power could not qualify as commercial activity for purposes of the sovereign immunities act. "[H]owever monstrous such abuse undoubtedly may be," he wrote, "a foreign state's exercise of the power of its police has long been understood . . . as peculiarly sovereign in nature."

White and Blackmun rejected Nelson's principal claims on a separate ground. They found that the alleged mistreatment lacked a sufficient connection to the United States to qualify for the exception. Only Stevens dissented from the decision to bar the bulk of Nelson's suit.

Kennedy, Blackmun, and Stevens joined, however, in voting to permit Nelson to proceed with a claim that the Saudi's U.S.-based company should have warned him of the possibility of mistreatment. Souter called this failure to warn claim "a semantic ploy." But Kennedy, who joined the rest of Souter's opinion, said Nelson should have a chance to pursue those counts of his complaint.

Labor Law

Labor Relations

Building and Construction Trades of the Metropolitan District v. Associated Builders and Contractors of Massachusetts/Rhode Island, Inc., decided by a 9-0 vote, March 8, 1993; Blackmun wrote the opinion.

Federal labor law does not prevent an independent state authority from entering into a labor agreement requiring employees on construction projects to be union members.

The National Labor Relations Act (NLRA) generally preempts state regulation of labor relations. The act also specifically authorizes employers in the construction industry to enter into so-called prehire collective bargaining agreements that require all employees to join the designated union within seven days of being hired. The Massachusetts Water

Resources Authority negotiated such an agreement with a trade union in 1988 for the $6.1-billion cleanup of the Boston Harbor. A group of nonunion contractors challenged the agreement, contending that the state agency's action amounted to improper regulation of labor matters.

The Court unanimously disagreed, saying that the state's role amounted to "proprietary conduct" rather than regulation. "When a State owns and manages property . . . ," Blackmun explained, it "is not subject to pre-emption by the NLRA, because pre-emption doctrines apply only to state *regulation.*"

Pensions and Benefits

Commissioner of Internal Revenue v. Keystone Consolidated Industries, Inc., decided by an 8-1 vote, May 24, 1993; Blackmun wrote the opinion; Stevens dissented.

Employers cannot satisfy their funding obligations under the federal pension protection law by contributing real estate instead of money to employee pension plans.

The nearly unanimous Court held that a section of the Employee Retirement Income Security Act of 1974 prohibited contributions of real estate to so-called defined-benefit pension plans even if the property is not subject to a mortgage or similar lien. A defined-benefit plan provides an employee a guaranteed level of benefits upon retirement.

Writing for the Court, Blackmun agreed with the Internal Revenue Service that real estate contributions could be subject to overvaluation and could impose investment risks and administrative burdens on pension plan trustees. The decision upheld a tax penalty on a Dallas-based company that had contributed real estate valued at $15 million to its employee pension plan.

In a dissent, Stevens said pension plan trustees should have discretion to decide whether to accept real estate instead of cash.

Concrete Pipe & Products of California, Inc. v. Construction Laborers Pension Trust for Southern California, decided by a 9-0 vote, June 14, 1993; Souter wrote the opinion.

The Court again upheld a federal law requiring employers who withdraw from an industrywide pension plan to pay their share of the plan's obligations before pulling out.

The unanimous decision rejected a due process challenge to provisions of the law making it difficult for employers to contest the determination of their "withdrawal liability." The Court had twice before, in 1984 and 1986, rejected broader challenges to the law, the Multiemployer Pension Plan Amendments Act. The law provided that the pension plan trustees initially determine how much an employer must pay before withdrawing from the plan, subject to review first by an arbitrator and then in court.

In the new challenge, a California construction company argued that the law's presumptions in favor of factual determinations by the trustees and their actuaries violated its right to an impartial adjudication. The Court rejected the arguments. "[T]he statutory presumptions work no deprivation of procedural due process," Souter wrote.

The Court also rejected substantive due process arguments that the company was being required to pay more than its fair share of the pension plan's obligations.

The District of Columbia v. The Greater Washington Board of Trade, decided by an 8-1 vote, December 14, 1992; Thomas wrote the opinion; Stevens dissented.

Federal law prevents states from requiring employers to provide disabled workers the same health insurance they offer to other employees.

In a victory for business groups, the Court held that such a requirement is preempted by the federal Employee Retirement Income Security Act (ERISA), which regulates employee pension and benefits plans. The act states that its provisions "shall supersede" any state laws that "relate to any employee benefit plan" covered by the federal law.

The decision struck down a District of Columbia law aimed at maintaining health insurance benefits for injured employees. Business groups said the ruling would directly affect laws in eight other states.

Local 144 Nursing Home Pension Fund v. Demisay, decided by a 9-0 vote, June 14, 1993; Scalia wrote the opinion.

Federal courts have no general power to require union pension and welfare funds to be administered according to federal labor law.

The unanimous decision blocked an effort by an association of New York City nursing homes to force the trustees of two union funds to turn over a portion of their assets to two new funds established by the association.

The employers' group argued that a section of the the 1947 Labor Management Relations Act—the Taft-Hartley Act—authorized federal courts to prevent abuses of union trust funds. Writing for the Court, however, Scalia said that the section dealt only with specific violations of the act and did not provide general authority for a court to order a trust fund or its trustees to comply with the law.

Stevens, joined by White and Blackmun, concurred separately, saying that the law would not require the existing trust funds to transfer assets to the new funds even if courts had the power to issue such an order.

Mertens v. Hewitt Associates, decided by a 5-4 vote, June 1, 1993; Scalia wrote the opinion; White, Rehnquist, Stevens, and O'Connor dissented.

The federal pension protection law does not permit workers to obtain monetary damages from outside advisers for mismanagement.

The Court's narrow majority interpreted a provision of the Employee Retirement Income Security Act (ERISA) that permits suits against outside advisers for "appropriate equitable relief" to authorize injunctions or other court orders but not compensatory or punitive damages. The decision rejected a suit by retired Kaiser Steel Corporation employees against an actuarial firm that advised the company in setting up its pension plan. The employees claimed that because of the firm's poor advice, the pension plan was underfunded and was eventually terminated. The retired employees received the benefits guaranteed to them under ERISA, but not as much as they would have received under the pension plan. They sued the actuarial firm seeking to recover their losses. Separately, they sued the pension plan managers—the so-called "fiduciaries"—for breach of fiduciary duty.

Writing for the majority, Scalia said ERISA did not authorize damage suits against nonfiduciaries who knowingly participate in a fiduciary's breach of duty. He said the statutory language envisioned a distinction between "equitable" relief, such as an injunction, and the "legal" remedy of monetary damages.

In the dissenting opinion, White said the majority had misinterpreted the law "so as to *deprive* beneficiaries of remedies they enjoyed prior to the statute's enactment."

Public Employees

Moreau v. Klevenhagen, Sheriff of Harris County, Texas, decided by a 9-0 vote, May 3, 1993; Stevens wrote the opinion.

State and local governments that do not permit collective bargaining by public employees may unilaterally adopt overtime policies giving employees compensatory time off instead of premium pay.

The unanimous decision rejected an effort by a group of deputy sheriffs in Harris County (Houston), Texas, to require overtime policies to be negotiated with an association that represented them in some personnel matters. Texas law prohibited collective bargaining by public employees. The legal issue involved an ambiguous provision of amendments passed by Congress in 1985. They were aimed at easing the financial impact of a Supreme Court decision that upheld enforcement of the Fair Labor Standards Act against state and local governments.

Stevens said the amendments require overtime policies be negotiated with public employee unions if they have the power to engage in collective bargaining. But government employers that do not permit collective bargaining may adopt the policies as part of individual agreements with employees.

Workers' Compensation

Bath Iron Works Corp. v. Director, Office of Workers' Compensation Programs, decided by a 9-0 vote, January 12, 1993; Stevens wrote the opinion.

The Court interpreted a federal workers' compensation law covering shipbuilders and ship repairers to allow more generous benefits for some workers who are injured on the job but file for benefits only after retiring.

The dispute involved two different compensation systems under the federal Longshore and Harbor Workers' Compensation Act. One system provides scheduled benefits for a number of listed injuries, including hearing loss. Another system provides lower benefits to retired workers for "an occupational disease which does not immediately result in . . . disability." Congress created this scheme in 1984 to deal with asbestos-related injuries that may become evident long after exposure.

A retired ship riveter filed for benefits due to hearing loss in 1985. He sought the more generous benefits, but his former employer cited two federal appeals court rulings that required all retired workers to claim benefits only under the less generous system. The Supreme Court, however, ruled unanimously that an occupational hearing loss results in immediate disability and is therefore covered by the more generous benefits schedule even if a worker has retired.

States

Boundary Disputes

Mississippi v. Louisiana, decided by a 9-0 vote, December 14, 1992; Rehnquist wrote the opinion.

A federal statute that gives the Supreme Court "original and exclusive jurisdiction of all controversies" between two or more states prevents lower federal courts from determining a state boundary dispute as part of a lawsuit between private parties over property lines.

The ruling returned to a federal district court a suit brought by private landowners to settle ownership of land along the west bank of the Mississippi River along the border between Mississippi and Louisiana. The state of Louisiana sought to join the lawsuit and to bring the state of Mississippi into the action as well.

The Supreme Court ruled that the statutory provision giving it "exclusive" jurisdiction over disputes between states "necessarily denies jurisdiction of such cases to any other federal court." The justices said that the lower federal court could complete action on the private parties' lawsuit, but that the states would not be bound by the decision.

Immunity

Puerto Rico Aqueduct and Sewer Authority v. Metcalf & Eddy, Inc., decided by an 8-1 vote, January 12, 1993; White wrote the opinion; Stevens dissented.

States or state agencies may take an immediate appeal of a ruling that rejects their claim of immunity from federal court suit under the Eleventh Amendment.

The Court's decision allowed states to take advantage of the "collateral order doctrine," which permits an immediate appeal of some pretrial rulings. Most pretrial rulings cannot be appealed until after trial.

Puerto Rico's water and sewer authority was seeking to appeal a federal district court's ruling to permit a private engineering company to proceed with a federal court suit in a contract dispute. But the First U.S. Circuit Court of Appeals refused to consider the claim and returned the case for trial.

The Supreme Court, however, said the ruling on the immunity issue was immediately appealable. White said the appeal "involves a claim to a fundamental constitutional protection, whose resolution generally will have no bearing on the merits of the underlying action." An immediate appeal, he said, was important to "ensuring that the States' dignitary interests can be fully vindicated."

Taxation

Harper v. Virginia Department of Taxation, decided by a 7-2 vote, June 18, 1993; Thomas wrote the opinion; O'Connor and Rehnquist dissented.

The Court required retroactive application of a four-year-old decision entitling federal retirees to tax relief from states that had denied them a tax benefit granted to state and local government pensioners.

The immediate effect of the ruling was to force Virginia and fifteen other states to consider refunds or other relief totaling hundreds of millions of dollars for federal retirees who had been taxed on their pension benefits. The Court also used the case to announce a broad new rule that its decisions normally be given full retroactive effect in any kind of civil case.

Writing for a five-justice majority on the legal issue, Thomas said that the Court's decisions must be applied retroactively by all other federal and state tribunals unless the Court specifically chooses not to apply a new rule to the parties in the case before it. Blackmun, Stevens, Scalia, and Souter joined that part of the opinion.

The decision paralleled a retroactivity rule adopted for criminal cases in 1987. In civil cases, however, the Court in 1971 had adopted a balancing test allowing some decisions that changed existing law to be applied only to future cases.

The tax issue arose when the Court held in *Michigan v. Davis* (1989) that a state scheme taxing federal retirees' pensions while exempting benefits paid to state or local government retirees violated the doctrine of intergovernmental immunities. Virginia, which faced a tax refund of $440 million under the ruling, argued it should not be applied retroactively. Seven justices agreed that Virginia had to provide refunds or prospective tax relief to the federal retirees. White and Kennedy, however, refused to join in the Court's broad retroactivity rule.

O'Connor, in a dissent joined by Rehnquist, said the decision would "impose crushing and unnecessary liability on the States, precisely at a time when they can least afford it."

Itel Containers International Corp. v. Huddleston, Commissioner of Revenue of Tennessee, decided by an 8-1 vote, February 23, 1993; Kennedy wrote the opinion; Blackmun dissented.

States may impose sales taxes on a domestic company's leasing of cargo containers used in international shipping.

The Court rejected arguments by a California-based company that Tennessee's effort to tax cargo container leases within the state violated international treaties and constitutional prohibitions on state interference with foreign commerce. Writing for the nearly unanimous Court, Kennedy said Tennessee had a "legitimate interest in taxing the transaction" and did not "attempt to interfere with the free flow of commerce, be it foreign or domestic."

Oklahoma Tax Commission v. Sac and Fox Nation, decided by a 9-0 vote, May 17, 1993; O'Connor wrote the opinion.

The Court strengthened the rule against state taxation of Indian tribal members by extending the exemption to Native Americans living in Indian communities but outside formal reservations.

The unanimous Court held that without explicit congressional authority, a state may not tax tribal members who live and work in "Indian country." The Court said that Congress had defined Indian country to include formal or informal reservations, allotted lands, and dependent Indian communities.

The decision came in a dispute between the state of Oklahoma and the 2,500-member Sac and Fox Nation. Oklahoma authorities had sought to impose income and motor vehicle excise taxes on tribe members. The ruling returned the case to lower federal courts to determine whether the tribal members live in Indian country as defined by the Court.

United States v. California, decided by a 9-0 vote, April 26, 1993; O'Connor wrote the opinion.

The federal government was blocked from recovering state sales taxes that it said the state had wrongfully assessed against a federal contractor.

Williams Brothers Engineering Co. managed an oil drilling operation at the federal Naval Petroleum Reserve in Kern County, California. The state levied $14 million in sales taxes against the company for tax years 1975 through 1981. The company contested the tax, but dropped its administrative challenge after the state agreed to a $3 million refund.

The company's agreement with the federal government required the government to reimburse it for any state taxes. After the state administrative proceedings had ended, the federal government brought a contract-type suit against the state in federal court in 1988 to try to recover the taxes the company had paid.

The Court, however, ruled that the government had no right to recover the money merely because federal funds were involved and that the government had waited too long to bring the suit. The Court suggested the government could avoid similar problems in the future by requiring federal contractors to assume responsibility for any wrongfully assessed state taxes.

Water Rights

Nebraska v. Wyoming, decided by a 9-0 vote, April 20, 1993; O'Connor wrote the opinion.

The Court upheld a special master's recommendations resolving parts of a water rights dispute among Nebraska, Wyoming, and the federal government involving the North Platte River and its tributaries.

The dispute involved a 1945 Supreme Court decree that had allotted 75 percent of the North Platte's flow to Nebraska during the irrigation season and 25 percent to Wyoming. The unanimous Court backed Nebraska and the federal Bureau of Reclamation in diverting and storing water in irrigation reservoirs in western Nebraska. It also allowed Nebraska to proceed with a challenge to a new reservoir on the tributary Deer Creek. Wyoming said the reservoir was intended for municipal water supplies and was exempted from the terms of the decree.

The Court rejected for the time being, however, Nebraska's challenge to an electric power plant and irrigation system planned for the tributary Laramie River in Wyoming. The Court said there was no evidence that Nebraska would be injured by the two projects.

United States v. Idaho ex rel. Director, Idaho Department of Water Resources, decided by a 9-0 vote, May 3, 1993; Rehnquist wrote the opinion.

The federal government cannot be required to pay a filing fee when a state joins it as a defendant in a state court proceeding to adjudicate water rights.

The state of Idaho initiated a proceeding to adjudicate water rights in the Snake River Basin and invoked a federal law known as the McCarran Amendment to bring the United States into the proceeding. A state law designed to shift the cost of such litigation to water users required all water rights claimants to pay "filing fees." The United States filed claims in the case, but refused to pay filing fees, which it estimated would total $10 million.

In a brief unanimous decision, the Court said the McCarran Amendment did not permit imposition of the fees against the United States. Rehnquist noted that the amendment provided that no "costs" could be imposed on the federal government and that the distinction between fees and costs in this proceeding "is blurred, indeed."

Miscellaneous State Case

Delaware v. New York, decided by a 6-3 vote, March 30, 1993; Thomas wrote the opinion; White, Blackmun, and Stevens dissented.

Delaware won a lucrative victory in a dispute with New York over which state could claim hundreds of millions of dollars in unclaimed stock dividends.

The Court ruled that dividends that cannot be traced to individual owners can be claimed by the state where the bank or brokerage firm holding the money is incorporated. Many of the nation's largest brokerage houses are incorporated in Delaware. New York had taken $360 million in funds of abandoned securities between 1985 and 1989, according to the Court's opinion. Delaware brought an original action in the Supreme Court in 1988 to recover the funds.

A law professor named by the Court as a "special master" to hear the case recommended that the unclaimed funds go to the state where the company issuing the stock had its principal offices. But Thomas said the Court's precedents had adopted the simpler rule of using the place of incorporation to determine rights to abandoned intangible property.

New York could keep some of the money it had collected, however, because some major banks are incorporated in the state. The big losers were the forty-eight other states and the District of Columbia, which stood to share in the funds if the special master's approach had been adopted.

The dissenting justices said the special master's recommendation "did no violence to our precedents" and would produce "a more equitable result."

Torts

Federal Tort Claims Act

McNeil v. United States, decided by a 9-0 vote, May 17, 1993; Stevens wrote the opinion.

The Court refused to create an exception to the Federal Tort Claims Act's requirement that an individual exhaust administrative remedies before instituting a claim.

The short unanimous decision said that the exhaustion requirement applied even if the claim was presented and rejected before any substantial progress had been made in the litigation. Some federal appeals courts had approved an exception to the requirement in such cases. "The interest in orderly administration of this body of litigation is best served by adherence to the straight-forward statutory command," Stevens wrote.

Smith v. United States, decided by an 8-1 vote, March 8, 1993; Rehnquist wrote the opinion; Stevens dissented.

The Federal Tort Claims Act (FTCA) does not authorize lawsuits against the United States government for negligent actions or omissions occurring in Antarctica.

The decision barred a wrongful death action by the widow of a man who died in a fall in Antarctica, where he had been working for a construction company on contract to the federal National Science Foundation. The FTCA waives the federal government's sovereign immunity for certain tort claims, but it does not apply to "[a]ny claim arising in a foreign country." In a brief opinion, the Court held that Antarctica comes within that exception even though it has no recognized government.

In a dissent, Stevens warned that the Court's rationale could also limit suits under the FTCA for injuries sustained by astronauts during exploration of outer space.

Punitive Damages

TXO Production Corp. v. Alliance Resources Corp., decided by a 6-3 vote, June 25, 1993; Stevens wrote the main opinion; O'Connor, White, and Souter dissented.

In a blow to business groups and other critics of the civil justice system, the Court refused for the fifth time in recent years to set strict guidelines for juries to follow in awarding punitive damages.

The justices upheld a $10 million punitive damage award that a West Virginia jury voted against a Texas corporation in a dispute with a West Virginia company over oil and gas drilling rights. The defendant,

TXO Production Corp., argued the award was grossly excessive when compared to the jury's $19,000 award for compensatory damages.

The six justices who rejected TXO's due process challenge produced three opinions that took radically different approaches to reviewing punitive damages. Stevens, joined by Rehnquist and Blackmun, said that punitive damage awards must satisfy "a general concern of reasonableness," but did not specify factors to be used under that standard. Kennedy called for reviewing a jury's verdict to assure that it did not result from bias, passion, or prejudice. All four justices agreed that the jury had some basis for imposing the punitive damage award against TXO. They cited evidence that the company had devised a fraudulent scheme to try to renegotiate a royalty agreement with Alliance Resources and other West Virginia landowners.

Scalia, joined by Thomas, called for a more limited review of punitive damages. He said federal courts should determine only whether proper procedures were followed.

Dissenting justices called the award "monstrous" and faulted the majority for failing to provide "a single guidepost" for lower courts to use in reviewing punitive damages. O'Connor complained that the decision retreated from the Court's 1991 ruling, *Pacific Mutual Insurance Co. v. Haslip,* that had hinted at numerical guidelines to be used in comparing punitive and compensatory damage awards.

Racketeering

Reves v. Ernst & Young, decided by a 7-2 vote, March 3, 1993; Blackmun wrote the opinion; Souter and White dissented.

The federal antiracketeering law can be used only against persons who participate in the operation or management of an illegal enterprise. It cannot be wielded against outside advisers such as accountants or lawyers who do not have a part in directing the enterprise's affairs.

The ruling marked the first time the Court had narrowed the controversial Racketeer Influenced and Corrupt Organizations Act (RICO), which provides stiff civil and criminal penalties for conducting unlawful activities through businesses or other organizations.

Writing for the majority, Blackmun adopted a narrow construction of RICO's central provision making it unlawful "to conduct or participate, directly or indirectly, in the conduct" of an illegal enterprise. "RICO liability is not limited to those with primary responsibility for the enterprise's affairs, . . . but *some* part in directing the enterprise's affairs is required," he wrote.

The decision upheld a federal appeals court's ruling that cleared the accounting firm of Ernst & Young of civil liability for concealing from investors the shaky financial condition of an agricultural cooperative that later went bankrupt. The Court's holding applied equally, however, to criminal RICO prosecutions.

4 | *Opinion Excerpts*

Following are excerpts from some of the most important rulings of the Supreme Court's 1992-1993 term. They appear in the order in which they were announced.

No. 90-985

Jayne Bray, et al., Petitioners v. Alexandria Women's Health Clinic et al.

On writ of certiorari to the United States Court of Appeals for the Fourth Circuit

[January 13, 1993]

JUSTICE SCALIA delivered the opinion of the Court.

This case presents the question whether the first clause of Rev. Stat. § 1980, 42 U.S.C. § 1985(3)—the surviving version of § 2 of the Civil Rights Act of 1871—provides a federal cause of action against persons obstructing access to abortion clinics. Respondents are clinics that perform abortions, and organizations that support legalized abortion and that have members who may wish to use abortion clinics. Petitioners are Operation Rescue, an unincorporated association whose members oppose abortion, and six individuals. Among its activities, Operation Rescue organizes antiabortion demonstrations in which participants trespass on, and obstruct general access to, the premises of abortion clinics. The individual petitioners organize and coordinate these demonstrations.

Respondents sued to enjoin petitioners from conducting demonstrations at abortion clinics in the Washington, D.C., metropolitan area. Following an expedited trial, the District Court ruled that petitioners had violated § 1985(3) by conspiring to deprive women seeking abortions of their right to interstate travel. The court also ruled for respondents on their pendent state-law claims of trespass and public nuisance. As relief on these three claims, the court enjoined petitioners from trespassing on, or obstructing access to, abortion clinics in specified Virginia counties and cities in the Washington, D.C., metropolitan area. *National Organization for Women v. Operation Rescue* (ED Va. 1989). . . .

The Court of Appeals for the Fourth Circuit affirmed, *National Organization for Women v. Operation Rescue* (1990), and we granted certiorari (1991). The case was argued in the October 1991 Term, and pursuant to our direction was reargued in the current Term.

I

Our precedents establish that in order to prove a private conspiracy in violation of the first clause of § 1985(3), a plaintiff must show, *inter alia,* (1) that "some racial, or perhaps otherwise class-based, invidiously discriminatory animus [lay] behind the conspirators' action," *Griffin v. Breckenridge* (1971), and (2) that the conspiracy "aimed at interfering with rights" that are "protected against private, as well as official, encroachment," *Carpenters v. Scott* (1983). We think neither showing has been made in the present case.

A

In *Griffin* this Court held, reversing a 20-year-old precedent, see *Collins v. Hardyman* (1951), that § 1985(3) reaches not only conspiracies under color of state law, but also purely private conspiracies. In finding that the text required that expanded scope, however, we recognized the "constitutional shoals that would lie in the path of interpreting § 1985(3) as a general federal tort law." *Griffin.* That was to be avoided, we said, "by requiring, as an element of the cause of action, the kind of invidiously discriminatory motivation stressed by the sponsors of the limiting amendment." ... We said that "[t]he language [of § 1985(3)] requiring intent to deprive of *equal* protection, or *equal* privileges and immunities, means that there must be some racial, or perhaps otherwise class-based, invidiously discriminatory animus behind the conspirators' action."

We have not yet had occasion to resolve the "perhaps"; only in *Griffin* itself have we addressed and upheld a claim under § 1985(3), and that case involved race discrimination. Respondents assert that there qualifies alongside race discrimination, as an "otherwise class-based, invidiously discriminatory animus" covered by the 1871 law, opposition to abortion. Neither common sense nor our precedents support this.

To begin with, we reject the apparent conclusion of the District Court (which respondents make no effort to defend) that opposition to abortion constitutes discrimination against the "class" of "women seeking abortion." Whatever may be the precise meaning of "class" for purposes of *Griffin's* speculative extension of § 1985(3) beyond race, the term unquestionably connotes something more than a group of individuals who share a desire to engage in conduct that the § 1985(3) defendant disfavors. Otherwise, innumerable tort plaintiffs would be able to assert causes of action under § 1985(3) by simply defining the aggrieved class as those seeking to engage in the activity the defendant has interfered with. This definitional ploy would convert the statute into the "general federal tort law" it was the very purpose of the animus requirement to avoid. . . .

Respondents' contention, however, is that the alleged class-based discrimination is directed not at "women seeking abortion" but at women in general. We find it unnecessary to decide whether *that* is a qualifying class under § 1985(3), since the claim that petitioners' opposition to abortion reflects an animus against women in general must be rejected. We do not think that the "animus" requirement can be met only by maliciously motivated, as opposed to assertedly benign (though objectively invidious), discrimination against women. It does demand, however, at least a purpose that focuses upon women *by reason of their sex*—for example (to use an illustration of assertedly benign discrimination), the purpose of "saving" women *because they are women* from a combative, aggressive profession such as the practice of law. The record in this case does not indicate that petitioners' demonstrations are motivated by a purpose (malevolent *or* benign) directed specifically at women as a class; to the contrary, the District Court found that petitioners define their "rescues" not with reference to women, but as physical intervention "between abortionists and the innocent victims," and that "all [petitioners] share a deep commitment to the goals of stopping the practice of abortion and reversing its legalization." Given this record, respondents' contention that a class-based animus has been established can be true only if one of two suggested propositions is true: (1) that opposition to abortion can reasonably be presumed to reflect a sex-based intent, or (2) that intent is irrelevant, and a class-based animus can be determined solely by effect. Neither proposition is supportable.

As to the first: Some activities may be such an irrational object of disfavor that, if they are targeted, and if they also happen to be engaged in exclusively or predominantly by a particular class of people, an intent to disfavor that class can readily be presumed. A tax on wearing yarmulkes is a tax on Jews. But opposition to voluntary abortion cannot possibly be considered such an irrational surrogate for opposition to (or paternalism towards) women. Whatever one thinks of abortion, it cannot be denied that there are common and respectable reasons for opposing it, other than hatred of or condescension toward (or indeed any view at all concerning) women as a class—as is evident from the fact that men and women are on both sides of the issue, just as men and women are on both sides of petitioners' unlawful demonstrations. . . .

Respondents' case comes down, then, to the proposition that intent is legally irrelevant; that since voluntary abortion is an activity engaged in only by women, to disfavor it is *ipso facto* to discriminate invidiously against women as a class. Our cases do not support that proposition. . . . Moreover, two of our cases deal specifically with the disfavoring of abortion, and establish conclusively that it is not *ipso facto* sex discrimination. In *Maher v. Roe* (1977) and *Harris v. McRae* (1980), we held that the constitutional test applicable to government abortion-funding restrictions is not the heightened-scrutiny standard that our cases demand for sex-based discrimination, see *Craig v. Boren* (1976), but the ordinary rationality standard. . . .

The nature of the "invidiously discriminatory animus" *Griffin* had in mind is suggested both by the language used in that phrase ("invidious . . . [t]ending to excite odium, ill will, or envy; likely to give offense; esp., unjustly and irritatingly discriminating," Webster's Second International Dictionary 1306 (1954)) and by the company in which the phrase is found ("there must be *some racial, or perhaps otherwise class-based,* invidiously discriminatory animus," *Griffin* (emphasis added)). Whether one agrees or disagrees with the goal of preventing abortion, that goal in itself (apart from the use of unlawful means to achieve it, which is not relevant to our discussion of animus) does not remotely qualify for such harsh description, and for such derogatory association with racism. To the contrary, we have said that "a value judgment favoring childbirth over abortion" is proper and reasonable enough to be implemented by the allocation of public funds, and Congress itself has, with our approval, discriminated against abortion in its provision of financial support for medical procedures. This is not the stuff out of which a § 1985(3) "invidiously discriminatory animus" is created.

B

Respondents' federal claim fails for a second, independent reason: A § 1985(3) private conspiracy "for the purpose of depriving . . . any person or class of persons of the equal protection of the laws, or of equal privileges and immunities under the laws," requires an intent to deprive persons of a right guaranteed against private impairment. . . . No intent to deprive of such a right was established here.

Respondents, like the courts below, rely upon the right to interstate travel—which we have held to be, in at least some contexts, a right constitutionally protected against private interference. . . . But all that respondents can point to by way of connecting petitioners' actions with that particular right is the District Court's finding that "[s]ubstantial numbers of women seeking the services of [abortion] clinics in the Washington Metropolitan area travel interstate to reach the clinics." That is not enough. . . . Our discussion in *Carpenters* makes clear that it does not suffice for application of § 1985(3) that a protected right be incidentally affected. A conspiracy is not "for the purpose" of denying equal protection simply because it has an effect upon a protected right. The right must be *"aimed at"*; its impairment must be a conscious objective of the enterprise. Just as the "invidiously discriminatory animus" requirement, discussed above, requires that the defendant have taken his action "at least in part 'because of,' not merely 'in spite of,' its adverse effects upon an identifiable group," so also the "intent to deprive of a right" requirement demands that the defendant do more than merely be aware of a deprivation of right that he causes, and more than merely accept it; he must act at least in part for the very purpose of producing it. That was not shown to be the case here, and is on its face implausible. Petitioners oppose abortion, and it is irrelevant to their opposition whether the abortion is performed after interstate travel.

Respondents have failed to show a conspiracy to violate the right of interstate travel for yet another reason: petitioners' proposed demonstrations would not implicate that right. The federal guarantee of interstate travel does not transform state-law torts into federal offenses when they are intentionally committed against interstate travelers. Rather, it protects interstate travelers against two sets of burdens: "the erection of actual barriers to interstate movement" and "being treated differently" from intrastate travelers. *Zobel v. Williams* (1982). . . . As far as appears from this record, the only "actual barriers to movement" that would have resulted from Petitioners' proposed demonstrations would have been in the immediate vicinity of the abortion clinics, restricting movement from one portion of the Commonwealth of Virginia to another. Such a purely intrastate restriction does not implicate the right of interstate travel, even if it is applied intentionally against travelers from other States, unless it is applied *discriminatorily* against them. That would not be the case here, as respondents conceded at oral argument.

The other right alleged by respondents to have been intentionally infringed is the right to abortion. The District Court declined to rule on this contention, relying exclusively upon the right-of-interstate-travel theory; in our view it also is an inadequate basis for respondents' § 1985(3) claim. Whereas, unlike the right of interstate travel, the asserted right to abortion was assuredly "aimed at" by the petitioners, deprivation of that federal right (whatever its contours) cannot be the object of a purely private conspiracy. In *Carpenters,* we rejected a claim that an alleged private conspiracy to infringe First Amendment rights violated § 1985(3). The statute does not apply, we said, to private conspiracies that are "aimed at a right that is by definition a right only against state interference," but applies only to such conspiracies as are "aimed at interfering with rights ... protected against private, as well as official, encroachment." There are few such rights (we have hitherto recognized only the Thirteenth Amendment right to be free from involuntary servitude ... and, in the same Thirteenth Amendment context, the right of interstate travel. . . . The right to abortion is not among them. It would be most peculiar to accord it that preferred position, since it is much less explicitly protected by the Constitution than, for example, the right of free speech rejected for such status in *Carpenters*. Moreover, the right to abortion has been described in our opinions as one element of a more general right of privacy, see *Roe v. Wade* (1973), or of Fourteenth Amendment liberty, see *Planned Parenthood of Southeastern Pennsylvania* [*v. Casey*, 1992], and the other elements of those more general rights are obviously not protected against private infringement. (A burglar does not violate the Fourth Amendment, for example, nor does a mugger violate the Fourteenth.) Respondents' § 1985(3) "deprivation" claim must fail, then, because they have identified no right protected against private action that has been the object of the alleged conspiracy.

II

Two of the dissenters claim that respondents have established a violation of the second, "hindrance" clause of § 1985(3), which covers conspiracies "for the purpose of preventing or hindering the constituted authorities of any State or Territory from giving or securing to all persons within such State or Territory the equal protection of the laws."

This "claim" could hardly be presented in a posture less suitable for our review. As respondents frankly admitted at both argument and reargument, their complaint did not set forth a claim under the "hindrance" clause. Not surprisingly, therefore, neither the District Court nor the Court of Appeals considered the application of that clause to the current facts. The "hindrance"-clause issue is not fairly included within the questions on which petitioners sought certiorari, which is alone enough to exclude it from our consideration. Nor is it true that "[t]he issue was briefed, albeit sparingly, by the parties prior to the first oral argument in this case." To the contrary, neither party initiated even the slightest suggestion that the "hindrance" question was an issue to be argued and decided here. That possibility was suggested for the first time by questions from the bench during argument, and was reintroduced, again from the bench, during reargument. . . .

The dissenters' zeal to reach the question whether there was a "hindrance"-clause violation would be more understandable, perhaps, if the affirmative answer they provided were an easy one. It is far from that. Judging from the statutory text, a cause of action under the "hindrance" clause would seem to require the same "class-based, invidiously discriminatory animus" that the "deprivation" clause requires, and that we have found lacking here. . . .

Even, moreover, if the "hindrance"-clause claim did not fail for lack of class-based animus, it would still fail unless the "hindrance" clause applies to a private conspiracy aimed at rights that are constitutionally protected only against official (as opposed to private) encroachment. . . . To the extent that case illuminates this question at all, it is clearly contrary to the dissent's view, holding that the "deprivation" clause, at least, does not cover private conspiracies aimed at rights protected only against state encroachment. . . .

III

Because respondents were not entitled to relief under § 1985(3), they were also not entitled to attorney's fees and costs under 42 U.S.C. § 1988. We therefore vacate that award.

Petitioners seek even more. They contend that respondents' § 1985(3) claims were so insubstantial that the District Court lacked subject-matter jurisdiction over the action, including the pendent state claims; and that the injunction should therefore be vacated and the entire action dismissed. We do not agree. While respondents' § 1985(3) causes of action fail, they were not, prior to our deciding of this case, "wholly insubstantial and frivolous," *Bell v. Hood* (1946), so as to deprive the District Court of jurisdiction.

It may be, of course, that even though the District Court had jurisdiction over the state-law claims, judgment on those claims alone cannot support the injunction that was entered. We leave that question for consideration on remand.

JUSTICE STEVENS' dissent observes that this is "a case about the exercise of federal power to control an interstate conspiracy to commit illegal acts" and involves "no ordinary trespass," or "picketing of a local retailer," but "the kind of zealous, politically motivated, lawless conduct that led to the enactment of the Ku Klux Act in 1871 and gave it its name." Those are certainly evocative assertions, but as far as the point of law we have been asked to decide is concerned, they are irrelevant. We construe the statute, not the views of "most members of the citizenry." By its terms, § 1985(3) covers concerted action by as few as two persons, and does not require even interstate (much less nationwide) scope. It applies no more and no less to completely local action by two part-time protesters than to nationwide action by a full-time force of thousands. And under our precedents it simply does not apply to the sort of action at issue here.

Trespassing upon private property is unlawful in all States, as is, in many States and localities, intentionally obstructing the entrance to private premises. These offenses may be prosecuted criminally under state law, and may also be the basis for state civil damages. They do not, however, give rise to a federal cause of action simply because their objective is to prevent the performance of abortions, any more than they do so (as we have held) when their objective is to stifle free speech.

The judgment of the Court of Appeals is reversed in part and vacated in part, and the case is remanded for further proceedings consistent with this opinion.

It is so ordered.

JUSTICE KENNEDY, concurring.

In joining the opinion of the Court, I make these added observations.

The three separate dissenting opinions in this case offer differing interpretations of the statute in question, 42 U.S.C. § 1985(3). Given the difficulty of the question, this is understandable, but the dissenters' inability to agree on a single rationale confirms, in my view, the correctness of the Court's opinion. . . .

Of course, the wholesale commission of common state-law crimes creates dangers that are far from ordinary. Even in the context of political protest, persistent, organized, premeditated lawlessness menaces in a unique way the capacity of a State to maintain order and preserve the rights of its citizens. Such actions are designed to inflame, not inform. They subvert the civility and mutual respect that are the essential preconditions for the orderly resolution of social conflict in a free society. For this reason, it is important to note that another federal statute offers the possibility of powerful federal assistance for persons who are injured or threatened by organized lawless conduct that falls within the primary jurisdiction of the States and their local governments.

Should state officials deem it necessary, law enforcement assistance is authorized upon request by the State to the Attorney General of the United States, pursuant to 42 U.S.C. § 10501. In the event of a law enforcement emergency as to which "State and local resources are inadequate to protect the lives and property of citizens or to enforce the criminal law," § 10502(3), the Attorney General is empowered to put the full range of federal law enforcement resources at the disposal of the State, including the resources of the United States Marshals Service, which was presumably the principal practical advantage to respondents of seeking a federal injunction under § 1985(3). . . .

. . . Thus, even if, after proceedings on remand, the ultimate result is dismissal of the action, local authorities retain the right and the ability to request federal assistance, should they deem it warranted.

JUSTICE SOUTER, concurring in the judgment in part and dissenting in part.

I

This case turns on the meaning of two clauses of 42 U.S.C. § 1985(3) which render certain conspiracies civilly actionable. The first clause (the deprivation clause) covers conspiracies

"for the purpose of depriving, either directly or indirectly, any person or class of persons of the equal protection of the laws, or of equal privileges and immunities under the laws";

the second (the prevention clause), conspiracies

"for the purpose of preventing or hindering the constituted authorities of any State or Territory from giving or securing to all persons within such State or Territory the equal protection of the laws. . . ."

For liability in either instance the statute requires an "act in furtherance of the . . . conspiracy, whereby [a person] is injured in his person or property, or deprived of . . . any right or privilege of a citizen of the United States. . . ."

Prior cases giving the words "equal protection of the laws" in the deprivation clause an authoritative construction have limited liability under that clause by imposing two conditions not found in the terms of the text. An actionable conspiracy must have some racial or perhaps other class-based motivation, *Griffin v. Breckenridge* (1971), and, if it is "aimed at" the deprivation of a constitutional right, the right must be one secured not only against official infringement, but against private action as well. *Carpenters v. Scott* (1983). The Court follows these cases in applying the deprivation clause today, and to this extent I take no exception to its conclusion. . . .

II

The meaning of the prevention clause is not thus settled, however. . . .

[III Omitted]

IV

. . . I conclude that the prevention clause may be applied to a conspiracy intended to hobble or overwhelm the capacity of duly constituted state police authorities to secure equal protection of the laws, even when the conspirators' animus is not based on race or a like class characteristic, and even when the ultimate object of the conspiracy is to violate a constitutional guarantee that applies solely against state action. . . .

JUSTICE STEVENS, with whom JUSTICE BLACKMUN joins, dissenting.

After the Civil War, Congress enacted legislation imposing on the Federal Judiciary the responsibility to remedy both abuses of power by persons acting under color of state law and lawless conduct that state courts are neither fully competent, nor always certain, to prevent. The Ku Klux Act of 1871 was a response to the massive, organized lawlessness that infected our Southern States during the post-Civil War era. When a question concerning this statute's coverage arises, it is appropriate to consider whether the controversy has a purely local character or the kind of federal dimension that gave rise to the legislation.

Based on detailed, undisputed findings of fact, the District Court concluded that the portion of § 2 of the Ku Klux Act now codified at 42 U.S.C. § 1985(3) provides a federal remedy for petitioners' violent concerted activities on the public streets and private property of law-abiding citizens. *National Organization for Women v. Operation Rescue* (ED Va. 1989). The Court of Appeals affirmed. *National Organization for Women v. Operation Rescue* (CA4 1990). The holdings of the courts below are supported by the text and the legislative history of the statute and are fully consistent with this Court's precedents. Admittedly, important questions concerning the meaning of § 1985(3) have been left open in our prior cases, including whether the statute covers gender-based discrimination and whether it provides a remedy for the kind of interference with a woman's right to travel to another State to obtain an abortion revealed by this record. Like the overwhelming majority of federal judges who have spoken to the issue, I am persuaded that traditional principles of statutory construction readily provide affirmative answers to these questions.

It is unfortunate that the Court has analyzed this case as though it presented an abstract question of logical deduction rather than a question concerning the exercise and allocation of power in our federal system of government. The Court ignores the obvious (and entirely constitutional) congressional intent behind § 1985(3) to protect this Nation's citizens from what amounts to the theft of their constitutional rights by organized and violent mobs across the country. . . .

I

Petitioners are dedicated to a cause that they profoundly believe is far more important than mere obedience to the laws of the Commonwealth of Virginia or the police power of its cities. To achieve their goals, the individual petitioners "have agreed and combined with one another and with defendant Operation Rescue to organize, coordinate and participate in 'rescue' demonstrations at abortion clinics in various parts of the country, including the Washington Metropolitan area. The purpose of these 'rescue' demonstrations is to disrupt operations at the target clinic and indeed ultimately to cause the clinic to cease operations entirely."

The scope of petitioners' conspiracy is nationwide; it far exceeds the bounds or jurisdiction of any one State. They have blockaded clinics across the country, and their activities have been enjoined in New York, Pennsylvania, Washington, Connecticut, California, Kansas, and Nevada, as well as the District of Columbia metropolitan area. They have carried out their "rescue" operations in the District of Columbia and Maryland in defiance of federal injunctions.

Pursuant to their overall conspiracy, petitioners have repeatedly engaged in "rescue" operations that violate local law and harm innocent women. Petitioners trespass on clinic property and physically block access to the clinic, preventing patients, as well as physicians and medical staff, from entering the clinic to render or receive medical or counseling services. Uncontradicted trial testimony demonstrates that petitioners' conduct created a "substantial risk that existing or prospective patients may suffer physical or mental harm." Petitioners make no claim that their conduct is a legitimate form of protected expression.

Petitioners' intent to engage in repeated violations of law is not contested. They trespass on private property, interfere with the ability of patients to obtain medical and counseling services, and incite others to engage in similar unlawful activity. They also engage in malicious conduct, such as defacing clinic signs, damaging clinic property, and strewing nails in clinic parking lots and on nearby public streets. This unlawful conduct is "vital to [petitioners'] avowed purposes and goals." They show no signs of abandoning their chosen method for advancing their goals.

Rescue operations effectively hinder and prevent the constituted authorities of the targeted community from providing local citizens with adequate protection. The lack of advance warning of petitioners' activities, combined with limited police department resources, makes it difficult for the police to prevent petitioners' ambush by "rescue" from closing a clinic for many hours at a time. The trial record is replete with examples of petitioners overwhelming local law enforcement officials by sheer force of numbers. In one "rescue" in Falls Church, Virginia, the demonstrators vastly outnumbered the police department's complement of 30 deputized officers. The police arrested 240 rescuers, but were unable to prevent the blockade from closing the clinic for more than six hours. Because of the large-scale, highly organized nature of petitioners' activities, the local authorities are unable to protect the victims of petitioners' conspiracy.

Petitioners' conspiracy had both the purpose and effect of interfering with interstate travel. The number of patients who cross state lines to obtain an abortion obviously depends, to some extent, on the location of the clinic and the quality of its services. In the Washington Metropolitan area, where interstate travel is routine, 20 to 30 percent of the patients at some clinics were from out of State, while at least one clinic obtained over half its patients from other States. . . .

To summarize briefly, the evidence establishes that petitioners engaged in a nationwide conspiracy; to achieve their goal they repeatedly occupied public streets and trespassed on the premises of private citizens in order to prevent or hinder the constituted authorities from protecting access to abortion clinics by women, a substantial number of whom traveled in interstate commerce to reach the destinations blockaded by petitioners. The case involves no ordinary trespass, nor anything remotely resembling the peaceful picketing of a local retailer. It presents a striking contemporary example of the kind of zealous, politically motivated, lawless conduct that led to the enactment of the Ku Klux Act in 1871 and gave it its name.

II

The text of the statute makes plain the reasons Congress considered a federal remedy for such conspiracies both necessary and appropriate. . . .

The plain language of the statute is surely broad enough to cover petitioners' conspiracy. Their concerted activities took place on both the public "highway" and the private "premises of another." The women targeted by their blockade fit comfortably within the statutory category described as "any person or class of persons." Petitioners' interference with police protection of women seeking access to abortion clinics "directly or indirectly" deprived them of equal protection of the laws and of their privilege of engaging in lawful travel. Moreover, a literal reading of the second clause of the statute describes petitioners' proven "purpose of preventing or hindering the constituted authorities of any State or Territory" from securing "to all persons within such State or Territory the equal protection of the laws."

No one has suggested that there would be any constitutional objection to the application of this statute to petitioners' nationwide conspiracy; it is obvious that any such constitutional claim would be frivolous. Accordingly, if, as it sometimes does, the Court limited its analysis to the statutory text, it would certainly affirm the judgment of the Court of Appeals. For both the first clause and the second clause of § 1985(3) plainly describe petitioners' conspiracy.

III

The Court bypasses the statute's history, intent, and plain language in its misplaced reliance on prior precedent. Of course, the Court has never before had occasion to construe the second clause of § 1985(3). The first clause, however, has been narrowly construed in *Collins v. Hardyman* (1951), *Griffin v. Breckenridge,* (1971), and *Carpenters v. Scott* (1983). In the first of these decisions, the Court held that § 1985(3) did not apply to wholly private conspiracies. In *Griffin* the Court rejected that view but limited the application of the statute's first clause to conspiracies motivated by discriminatory intent to deprive plaintiffs of rights constitutionally protected against private (and not just governmental) deprivation. Finally, *Carpenters* re-emphasized that the first clause of § 1985(3) offers no relief from the violation of rights protected against only state interference. To date, the Court has recognized as rights protected against private encroachment (and, hence, by § 1985(3)) only the constitutional right of interstate travel and rights granted by the Thirteenth Amendment.

For present purposes, it is important to note that in each of these cases the Court narrowly construed § 1985(3) to avoid what it perceived as serious constitutional problems with the statute itself. Because those problems are not at issue here, it is even more important to note a larger point about our precedent. In the course of applying Civil War era legislation to civil rights issues unforeseeable in 1871, the Court has adopted a flexible approach, interpreting the statute to reach current concerns without exceeding the bounds of its intended purposes or the constitutional powers of Congress. We need not exceed those bounds to apply the statute to these facts.

The facts and decision in *Griffin* are especially instructive here. In overruling an important part of *Collins,* the Court found that the conduct the plaintiffs alleged—a Mississippi highway attack on a white man suspected of being a civil rights worker and the two black men who were passengers in his car—was emblematic of the antiabolitionist violence that § 1985(3) was intended to prevent. A review of the legislative history demonstrated, on the one hand, that Congress intended the coverage of § 1985(3) to reach purely private conspiracies, but on the other hand, that it wanted to avoid the "constitutional shoals" that would lie in the path of a general federal tort law punishing an ordinary assault and battery committed by two or more persons. The racial motivation for the battery committed by the defendants in the case before the Court placed their conduct "close to the core of the coverage intended by Congress." It therefore satisfied the limiting construction that the Court placed on the reference to a deprivation of "equal" privileges and immunities in the first clause of the Act. . . .

A footnote carefully left open the question "whether a conspiracy motivated by invidiously discriminatory intent other than racial bias would be actionable *under the portion of § 1985 (3) before us.*" ([E]mphasis added.) Neither of our two more recent opinions construing § 1985 (3) has answered the question left open in *Griffin* or has involved the second clause of the statute.

After holding that the statute did apply to such facts, and that requiring a discriminatory intent would prevent its over-application, the *Griffin* Court held that § 1985(3) would be within the constitutional power of Congress if its coverage were limited to constitutional rights secured against private action. The facts in that case identified two such grounds.

One ground was § 2 of the Thirteenth Amendment. The other was the right to travel. The Court explained how the petitioners could show a violation of the latter. As with the class-based animus requirement, the Court was less concerned with the specifics of that showing than with the constitutionality of § 1985(3); it emphasized that whatever evidence they presented had to "make it clear that the petitioners had suffered from conduct that Congress may reach under its power to protect the right of interstate travel."

The concerns that persuaded the Court to adopt a narrow reading of the text of § 1985(3) in *Griffin* are not presented in this case. Giving effect to the plain language of § 1985(3) to provide a remedy against the violent interference with women exercising their privilege—indeed, their right— to engage in interstate travel to obtain an abortion presents no danger of turning the statute into a general tort law. Nor does anyone suggest that such relief calls into question the constitutional powers of Congress. . . . Once concerns about the constitutionality of § 1985(3) are properly put aside, we can focus more appropriately on giving the statute its intended effect. On the facts disclosed by this record, I am convinced that both the text of the statute and its underlying purpose support the conclusion that petitioners' conspiracy was motivated by a discriminatory animus and violated respondents' protected right to engage in interstate travel.

IV

The question left open in *Griffin*—whether the coverage of § 1985(3) is limited to cases involving racial bias—is easily answered. The text of the statute provides no basis for excluding from its coverage any cognizable class of persons who are entitled to the equal protection of the laws. . . .

The legislative history of the Act confirms the conclusion that even though it was primarily motivated by the lawless conduct directed at the recently emancipated citizens, its protection extended to "all the thirty-eight millions of the citizens of this nation." Cong. Globe, 42d Cong., 1st Sess. 484 (1871). Given then prevailing attitudes about the respective roles of males and females in society, it is possible that the enacting legislators did not anticipate protection of women against class-based discrimination.

That, however, is not a sufficient reason for refusing to construe the statutory text in accord with its plain meaning, particularly when that construction fulfills the central purpose of the legislation. . . .

V

The terms "animus" and "invidious" are susceptible to different interpretations. The Court today announces that it could find class-based animus in petitioners' mob violence "only if one of two suggested propositions is true: (1) that opposition to abortion can reasonably be presumed to reflect a sex-based intent, or (2) that intent is irrelevant, and a class-based animus can be determined solely by effect." . . .

Both forms of class-based animus that the Court proposes are present in this case.

Sex-Based Discrimination

. . . To satisfy the class-based animus requirement of § 1985(3), the conspirators' conduct need not be motivated by hostility toward individual women. As women are unquestionably a protected class, that requirement—as well as the central purpose of the statute—is satisfied if the conspiracy is aimed at conduct that only members of the protected class have the capacity to perform. It is not necessary that the intended effect upon women be the sole purpose of the conspiracy. It is enough that the conspiracy be motivated "at least in part" by its adverse effects upon women. . . . The immediate and intended effect of this conspiracy was to prevent women from obtaining abortions. Even assuming that the ultimate and indirect consequence of petitioners' blockade was the legitimate and nondiscriminatory goal of saving potential life, it is undeniable that the conspirators' immediate purpose was to affect the conduct of women. Moreover, petitioners target women *because of* their sex, specifically, because of their capacity to become pregnant and to have an abortion.

It is also obvious that petitioners' conduct was motivated "at least in part" by the invidious belief that individual women are not capable of deciding whether to terminate a pregnancy, or that they should not be allowed to act on such a decision. Petitioners' blanket refusal to allow any women access to an abortion clinic overrides the individual class member's choice, no matter whether she is the victim of rape or incest, whether the abortion may be necessary to save her life, or even whether she is merely seeking advice or information about her options. Petitioners' conduct is designed to deny *every* woman the opportunity to exercise a constitutional right that *only* women possess. Petitioners' conspiracy, which combines massive defiance of the law with violent obstruction of the constitutional rights of their fellow citizens, represents a paradigm of the kind of conduct that the statute was intended to cover. . . .

Statutory Relief from Discriminatory Effects

As for the second definition of class-based animus, disdainfully proposed by the Court, there is no reason to insist that a statutory claim under § 1985(3) must satisfy the restrictions we impose on constitutional claims under the Fourteenth Amendment. A congressional statute may offer relief from discriminatory effects even if the Fourteenth Amendment prevents only discriminatory intent. . . .

VI

Respondents' right to engage in interstate travel is inseparable from the right they seek to exercise. That right, unduly burdened and frustrated by petitioners' conspiracy, is protected by the Federal Constitution. . . .

The District Court's conclusion that petitioners intended to interfere with the right to engage in interstate travel is well-supported by the record. Interference with a woman's ability to visit another State to obtain an abortion is essential to petitioners' achievement of their ultimate goal— the complete elimination of abortion services throughout the United States. . . .

VII

Respondents have unquestionably established a claim under the second clause of § 1985(3), the state hindrance provision. The record amply demonstrates petitioners' successful efforts to overpower local law enforcement officers. During the "rescue" operations, the duly constituted authorities are rendered ineffective, and mob violence prevails. A conspiracy that seeks by force of numbers to prevent local officials from protecting the victims' constitutional rights presents exactly the kind of pernicious combination that the second clause of § 1985(3) was designed to counteract. As we recognized in *Griffin,* the second clause of § 1985(3) explicitly concerns such interference with state officials and for that reason does not duplicate the coverage of the first clause. . . .

Petitioners' conspiracy hinders the lawful authorities from protecting women's constitutionally protected right to choose whether to end their pregnancies. Though this may be a right that is protected only against state infringement, it is clear that by preventing government officials from safeguarding the exercise of that right, petitioners' conspiracy effects a deprivation redressable under § 1985(3). . . . A conspiracy that seeks to interfere with law enforcement officers' performance of their duties entails sufficient involvement with the State to implicate the federally protected right to choose an abortion and to give rise to a cause of action under § 1985(3).

We have not previously considered whether class-based animus is an element of a claim under the second clause of § 1985(3). . . .

. . . The justification for a narrow reading of *Griffin*'s judicially crafted requirement of class-based animus simply does not apply to the state hindrance clause. An action under that clause entails both a violation of the victims' constitutional rights and state involvement. This situation is so far removed from the question whether facially neutral legislation constitutes a violation of the Equal Protection Clause that the strict intent standards developed in that area can have no application.

In the context of a conspiracy that hinders state officials and violates respondents' constitutional rights, class-based animus can be inferred if the conspirators' conduct burdens an activity engaged in predominantly by members of the class. Indeed, it would be faithful both to *Griffin* and to the text of the state hindrance clause to hold that the clause proscribes conspiracies to prevent local law enforcement authorities from protecting activities that are performed exclusively by members of a protected class, even if the conspirators' animus were directed at the activity rather than at the class members. Thus, even if yarmulkes, rather than Jews, were the object of the conspirators' animus, the statute would prohibit a conspiracy to hinder the constituted authorities from protecting access to a synagogue or other place of worship for persons wearing yarmulkes. Like other civil rights legislation, this statute should be broadly construed to provide federal protection against the kind of disorder and anarchy that the States are unable to control effectively.

With class-based animus understood as I have suggested, the conduct covered by the state hindrance clause would be as follows: a large-scale conspiracy that violates the victims' constitutional rights by overwhelming the local authorities and that, by its nature, victimizes predominantly members of a particular class. I doubt whether it would be possible to describe conduct closer to the core of § 1985(3)'s coverage. This account would perfectly describe the conduct of the Ku Klux Klan, the group whose activities prompted the enactment of the statute. This description also applies to petitioners, who have conspired to deprive women of their constitutional right to choose an abortion by overwhelming the local police and by blockading clinics with the intended effect of preventing women from exercising a right only they possess. The state hindrance clause thus provides an independent ground for affirmance. . . .

JUSTICE O'CONNOR, with whom JUSTICE BLACKMUN joins, dissenting.

Petitioners act in organized groups to overwhelm local police forces and physically blockade the entrances to respondents' clinics with the purpose of preventing women from exercising their legal rights. Title 42 U.S.C. § 1985(3) provides a federal remedy against private conspiracies aimed at depriving any person or class of persons of the "equal protection of the laws," or of "equal privileges and immunities under the laws." In my view, respondents' injuries and petitioners' activities fall squarely within the ambit of this statute. . . .

No. 91-7328

Leonel Torres Herrera, Petitioner v. James A. Collins, Director, Texas Department of Criminal Justice, Institutional Division

On writ of certiorari to the United States Court of Appeals for the Fifth Circuit

[January 25, 1993]

CHIEF JUSTICE REHNQUIST delivered the opinion of the Court.

Petitioner Leonel Torres Herrera was convicted of capital murder and sentenced to death in January 1982. He unsuccessfully challenged the conviction on direct appeal and state collateral proceedings in the Texas state courts, and in a federal habeas petition. In February 1992—10 years after his conviction—he urged in a second federal habeas petition that he was "actually innocent" of the murder for which he was sentenced to death, and that the Eighth Amendment's prohibition against cruel and unusual punishment and the Fourteenth Amendment's guarantee of due process of law therefore forbid his execution. He supported this claim with affidavits tending to show that his now-dead brother, rather than he, had been the perpetrator of the crime. Petitioner urges us to hold that this showing of innocence entitles him to relief in this federal habeas proceeding. We hold that it does not.

Shortly before 11 p.m. on an evening in late September 1981, the body of Texas Department of Public Safety Officer David Rucker was found by a passerby on a stretch of highway about six miles east of Los Fresnos, Texas, a few miles north of Brownsville in the Rio Grande

Valley. Rucker's body was lying beside his patrol car. He had been shot in the head.

At about the same time, Los Fresnos Police Officer Enrique Carrisalez observed a speeding vehicle traveling west towards Los Fresnos, away from the place where Rucker's body had been found, along the same road. Carrisalez, who was accompanied in his patrol car by Enrique Hernandez, turned on his flashing red lights and pursued the speeding vehicle. After the car had stopped briefly at a red light, it signaled that it would pull over and did so. The patrol car pulled up behind it. Carrisalez took a flashlight and walked toward the car of the speeder. The driver opened his door and exchanged a few words with Carrisalez before firing at least one shot at Carrisalez' chest. The officer died nine days later.

Petitioner Herrera was arrested a few days after the shootings and charged with the capital murder of both Carrisalez and Rucker. He was tried and found guilty of the capital murder of Carrisalez in January 1982, and sentenced to death. In July 1982, petitioner pleaded guilty to the murder of Rucker.

At petitioner's trial for the murder of Carrisalez, Hernandez, who had witnessed Carrisalez' slaying from the officer's patrol car, identified petitioner as the person who had wielded the gun. A declaration by Officer Carrisalez to the same effect, made while he was in the hospital, was also admitted. Through a license plate check, it was shown that the speeding car involved in Carrisalez' murder was registered to petitioner's "live-in" girlfriend. Petitioner was known to drive this car, and he had a set of keys to the car in his pants pocket when he was arrested. Hernandez identified the car as the vehicle from which the murderer had emerged to fire the fatal shot. He also testified that there had been only one person in the car that night.

The evidence showed that Herrera's Social Security card had been found alongside Rucker's patrol car on the night he was killed. Splatters of blood on the car identified as the vehicle involved in the shootings, and on petitioner's blue jeans and wallet were identified as type A blood—the same type which Rucker had. (Herrera has type O blood.) Similar evidence with respect to strands of hair found in the car indicated that the hair was Rucker's and not Herrera's. A handwritten letter was also found on the person of petitioner when he was arrested, which strongly implied that he had killed Rucker.

Petitioner appealed his conviction and sentence, arguing, among other things, that Hernandez' and Carrisalez' identifications were unreliable and improperly admitted. The Texas Court of Criminal Appeals affirmed, . . . and we denied certiorari. . . . Petitioner's application for state habeas relief was denied. Petitioner then filed a federal habeas petition, again challenging the identifications offered against him at trial. This petition was denied, and we again denied certiorari.

Petitioner next returned to state court and filed a second habeas petition, raising, among other things, a claim of "actual innocence" based on newly discovered evidence. In support of this claim petitioner presented the affidavits of Hector Villarreal, an attorney who had represented petitioner's brother, Raul Herrera, Sr., and of Juan Franco Palacious, one of Raul Sr.'s former cellmates. Both individuals claimed that Raul Sr., who died in 1984, had told them that he—and not petitioner—had killed Officers Rucker and Carrisalez. The State District Court denied this application, finding that "no evidence at trial remotely suggest[ed] that anyone other than [petitioner] committed the offense." . . . The Texas Court of Criminal Appeals affirmed, . . . and we denied certiorari. . . .

In February 1992, petitioner lodged the instant habeas petition—his second—in federal court, alleging, among other things, that he is innocent of the murders of Rucker and Carrisalez, and that his execution would thus violate the Eighth and Fourteenth Amendments. In addition to proffering the above affidavits, petitioner presented the affidavits of Raul Herrera, Jr., Raul Sr.'s son, and Jose Ybarra, Jr., a schoolmate of the Herrera brothers. Raul Jr. averred that he had witnessed his father shoot Officers Rucker and Carrisalez and petitioner was not present. Raul Jr. was nine years old at the time of the killings. Ybarra alleged that Raul Sr. told him one summer night in 1983 that he had shot the two police officers. Petitioner alleged that law enforcement officials were aware of this evidence, and had withheld it in violation of *Brady v. Maryland* (1963).

The District Court dismissed most of petitioner's claims as an abuse of the writ. However, "in order to ensure that Petitioner can assert his constitutional claims and out of a sense of fairness and due process," the District Court granted petitioner's request for a stay of execution so that he could present his claim of actual innocence, along with the Raul Jr. and Ybarra affidavits, in state court. Although it initially dismissed petitioner's *Brady* claim on the ground that petitioner had failed to present "any evidence of withholding exculpatory material by the prosecution," the District Court also granted an evidentiary hearing on this claim after reconsideration.

The Court of Appeals vacated the stay of execution. It agreed with the District Court's initial conclusion that there was no evidentiary basis for petitioner's *Brady* claim, and found disingenuous petitioner's attempt to couch his claim of actual innocence in *Brady* terms. Absent an accompanying constitutional violation, the Court of Appeals held that petitioner's claim of actual innocence was not cognizable because, under *Townsend v. Sain* (1963), "the existence merely of newly discovered evidence relevant to the guilt of a state prisoner is not a ground for relief on federal habeas corpus." We granted certiorari (1992), and the Texas Court of Criminal Appeals stayed petitioner's execution. We now affirm.

Petitioner asserts that the Eighth and Fourteenth Amendments to the United States Constitution prohibit the execution of a person who is innocent of the crime for which he was convicted. This proposition has an elemental appeal, as would the similar proposition that the Constitution prohibits the imprisonment of one who is innocent of the crime for which he was convicted. After all, the central purpose of any system of criminal justice is to convict the guilty and free the innocent.... But the evidence upon which petitioner's claim of innocence rests was not produced at his trial, but rather eight years later. In any system of criminal justice, "innocence" or "guilt" must be determined in some sort of a judicial proceeding. Petitioner's showing of innocence, and indeed his constitutional claim for relief based upon that showing, must be evaluated in the light of the previous proceedings in this case, which have stretched over a span of 10 years.

A person when first charged with a crime is entitled to a presumption of innocence, and may insist that his guilt be established beyond a reasonable doubt. *In re Winship* (1970)....

Once a defendant has been afforded a fair trial and convicted of the offense for which he was charged, the presumption of innocence disappears.... Here, it is not disputed that the State met its burden of proving at trial that petitioner was guilty of the capital murder of Officer Carrisalez beyond a reasonable doubt. Thus, in the eyes of the law, petitioner does not come before the Court as one who is "innocent," but on the contrary as one who has been convicted by due process of law of two brutal murders.

Based on affidavits here filed, petitioner claims that evidence never presented to the trial court proves him innocent notwithstanding the verdict reached at his trial. Such a claim is not cognizable in the state courts of Texas. For to obtain a new trial based on newly discovered evidence, a defendant must file a motion within 30 days after imposition or suspension of sentence. The Texas courts have construed this 30-day time limit as jurisdictional....

Claims of actual innocence based on newly discovered evidence have never been held to state a ground for federal habeas relief absent an independent constitutional violation occurring in the underlying state criminal proceeding. Chief Justice Warren made this clear in *Townsend v. Sain* (emphasis added):

> "Where newly discovered evidence is alleged in a habeas application, evidence which could not reasonably have been presented to the state trier of facts, the federal court must grant an evidentiary hearing. Of course, such evidence must bear upon the constitutionality of the applicant's detention; *the existence merely of newly discovered evidence relevant to the guilt of a state prisoner is not a ground for relief on federal habeas corpus.*"

This rule is grounded in the principle that federal habeas courts sit to ensure that individuals are not imprisoned in violation of the Constitution—not to correct errors of fact....

... Few rulings would be more disruptive of our federal system than to provide for federal habeas review of free-standing claims of actual innocence.

Our decision in *Jackson v. Virginia* (1979) comes as close to authorizing evidentiary review of a state court conviction on federal habeas as any of our cases. There, we held that a federal habeas court may review a claim that the evidence adduced at a state trial was not sufficient to convict a criminal defendant beyond a reasonable doubt....

The type of federal habeas review sought by petitioner here is different in critical respects than that authorized by *Jackson*. First, the *Jackson* inquiry is aimed at determining whether there has been an independent constitutional violation—*i.e.*, a conviction based on evidence that fails to meet the *Winship* standard. Thus, federal habeas courts act in their historic capacity—to assure that the habeas petitioner is not being held in violation of his or her federal constitutional rights. Second, the sufficiency of the evidence review authorized by *Jackson* is limited to "record evidence." *Jackson* does not extend to nonrecord evidence, including newly discovered evidence. Finally, the *Jackson* inquiry does not focus on whether the trier of fact made the *correct* guilt or innocence determination, but rather whether it made a *rational* decision to convict or acquit....

The dissent would place the burden on petitioner to show that he is "probably" innocent. Although petitioner would not be entitled to discovery "as a matter of right," the District Court would retain its "discretion to order discovery ... when it would help the court make a reliable determination with respect to the prisoner's claim." And although the District Court would not be required to hear testimony from the witnesses who testified at trial or the affiants upon whom petitioner relies, it would allow the District Court to do so "if the petition warrants a hearing." At the end of the day, the dissent would have the District Court "make a case-by-case determination about the reliability of newly discovered evidence under the circumstances," and then "weigh the evidence in favor of the prisoner against the evidence of his guilt."

The dissent fails to articulate the relief that would be available if petitioner were to meets its "probable innocence" standard. Would it be commutation of petitioner's death sentence, new trial, or unconditional release from imprisonment? The typical relief granted in federal habeas corpus is a conditional order of release unless the State elects to retry the successful habeas petitioner, or in a capital case a similar conditional order vacating the death sentence. Were petitioner to satisfy the dissent's "probable innocence" standard, therefore, the District Court would presumably be required to grant a conditional order of relief, which would in effect require the State to retry petitioner 10 years after his first trial, not because of any constitutional violation which had occurred at the first trial, but simply because of a belief that in light of petitioner's new found evidence a jury might find him not guilty at a second trial.

Yet there is no guarantee that the guilt or innocence determination would be any more exact. To the contrary, the passage of time only diminishes the reliability of criminal adjudications. . . .

This is not to say that our habeas jurisprudence casts a blind eye towards innocence. In a series of cases culminating with *Sawyer v. Whitley* (1992), decided last Term, we have held that a petitioner otherwise subject to defenses of abusive or successive use of the writ may have his federal constitutional claim considered on the merits if he makes a proper showing of actual innocence. This rule, or fundamental miscarriage of justice exception, is grounded in the "equitable discretion" of habeas courts to see that federal constitutional errors do not result in the incarceration of innocent persons. . . . But this body of our habeas jurisprudence makes clear that a claim of "actual innocence" is not itself a constitutional claim, but instead a gateway through which a habeas petitioner must pass to have his otherwise barred constitutional claim considered on the merits. . . .

Petitioner asserts that this case is different because he has been sentenced to death. But we have "refused to hold that the fact that a death sentence has been imposed requires a different standard of review on federal habeas corpus." *Murray v. Giarratano* (1989) (plurality opinion). We have, of course, held that the Eighth Amendment requires increased reliability of the process by which capital punishment may be imposed. . . . But petitioner's claim does not fit well into the doctrine of these cases, since, as we have pointed out, it is far from clear that a second trial 10 years after the first trial would produce a more reliable result. . . .

Alternatively, petitioner invokes the Fourteenth Amendment's guarantee of due process of law in support of his claim that his showing of actual innocence entitles him to a new trial, or at least to a vacation of his death sentence. . . .

. . . [W]e cannot say that Texas' refusal to entertain petitioner's newly discovered evidence eight years after his conviction transgresses a principle of fundamental fairness "rooted in the traditions and conscience of our people." . . . This is not to say, however, that petitioner is left without a forum to raise his actual innocence claim. For under Texas law, petitioner may file a request for executive clemency. . . . Clemency is deeply rooted in our Anglo-American tradition of law, and is the historic remedy for preventing miscarriages of justice where judicial process has been exhausted. . . .

Executive clemency has provided the "fail safe" in our criminal justice system. . . . It is an unalterable fact that our judicial system, like the human beings who administer it, is fallible. But history is replete with examples of wrongfully convicted persons who have been pardoned in the wake of after-discovered evidence establishing their innocence. In his classic work, Professor Edwin Borchard compiled 65 cases in which it was later determined that individuals had been wrongfully convicted of crimes. Clemency provided the relief mechanism in 47 of these cases; the remaining cases ended in judgments of acquittals after new trials. . . . Recent authority confirms that over the past century clemency has been exercised frequently in capital cases in which demonstrations of "actual innocence" have been made. . . .

In Texas, the Governor has the power, upon the recommendation of a majority of the Board of Pardons and Paroles, to grant clemency. The board's consideration is triggered upon request of the individual sentenced to death, his or her representative, or the Governor herself. In capital cases, a request may be made for a full pardon, a commutation of death sentence to life imprisonment or appropriate maximum penalty, or a reprieve of execution. The Governor has the sole authority to grant one reprieve in any capital case not exceeding 30 days.

The Texas clemency procedures contain specific guidelines for pardons on the ground of innocence. The board will entertain applications for a recommendation of full pardon because of innocence upon receipt of the following: "(1) a written unanimous recommendation of the current trial officials of the court of conviction; and/or (2) a certified order or judgment of a court having jurisdiction accompanied by certified copy of the findings of fact (if any); and (3) affidavits of witnesses upon which the finding of innocence is based." In this case, petitioner has apparently sought a 30-day reprieve from the Governor, but has yet to apply for a pardon, or even a commutation, on the ground of innocence or otherwise.

As the foregoing discussion illustrates, in state criminal proceedings the trial is the paramount event for determining the guilt or innocence of the defendant. Federal habeas review of state convictions has traditionally been limited to claims of constitutional violations occurring in the course of the underlying state criminal proceedings. Our federal habeas cases have treated claims of "actual innocence," not as an independent constitutional claim, but as a basis upon which a habeas petitioner may have an independent constitutional claim considered on the merits, even though his habeas petition would otherwise be regarded as successive or abusive. History shows that the traditional remedy for claims of innocence based on new evidence, discovered too late in the day to file a new trial motion, has been executive clemency.

We may assume, for the sake of argument in deciding this case, that in a capital case a truly persuasive demonstration of "actual innocence" made after trial would render the execution of a defendant unconstitutional, and warrant federal habeas relief if there were no state avenue open to process such a claim. But because of the very disruptive effect that entertaining claims of actual innocence would have on the need for finality in capital cases, and the enormous burden that having to retry cases based on often stale evidence would place on the States, the threshold showing for such an assumed right would necessarily be extraordinarily high. The showing made by petitioner in this case falls far short of any such threshold. . . .

The judgment of the Court of Appeals is

Affirmed.

JUSTICE O'CONNOR, with whom JUSTICE KENNEDY joins, concurring.

I cannot disagree with the fundamental legal principle that executing the innocent is inconsistent with the Constitution. . . . [T]he execution of a legally and factually innocent person would be a constitutionally intolerable event. Dispositive to this case, however, is an equally fundamental fact: Petitioner is not innocent, in any sense of the word. . . .

Ultimately, two things about this case are clear. First is what the Court does *not* hold. Nowhere does the Court state that the Constitution permits the execution of an actually innocent person. Instead, the Court assumes for the sake of argument that a truly persuasive demonstration of actual innocence would render any such execution unconstitutional and that federal habeas relief would be warranted if no state avenue were open to process the claim. Second is what petitioner has not demonstrated. Petitioner has failed to make a persuasive showing of actual innocence. Not one judge—no state court judge, not the District Court Judge, none of the three Judges of the Court of Appeals, and none of the Justices of this Court—has expressed doubt about petitioner's guilt. Accordingly, the Court has no reason to pass on, and appropriately reserves, the question whether federal courts may entertain convincing claims of actual innocence. That difficult question remains open. If the Constitution's guarantees of fair procedure and the safeguards of clemency and pardon fulfill their historical mission, it may never require resolution at all.

JUSTICE SCALIA, with whom JUSTICE THOMAS joins, concurring.

We granted certiorari on the question whether it violates due process or constitutes cruel and unusual punishment for a State to execute a person who, having been convicted of murder after a full and fair trial, later alleges that newly discovered evidence shows him to be "actually innocent." I would have preferred to decide that question, particularly since, as the Court's discussion shows, it is perfectly clear what the answer is: There is no basis in text, tradition, or even in contemporary practice (if that were enough), for finding in the Constitution a right to demand

judicial consideration of newly discovered evidence of innocence brought forward after conviction. In saying that such a right exists, the dissenters apply nothing but their personal opinions to invalidate the rules of more than two thirds of the States, and a Federal Rule of Criminal Procedure for which this Court itself is responsible. If the system that has been in place for 200 years (and remains widely approved) "shocks" the dissenters' consciences, perhaps they should doubt the calibration of their consciences, or, better still, the usefulness of "conscience-shocking" as a legal test.

I nonetheless join the entirety of the Court's opinion, including the final portion because there is no legal error in deciding a case by assuming *arguendo* that an asserted constitutional right exists, and because I can understand, or at least am accustomed to, the reluctance of the present Court to admit publicly that Our Perfect Constitution lets stand any injustice, much less the execution of an innocent man who has received, though to no avail, all the process that our society has traditionally deemed adequate. With any luck, we shall avoid ever having to face this embarrassing question again, since it is improbable that evidence of innocence as convincing as today's opinion requires would fail to produce an executive pardon. . . .

JUSTICE WHITE, concurring in the judgment.

In voting to affirm, I assume that a persuasive showing of "actual innocence" made after trial, even though made after the expiration of the time provided by law for the presentation of newly discovered evidence, would render unconstitutional the execution of petitioner in this case. To be entitled to relief, however, petitioner would at the very least be required to show that based on proffered newly discovered evidence and the entire record before the jury that convicted him, "no rational trier of fact could [find] proof of guilt beyond a reasonable doubt." *Jackson v. Virginia* (1979). For the reasons stated in the Court's opinion, petitioner's showing falls far short of satisfying even that standard, and I therefore concur in the judgment.

JUSTICE BLACKMUN, with whom JUSTICE STEVENS and JUSTICE SOUTER join with respect to Parts I-IV, dissenting.

Nothing could be more contrary to contemporary standards of decency, see *Ford v. Wainwright* (1986), or more shocking to the conscience, see *Rochin v. California* (1952), than to execute a person who is actually innocent.

I therefore must disagree with the long and general discussion that precedes the Court's disposition of this case. That discussion, of course, is dictum because the Court assumes, "for the sake of argument in deciding this case, that in a capital case a truly persuasive demonstration of 'actual innocence' made after trial would render the execution of a defendant unconstitutional." Without articulating the standard it is applying, however, the Court then decides that this petitioner has not made a sufficiently persuasive case. Because I believe that in the first instance the District Court should decide whether petitioner is entitled to a hearing and whether he is entitled to relief on the merits of his claim, I would reverse the order of the Court of Appeals and remand this case for further proceedings in the District Court.

I

The Court's enumeration of the constitutional rights of criminal defendants surely is entirely beside the point. These protections sometimes fail. We really are being asked to decide whether the Constitution forbids the execution of a person who has been validly convicted and sentenced but who, nonetheless, can prove his innocence with newly discovered evidence. Despite the State of Texas' astonishing protestation to the contrary, I do not see how the answer can be anything but "yes."

A

The Eighth Amendment prohibits "cruel and unusual punishments." This proscription is not static but rather reflects evolving standards of decency. . . . I think it is crystal clear that the execution of an innocent person is "at odds with contemporary standards of fairness and decency.". . . Indeed, it is at odds with any standard of decency that I can imagine.

This Court has ruled that punishment is excessive and unconstitutional if it is "nothing more than the purposeless and needless imposition of pain and suffering," or if it is "grossly out of proportion to the severity of the crime." . . . It has held that death is an excessive punishment for rape, *Coker v. Georgia* [1977], and for mere participation in a robbery during which a killing takes place. *Enmund v. Florida* (1982). If it is violative of the Eighth Amendment to execute someone who is guilty of those crimes, then it plainly is violative of the Eighth Amendment to execute a person who is actually innocent. Executing an innocent person epitomizes "the purposeless and needless imposition of pain and suffering." . . .

The protection of the Eighth Amendment does not end once a defendant has been validly convicted and sentenced. In *Johnson v. Mississippi* (1988), the petitioner had been convicted of murder and sentenced to death on the basis of three aggravating circumstances. One of those circumstances was that he previously had been convicted of a violent felony in the State of New York. After Johnson had been sentenced to death, the New York Court of Appeals reversed his prior conviction. Although there was no question that the prior conviction was valid at the time of Johnson's sentencing, this Court held that the Eighth Amendment required review of the sentence because "the jury was allowed to consider evidence that has been revealed to be materially inaccurate." In *Ford v. Wainwright,* the petitioner had been convicted of murder and sentenced to death. There was no suggestion that he was incompetent at the time of his offense, at trial, or at sentencing, but subsequently he exhibited changes in behavior that raised doubts about his sanity. This Court held that Florida was required under the Eighth Amendment to provide an additional hearing to determine whether Ford was mentally competent, and that he could not be executed if he were incompetent. Both *Johnson* and *Ford* recognize that capital defendants may be entitled to further proceedings because of an intervening development even though they have been validly convicted and sentenced to death.

Respondent and the United States as *amicus curiae* argue that the Eighth Amendment does not apply to petitioner because he is challenging his guilt, not his punishment. The majority attempts to distinguish *Ford* on that basis. Such reasoning, however, not only contradicts our decision in *Beck v. Alabama* (1980), but also fundamentally misconceives the nature of petitioner's argument. Whether petitioner is viewed as challenging simply his death sentence or also his continued detention, he still is challenging the State's right to punish him. Respondent and the United States would impose a clear line between guilt and punishment, reasoning that every claim that concerns guilt necessarily does not involve punishment. Such a division is far too facile. What respondent and the United States fail to recognize is that the legitimacy of punishment is inextricably intertwined with guilt. . . .

The Court also suggests that allowing petitioner to raise his claim of innocence would not serve society's interest in the reliable imposition of the death penalty because it might require a new trial that would be less accurate than the first. This suggestion misses the point entirely. The question is not whether a second trial would be more reliable than the first but whether, in light of new evidence, the result of the first trial is sufficiently reliable for the State to carry out a death sentence. Furthermore, it is far from clear that a State will seek to retry the rare prisoner who prevails on a claim of actual innocence. As explained in part III, I believe a prisoner must show not just that there was probably a reasonable doubt about his guilt but that he is probably actually innocent. I find it difficult to believe that any State would chose to retry a person who meets this standard.

I believe it contrary to any standard of decency to execute someone who is actually innocent. Because the Eighth Amendment applies to questions of guilt or innocence, . . . and to persons upon whom a valid sentence of death has been imposed, . . . I also believe that petitioner may raise an Eighth Amendment challenge to his punishment on the ground that he is actually innocent.

B

Execution of the innocent is equally offensive to the Due Process Clause of the Fourteenth Amendment. The majority's discussion misinterprets petitioner's Fourteenth Amendment claim as raising a procedural rather than a substantive due process challenge. . . .

Petitioner's claim fails within our due process precedents. In *Rochin* [*v. California,* 1952] deputy sheriffs investigating narcotics sales broke into Rochin's room and observed him put two capsules in his mouth. The deputies attempted to remove the capsules from his mouth and, having failed, took Rochin to a hospital and had his stomach pumped. The capsules were found to contain morphine. The Court held that the deputies' conduct "shock[ed] the conscience" and violated due process. . . . The lethal injection that petitioner faces as an allegedly innocent person is certainly closer to the rack and the screw than the stomach pump condemned in *Rochin.* Execution of an innocent person is the ultimate " 'arbitrary impositio[n].' " . . . It is an imposition from which one never recovers and for which one can never be compensated. Thus, I also believe that petitioner may raise a substantive due process challenge to his punishment on the ground that he is actuality innocent.

C

Given my conclusion that it violates the Eighth and Fourteenth Amendments to execute a person who is actually innocent, I find no bar in *Townsend v. Sain* (1963), to consideration of an actual innocence claim. Newly discovered evidence of petitioner's innocence does bear on the constitutionality of his execution. Of course, it could be argued this is in some tension with *Townsend*'s statement that "the existence merely of newly discovered evidence relevant to the guilt of a state prisoner is not a ground for relief on federal habeas corpus." That statement, however, is no more than distant dictum here, for we never had been asked to consider whether the execution of an innocent person violates the Constitution.

II

The majority's discussion of petitioner's constitutional claims is even more perverse when viewed in the light of this Court's recent habeas jurisprudence. Beginning with a trio of decisions in 1986, this Court shifted the focus of federal habeas review of successive, abusive, or defaulted claims away from the preservation of constitutional rights to a fact-based inquiry into the habeas petitioner's guilt or innocence. . . . The Court sought to strike a balance between the State's interest in the finality of its criminal judgments and the prisoner's interest in access to a forum to test the basic justice of his sentence. . . . In striking this balance, the Court adopted the view of Judge Friendly that there should be an exception to the concept of finality when a prisoner can make a claim of actual innocence. . . .

Having adopted an "actual innocence" requirement for review of abusive, successive, or defaulted claims, however, the majority would now take the position that "the claim of 'actual innocence' is not itself a constitutional claim, but instead a gateway through which a habeas petitioner must pass to have his otherwise barred constitutional claim considered on the merits." In other words, having held that a prisoner who is incarcerated in violation of the Constitution must show he is actually innocent to obtain relief, the majority would now hold that a prisoner who is actually innocent must show a constitutional violation to obtain relief. The only principle that would appear to reconcile these two positions is the principle that habeas relief should be denied whenever possible.

III

The Eighth and Fourteenth Amendments, of course, are binding on the States, and one would normally expect the States to adopt procedures to consider claims of actual innocence based on newly discovered evidence. . . . The majority's disposition of this case, however, leaves the States uncertain of their constitutional obligations.

A

Whatever procedures a State might adopt to hear actual innocence claims, one thing is certain: The possibility of executive clemency is not sufficient to satisfy the requirements of the Eighth and Fourteenth Amendments. The majority correctly points out: "A pardon is an act of grace." The vindication of rights guaranteed by the Constitution has never been made to turn on the unreviewable discretion of an executive official or administrative tribunal. Indeed, in *Ford v. Wainwright*, we explicitly rejected the argument that executive clemency was adequate to vindicate the Eighth Amendment right not to be executed if one is insane. . . .

[B Omitted]

C

The question that remains is what showing should be required to obtain relief on the merits of an Eighth or Fourteenth Amendment claim of actual innocence. . . .

In articulating the "actual-innocence" exception in our habeas jurisprudence, this Court has adopted a standard requiring the petitioner to show a " 'fair probability that, in light of all the evidence . . . , the trier of facts would have entertained a reasonable doubt of his guilt.' " . . . In other words, the habeas petitioner must show that there probably would be a reasonable doubt. . . .

I think the standard for relief on the merits of an actual-innocence claim must be higher than the threshold standard for merely reaching that claim or any other claim that has been procedurally defaulted or is successive or abusive. I would hold that, to obtain relief on a claim of actual innocence, the petitioner must show that he probably is innocent. This standard is supported by several considerations. First, new evidence of innocence may be discovered long after the defendant's conviction. Given the passage of time, it may be difficult for the State to retry a defendant who obtains relief from his conviction or sentence on an actual-innocence claim. The actual-innocence proceeding thus may constitute the final word on whether the defendant may be punished. In light of this fact, an otherwise constitutionally valid conviction or sentence should not be set aside lightly. Second, conviction after a constitutionally adequate trial strips the defendant of the presumption of innocence. The government bears the burden of proving the defendant's guilt beyond a reasonable doubt, . . . but once the government has done so, the burden of proving innocence must shift to the convicted defendant. The actual-innocence inquiry is therefore distinguishable from review for sufficiency of the evidence, where the question is not whether the defendant is innocent but whether the government has met its constitutional burden of proving the defendant's guilt beyond a reasonable doubt. When a defendant seeks to challenge the determination of guilt after he has been validly convicted and sentenced, it is fair to place on him the burden of proving his innocence, not just raising doubt about his guilt.

In considering whether a prisoner is entitled to relief on an actual-innocence claim, a court should take all the evidence into account, giving due regard to its reliability. . . . Because placing the burden on the prisoner to prove innocence creates a presumption that the conviction is valid, it is not necessary or appropriate to make further presumptions about the reliability of newly discovered evidence generally. Rather, the court charged with deciding such a claim should make a case-by-case determination about the reliability of the newly discovered evidence under the circumstances. The court then should weigh the evidence in favor of the prisoner against the evidence of his guilt. Obviously, the stronger the evidence of the prisoner's guilt, the more persuasive the newly discovered evidence of innocence must be. A prisoner raising an actual-innocence claim in a federal habeas petition is not entitled to discovery as a matter of right. . . . The district court retains discretion to order discovery, however, when it would help the court make a reliable determination with respect to the prisoner's claim. . . .

It should be clear that the standard I would adopt would not convert the federal courts into " 'forums in which to relitigate state trials.' " It would not "require the habeas court to hear testimony from the witnesses who testified at the trial," though, if the petition warrants a hearing, it may require the habeas court to hear the testimony of "those who made the statements in the affidavits which petitioner has presented." I believe that if a prisoner can show that he is probably actually innocent, in light of all the evidence, then he has made "a truly persuasive demonstration," and his execution would violate the Constitution. I would so hold.

IV

In this case, the District Court determined that petitioner's newly discovered evidence warranted further consideration. Because the District Court doubted its own authority to consider the new evidence, it thought that petitioner's claim of actual innocence should be brought in state court, but it clearly did not think that petitioner's evidence was so insubstantial that it could be dismissed without any hearing at all. I would reverse the order of the Court of Appeals and remand the case to the District Court to consider whether petitioner has shown, in light of all the evidence, that he is probably actually innocent. . . .

V

I have voiced disappointment over this Court's obvious eagerness to do away with any restriction on the States' power to execute whomever and however they please. See *Coleman v. Thompson* (1991) (dissenting opinion). See also *Coleman v. Thompson* (1992) (dissent from denial of stay of execution). I have also expressed doubts about whether, in the absence of such restrictions, capital punishment remains constitutional at all. *Sawyer v. Whitley* [1992] (opinion concurring in the judgment). Of one thing, however, I am certain. Just as an execution without adequate safeguards is unacceptable, so too is an execution when the condemned prisoner can prove that he is innocent. The execution of a person who can show that he is innocent comes perilously close to simple murder.

□□□

No. 91-2024

Lamb's Chapel and John Steigerwald, Petitioners v. Center Moriches Union Free School District et al.

On writ of certiorari to the United States Court of Appeals for the Second Circuit

[June 7, 1993]

JUSTICE WHITE delivered the opinion of the Court.

Section 414 of the New York Education Law authorizes local school boards to adopt reasonable regulations for the use of school property for 10 specified purposes when the property is not in use for school purposes. Among the permitted uses is the holding of "social, civic and recreational meetings and entertainments, and other uses pertaining to the welfare of the community; but such meetings, entertainment and uses shall be non-exclusive and open to the general public." § 414(c). The list of permitted uses does not include meetings for religious purposes, and a New York appellate court in *Trietley v. Board of Ed. of Buffalo* (App. Div. 1978), ruled that local boards could not allow student bible clubs to meet on school property because "[r]eligious purposes are not included in the enumerated purposes for which a school may be used under section 414." . . .

Pursuant to § 414's empowerment of local school districts, the Board of Center Moriches Union Free School District (District) has issued rules and regulations with respect to the use of school property when not in use for school purposes. The rules allow only 2 of the 10 purposes authorized by § 414: social, civic, or recreational uses (Rule 10) and use by political organizations if secured in compliance with § 414 (Rule 8). Rule 7, however, consistent with the judicial interpretation of state law, provides that "[t]he school premises shall not be used by any group for religious purposes."

The issue in this case is whether, against this background of state law, it violates the Free Speech Clause of the First Amendment, made applicable to the States by the Fourteenth Amendment, to deny a church access to school premises to exhibit for public viewing and for assertedly religious purposes, a film dealing with family and child-rearing issues faced by parents today.

I

Petitioners (Church) are Lamb's Chapel, an evangelical church in the community of Center Moriches, and its pastor John Steigerwald. Twice the Church applied to the District for permission to use school facilities to show a six-part film series containing lectures by Doctor James Dobson. A brochure provided on request of the District identified Dr. Dobson as a licensed psychologist, former associate clinical professor of pediatrics at the University of Southern California, best-selling author, and radio commentator. The brochure stated that the film series would discuss Dr. Dobson's views on the undermining influences of the media that could only be counterbalanced by returning to traditional, Christian family values instilled at an early stage. . . . The District denied the first application, saying that "[t]his film does appear to be church related and therefore your request must be refused." The second application for permission to use school premises for showing the film, which described it as a "Family oriented movie—from the Christian perspective," was denied using identical language.

The Church brought suit in District Court, challenging the denial as a violation of the Freedom of Speech and Assembly Clauses, the Free Exercise Clause, and the Establishment Clause of the First Amendment, as well as the Equal Protection Clause of the Fourteenth Amendment. . . . The District Court granted summary judgment for respondents, rejecting all of the Church's claims. With respect to the free-speech claim under the First Amendment, the District Court characterized the District's facilities as a "limited public forum." The court noted that the enumerated purposes for which § 414 allowed access to school facilities did not include religious worship or instruction, that Rule 7 explicitly proscribes using school facilities for religious purposes, and that the Church had conceded that its showing of the film would be for religious purposes. The District Court stated that once a limited public forum is opened to a particular type of speech, selectively denying access to other activities of the same genre is forbidden. Noting that the District had not opened its facilities to organizations similar to Lamb's Chapel for religious purposes, the District Court held that the denial in this case was viewpoint neutral and, hence, not a violation of the Freedom of Speech Clause. The District Court also rejected the assertion by the Church that denying its application demonstrated a hostility to religion and advancement of nonreligion not justified under the Establishment of Religion Clause of the First Amendment.

The Court of Appeals affirmed the judgment of the District Court "in all respects." *Lamb's Chapel v. Center Moriches Union Free School Dist.* (CA2 1992). It held that the school property, when not in use for school purposes, was neither a traditional nor a designated public forum;

rather, it was a limited public forum open only for designated purposes, a classification that "allows it to remain non-public except as to specified uses." The court observed that exclusions in such a forum need only be reasonable and viewpoint neutral, and ruled that denying access to the Church for the purpose of showing its film did not violate this standard. Because the holding below was questionable under our decisions, we granted the petition for certiorari (1992), which in principal part challenged the holding below as contrary to the Free Speech Clause of the First Amendment.

II

There is no question that the District, like the private owner of property, may legally preserve the property under its control for the use to which it is dedicated. *Cornelius v. NAACP Legal Defense and Ed. Fund, Inc.* (1985); *Perry Ed. Assn. v. Perry Local Educators' Assn.* (1983). . . . It is also common ground that the District need not have permitted after-hours use of its property for any of the uses permitted by § 414 of the state education law. The District, however, did open its property for 2 of the 10 uses permitted by § 414. The Church argued below that because under Rule 10 of the rules issued by the District, school property could be used for "social, civic, and recreational" purposes, the District had opened its property for such a wide variety of communicative purposes that restrictions on communicative uses of the property were subject to the same constitutional limitations as restrictions in traditional public fora such as parks and sidewalks. Hence, its view was that subject-matter or speaker exclusions on District property were required to be justified by a compelling state interest and to be narrowly drawn to achieve that end. Both the District Court and the Court of Appeals rejected this submission, which is also presented to this Court. The argument has considerable force, for the District's property is heavily used by a wide variety of private organizations, including some that presented a "close question," which the Court of Appeals resolved in the District's favor, as to whether the District had in fact already opened its property for religious uses. We need not rule on this issue, however, for even if the courts below were correct in this respect—and we shall assume for present purposes that they were—the judgment below must be reversed.

With respect to public property that is not a designated public forum open for indiscriminate public use for communicative purposes, we have said that "[c]ontrol over access to a nonpublic forum can be based on subject matter and speaker identity so long as the distinctions drawn are reasonable in light of the purpose served by the forum and are viewpoint neutral." . . . The Court of Appeals appeared to recognize that the total ban on using District property for religious purposes could survive First Amendment challenge only if excluding this category of speech was reasonable and viewpoint neutral. The court's conclusion in this case was that Rule 7 met this test. We cannot agree with this holding, for Rule 7 was unconstitutionally applied in this case.

The Court of Appeals thought that the application of Rule 7 in this case was viewpoint neutral because it had been and would be applied in the same way to all uses of school property for religious purposes. That all religions and all uses for religious purposes are treated alike under Rule 7, however, does not answer the critical question whether it discriminates on the basis of viewpoint to permit school property to be used for the presentation of all views about family issues and child-rearing except those dealing with the subject matter from a religious standpoint.

There is no suggestion from the courts below or from the District or the State that a lecture or film about child-rearing and family values would not be a use for social or civic purposes otherwise permitted by Rule 10. That subject matter is not one that the District has placed off limits to any and all speakers. Nor is there any indication in the record before us that the application to exhibit the particular film involved here was or would have been denied for any reason other than the fact that the presentation would have been from a religious perspective. In our view, denial on that basis was plainly invalid under our holding in *Cornelius* that

> "[a]lthough a speaker may be excluded from a nonpublic forum if he wishes to address a topic not encompassed within the purpose of the forum ... or if he is not a member of the class of speakers for whose special benefit the forum was created ... the government violates the First Amendment when it denies access to a speaker solely to suppress the point of view he espouses on an otherwise includable subject."

The film involved here no doubt dealt with a subject otherwise permissible under Rule 10, and its exhibition was denied solely because the film dealt with the subject from a religious standpoint. The principle that has emerged from our cases "is that the First Amendment forbids the government to regulate speech in ways that favor some viewpoints or ideas at the expense of others." *City Council of Los Angeles v. Taxpayers for Vincent* (1984). That principle applies in the circumstances of this case; as Judge Posner said for the Seventh Circuit Court of Appeals, to discriminate "against a particular point of view ... would ... flunk the test ... [of] *Cornelius,* provided that the defendants have no defense based on the establishment clause." *May v. Evansville-Vanderburgh School Corp.* (1986).

The District, as a respondent, would save its judgment below on the ground that to permit its property to be used for religious purposes would be an establishment of religion forbidden by the First Amendment. This

Court suggested in *Widmar v. Vincent* (1981), that the interest of the State in avoiding an Establishment Clause violation "may be [a] compelling" one justifying an abridgment of free speech otherwise protected by the First Amendment; but the Court went on to hold that permitting use of University property for religious purposes under the open access policy involved there would not be incompatible with the Court's Establishment Clause cases.

We have no more trouble than did the *Widmar* Court in disposing of the claimed defense on the ground that the posited fears of an Establishment Clause violation are unfounded. The showing of this film would not have been during school hours, would not have been sponsored by the school, and would have been open to the public, not just to church members. The District property had repeatedly been used by a wide variety of private organizations. Under these circumstances, as in *Widmar,* there would have been no realistic danger that the community would think that the District was endorsing religion or any particular creed, and any benefit to religion or to the Church would have been no more than incidental. As in *Widmar,* permitting District property to be used to exhibit the film involved in this case would not have been an establishment of religion under the three-part test articulated in *Lemon v. Kurtzman* (1971): The challenged governmental action has a secular purpose, does not have the principal or primary effect of advancing or inhibiting religion, and does not foster an excessive entanglement with religion. . . .

We note that the Attorney General for the State of New York, a respondent here, . . . submits that the exclusion is justified because the purpose of the access rules is to promote the interests of the public in general rather than sectarian or other private interests. In light of the variety of the uses of District property that have been permitted under Rule 10, this approach has its difficulties. This is particularly so since Rule 10 states that District property may be used for social, civic, or recreational use "only if it can be nonexclusive and open to all residents of the school district that form a homogeneous group deemed relevant to the event." At least arguably, the Rule does not require that permitted uses need be open to the public at large. However that may be, this was not the basis of the judgment that we are reviewing. The Court of Appeals, as we understand it, ruled that because the District had the power to permit or exclude certain subject matters, it was entitled to deny use for any religious purpose, including the purpose in this case. The Attorney General also defends this as a permissible subject-matter exclusion rather than a denial based on viewpoint, a submission that we have already rejected. . . .

For the reasons stated in this opinion, the judgment of the Court of Appeals is

Reversed.

JUSTICE KENNEDY, concurring in part and concurring in the judgment.

Given the issues presented as well as the apparent unanimity of our conclusion that this overt, viewpoint-based discrimination contradicts the Speech Clause of the First Amendment and that there has been no substantial showing of a potential Establishment Clause violation, I agree with JUSTICE SCALIA that the Court's citation of *Lemon v. Kurtzman* (1971) is unsettling and unnecessary. The same can be said of the Court's use of the phrase "endorsing religion," which, as I have indicated elsewhere, cannot suffice as a rule of decision consistent with our precedents and our traditions in this part of our jurisprudence. . . .

JUSTICE SCALIA, with whom JUSTICE THOMAS joins, concurring in the judgment.

I join the Court's conclusion that the District's refusal to allow use of school facilities for petitioners' film viewing, while generally opening the schools for community activities, violates petitioners' First Amendment free-speech rights (as does N.Y. Educ. Law § 414) to the extent it compelled the District's denial. I also agree with the Court that allowing Lamb's Chapel to use school facilities poses "no realistic danger" of a violation of the Establishment Clause, but I cannot accept most of its reasoning in this regard. The Court explains that the showing of petitioners' film on school property after school hours would not cause the community to "think that the District was endorsing religion or any particular creed," and further notes that access to school property would not violate the three-part test articulated in *Lemon v. Kurtzman* (1971).

As to the Court's invocation of the *Lemon* test: Like some ghoul in a late-night horror movie that repeatedly sits up in its grave and shuffles abroad, after being repeatedly killed and buried, *Lemon* stalks our Establishment Clause jurisprudence once again, frightening the little children and school attorneys of Center Moriches Union Free School District. Its most recent burial, only last Term, was, to be sure, not fully six-feet under: our decision in *Lee v. Weisman* (1992) conspicuously avoided using the supposed "test" but also declined the invitation to repudiate it. Over the years, however, no fewer than five of the currently sitting Justices have, in their own opinions, personally driven pencils through the creature's heart (the author of today's opinion repeatedly), and a sixth has joined an opinion doing so. See, *e.g., Weisman* (SCALIA, J., joined by, *inter alios,* THOMAS, J., dissenting); *Allegheny County v. American Civil Liberties Union, Greater Pittsburgh Chapter* (1989) (KENNEDY, J., concurring in the judgment in part and dissenting in part); *Corporation of Presiding Bishop of Church of Jesus Christ of Latter-day Saints v. Amos* (1987) (O'CONNOR, J. concurring); *Wallace v. Jaffree* (1985) (REHNQUIST, J., dissenting); (WHITE, J., dissenting);

School Dist. of Grand Rapids v. Ball (1985) (WHITE, J. dissenting);
Widmar v. Vincent (1981) (WHITE, J., dissenting); *New York v.
Cathedral Academy* (1977) (WHITE, J., dissenting); *Roemer v. Mary-
land Bd. of Public Works* (1976) (WHITE, J., concurring in judgment);
Committee for Public Education & Religious Liberty v. Nyquist (1973)
(WHITE, J., dissenting).

The secret of the *Lemon* test's survival, I think, is that it is so easy to
kill. It is there to scare us (and our audience) when we wish it to do so, but
we can command it to return to the tomb at will. See, *e.g., Lynch v.
Donnelly* (1984) (noting instances in which Court has not applied *Lemon*
test). When we wish to strike down a practice it forbids, we invoke it, see,
e.g., Aguilar v. Felton (1985) (striking down state remedial education
program administered in part in parochial schools); when we wish to
uphold a practice it forbids, we ignore it entirely, see *Marsh v. Chambers*
(1983) (upholding state legislative chaplains). Sometimes, we take a middle
course, calling its three prongs "no more than helpful signposts," *Hunt v.
McNair* (1973). Such a docile and useful monster is worth keeping around,
at least in a somnolent state; one never knows when one might need him.

For my part, I agree with the long list of constitutional scholars who
have criticized *Lemon* and bemoaned the strange Establishment Clause
geometry of crooked lines and wavering shapes its intermittent use has
produced. . . . I will decline to apply *Lemon*—whether it validates or
invalidates the government action in question—and therefore cannot join
the opinion of the Court today.

I cannot join for yet another reason: the Court's statement that the
proposed use of the school's facilities is constitutional because (among
other things) it would not signal endorsement of religion in general. What
a strange notion, that a Constitution which *itself* gives "religion in
general" preferential treatment (I refer to the Free Exercise Clause)
forbids endorsement of religion in general. The Attorney General of New
York not only agrees with that strange notion, he has an explanation for
it: "Religious advocacy," he writes, "serves the community only in the eyes
of its adherents and yields a benefit only to those who already believe."
That was *not* the view of those who adopted our Constitution, who
believed that the public virtues inculcated by religion are a public good. It
suffices to point out that during the summer of 1789, when it was in the
process of drafting the First Amendment, Congress enacted the famous
Northwest Territory Ordinance of 1789, Article III of which provides,
"Religion, morality, and knowledge, *being necessary to good government
and the happiness of mankind,* schools and the means of education shall
forever be encouraged." Unsurprisingly, then, indifference to "religion in
general" is not what our cases, both old and recent, demand. . . .

For the reasons given by the Court, I agree that the Free Speech
Clause of the First Amendment forbids what respondents have done here.

As for the asserted Establishment Clause justification, I would hold, simply and clearly, that giving Lamb's Chapel nondiscriminatory access to school facilities cannot violate that provision because it does not signify state or local embrace of a particular religious sect.

□□□

No. 92-515

Wisconsin, Petitioner v. Todd Mitchell

On writ of certiorari to the Supreme Court of Wisconsin

[June 11, 1993]

CHIEF JUSTICE REHNQUIST delivered the opinion of the Court.

Respondent Todd Mitchell's sentence for aggravated battery was enhanced because he intentionally selected his victim on account of the victim's race. The question presented in this case is whether this penalty enhancement is prohibited by the First and Fourteenth Amendments. We hold that it is not.

On the evening of October 7, 1989, a group of young black men and boys, including Mitchell, gathered at an apartment complex in Kenosha, Wisconsin. Several members of the group discussed a scene from the motion picture "Mississippi Burning," in which a white man beat a young black boy who was praying. The group moved outside and Mitchell asked them: " 'Do you all feel hyped up to move on some white people?' " Shortly thereafter, a young white boy approached the group on the opposite side of the street where they were standing. As the boy walked by, Mitchell said: " 'You all want to fuck somebody up? There goes a white boy; go get him.' " Mitchell counted to three and pointed in the boy's direction. The group ran towards the boy, beat him severely, and stole his tennis shoes. The boy was rendered unconscious and remained in a coma for four days.

After a jury trial in the Circuit Court for Kenosha County, Mitchell was convicted of aggravated battery. Wis. Stat. §§ 939.05 and 940.19(1m) (1989-1990). That offense ordinarily carries a maximum sentence of two years' imprisonment. §§ 940.19(1m) and 939.50(3)(e). But because the jury found that Mitchell had intentionally selected his victim because of the boy's race, the maximum sentence for Mitchell's offense was increased to seven years under § 939.645. That provision enhances the maximum penalty for an offense whenever the defendant "[i]ntentionally selects the person against whom the crime . . . is committed . . . because of the race, religion, color, disability, sexual orientation, national origin or ancestry of that person. . . ." § 939.645(1)(b). The Circuit Court sentenced Mitchell to four years' imprisonment for the aggravated battery.

Mitchell unsuccessfully sought postconviction relief in the Circuit Court. Then he appealed his conviction and sentence, challenging the constitutionality of Wisconsin's penalty-enhancement provision on First Amendment grounds. The Wisconsin Court of Appeals rejected Mitchell's challenge (1991), but the Wisconsin Supreme Court reversed. The Supreme Court held that the statute "violates the First Amendment directly by punishing what the legislature has deemed to be offensive thought." (1992). It rejected the State's contention "that the statute punishes only the 'conduct' of intentional selection of a victim." According to the court, "[t]he statute punishes the 'because of' aspect of the defendant's selection, the *reason* the defendant selected the victim, the *motive* behind the selection." ([E]mphasis in original.) And under *R.A.V. v. St. Paul* (1992), "the Wisconsin legislature cannot criminalize bigoted thought with which it disagrees."

The Supreme Court also held that the penalty-enhancement statute was unconstitutionally overbroad. It reasoned that, in order to prove that a defendant intentionally selected his victim because of the victim's protected status, the State would often have to introduce evidence of the defendant's prior speech, such as racial epithets he may have uttered before the commission of the offense. This evidentiary use of protected speech, the court thought, would have a "chilling effect" on those who feared the possibility of prosecution for offenses subject to penalty enhancement. Finally, the court distinguished antidiscrimination laws, which have long been held constitutional, on the ground that the Wisconsin statute punishes the "subjective mental process" of selecting a victim because of his protected status, whereas antidiscrimination laws prohibit "objective acts of discrimination."

We granted certiorari because of the importance of the question presented and the existence of a conflict of authority among state high courts on the constitutionality of statutes similar to Wisconsin's penalty-enhancement provision (1992). We reverse. . . .

The State argues that the statute does not punish bigoted thought, as the Supreme Court of Wisconsin said, but instead punishes only conduct. While this argument is literally correct, it does not dispose of Mitchell's First Amendment challenge. . . .

. . . [U]nder the Wisconsin statute the same criminal conduct may be more heavily punished if the victim is selected because of his race or other protected status than if no such motive obtained. Thus, although the statute punishes criminal conduct, it enhances the maximum penalty for conduct motivated by a discriminatory point of view more severely than the same conduct engaged in for some other reason or for no reason at all.

Because the only reason for the enhancement is the defendant's discriminatory motive for selecting his victim, Mitchell argues (and the Wisconsin Supreme Court held) that the statute violates the First Amendment by punishing offenders' bigoted beliefs.

Traditionally, sentencing judges have considered a wide variety of factors in addition to evidence bearing on guilt in determining what sentence to impose on a convicted defendant. See *Payne v. Tennessee* (1991); *United States v. Tucker* (1972); *Williams v. New York* (1949). The defendant's motive for committing the offense is one important factor. . . . Thus, in many States the commission of a murder, or other capital offense, for pecuniary gain is a separate aggravating circumstance under the capital-sentencing statute.

But it is equally true that a defendant's abstract beliefs, however obnoxious to most people, may not be taken into consideration by a sentencing judge. *Dawson v. Delaware* (1992). In *Dawson,* the State introduced evidence at a capital-sentencing hearing that the defendant was a member of a white supremacist prison gang. Because "the evidence proved nothing more than [the defendant's] abstract beliefs," we held that its admission violated the defendant's First Amendment rights. In so holding, however, we emphasized that "the Constitution does not erect a *per se* barrier to the admission of evidence concerning one's beliefs and associations at sentencing simply because those beliefs and associations are protected by the First Amendment." Thus, in *Barclay v. Florida* (1983) (plurality opinion), we allowed the sentencing judge to take into account the defendant's racial animus towards his victim. The evidence in that case showed that the defendant's membership in the Black Liberation Army and desire to provoke a "race war" were related to the murder of a white man for which he was convicted. Because "the elements of racial hatred in [the] murder" were relevant to several aggravating factors, we held that the trial judge permissibly took this evidence into account in sentencing the defendant to death.

Mitchell suggests that *Dawson* and *Barclay* are inapposite because they did not involve application of a penalty-enhancement provision. But in *Barclay* we held that it was permissible for the sentencing court to consider the defendant's racial animus in determining whether he should be sentenced to death, surely the most severe "enhancement" of all. And the fact that the Wisconsin Legislature has decided, as a general matter, that bias-motivated offenses warrant greater maximum penalties across the board does not alter the result here. For the primary responsibility for fixing criminal penalties lies with the legislature. . . .

Mitchell argues that the Wisconsin penalty-enhancement statute is invalid because it punishes the defendant's discriminatory motive, or reason, for acting. But motive plays the same role under the Wisconsin statute as it does under federal and state antidiscrimination laws, which we have previously upheld against constitutional challenge. . . .

Nothing in our decision last Term in *R.A.V.* compels a different result here. That case involved a First Amendment challenge to a municipal ordinance prohibiting the use of " 'fighting words' that insult, or provoke violence, 'on the basis of race, color, creed, religion or gender.' " Because the ordinance only proscribed a class of "fighting words" deemed particularly offensive by the city—*i.e.,* those "that contain . . . messages of 'bias-motivated' hatred," we held that it violated the rule against content-based discrimination. But whereas the ordinance struck down in *R.A.V.* was explicitly directed at expression (*i.e.,* "speech" or "messages"), the statute in this case is aimed at conduct unprotected by the First Amendment.

Moreover, the Wisconsin statute singles out for enhancement bias-inspired conduct because this conduct is thought to inflict greater individual and societal harm. For example, according to the State and its *amici,* bias-motivated crimes are more likely to provoke retaliatory crimes, inflict distinct emotional harms on their victims, and incite community unrest. The State's desire to redress these perceived harms provides an adequate explanation for its penalty-enhancement provision over and above mere disagreement with offenders' beliefs or biases. . . .

Finally, there remains to be considered Mitchell's argument that the Wisconsin statute is unconstitutionally overbroad because of its "chilling effect" on free speech. Mitchell argues (and the Wisconsin Supreme Court agreed) that the statute is "overbroad" because evidence of the defendant's prior speech or associations may be used to prove that the defendant intentionally selected his victim on account of the victim's protected status. Consequently, the argument goes, the statute impermissibly chills free expression with respect to such matters by those concerned about the possibility of enhanced sentences if they should in the future commit a criminal offense covered by the statute. We find no merit in this contention.

The sort of chill envisioned here is far more attenuated and unlikely than that contemplated in traditional "overbreadth" cases. We must conjure up a vision of a Wisconsin citizen suppressing his unpopular bigoted opinions for fear that if he later commits an offense covered by the statute, these opinions will be offered at trial to establish that he selected his victim on account of the victim's protected status, thus qualifying him for penalty-enhancement. To stay within the realm of rationality, we must surely put to one side minor misdemeanor offenses covered by the statute, such as negligent operation of a motor vehicle; for it is difficult, if not impossible, to conceive of a situation where such offenses would be racially motivated. We are left, then, with the prospect of a citizen suppressing his bigoted beliefs for fear that evidence of such beliefs will be introduced against him at trial if he commits a more serious offense against person or property. This is simply too speculative a hypothesis to support Mitchell's overbreadth claim.

The First Amendment, moreover, does not prohibit the evidentiary use of speech to establish the elements of a crime or to prove motive or intent. Evidence of a defendant's previous declarations or statements is commonly admitted in criminal trials subject to evidentiary rules dealing with relevancy, reliability, and the like. . . .

For the foregoing reasons, we hold that Mitchell's First Amendment rights were not violated by the application of the Wisconsin penalty-enhancement provision in sentencing him. The judgment of the Supreme Court of Wisconsin is therefore reversed, and the case is remanded for further proceedings not inconsistent with this opinion.

It is so ordered.

No. 92-94

Larry Zobrest, et ux., et al., Petitioners v. Catalina Foothills School District

On writ of certiorari to the United States Court of Appeals
for the Ninth Circuit

[June 18, 1993]

CHIEF JUSTICE REHNQUIST delivered the opinion of the Court.

Petitioner James Zobrest, who has been deaf since birth, asked respondent school district to provide a sign-language interpreter to accompany him to classes at a Roman Catholic high school in Tucson, Arizona, pursuant to the Individuals with Disabilities Education Act (IDEA), 20 U.S.C. § 1400 *et seq.,* and its Arizona counterpart, Ariz. Rev. Stat. Ann. § 15-761 *et seq.* (1991 and Supp. 1992). The United States Court of Appeals for the Ninth Circuit decided, however, that provision of such a publicly employed interpreter would violate the Establishment Clause of the First Amendment. We hold that the Establishment Clause does not bar the school district from providing the requested interpreter.

James Zobrest attended grades one through five in a school for the deaf, and grades six through eight in a public school operated by respondent. While he attended public school, respondent furnished him with a sign-language interpreter. For religious reasons, James' parents (also petitioners here) enrolled him for the ninth grade in Salpointe

Catholic High School, a sectarian institution. When petitioners requested that respondent supply James with an interpreter at Salpointe, respondent referred the matter to the County Attorney, who concluded that providing an interpreter on the school's premises would violate the United States Constitution. Pursuant to Ariz. Rev. Stat. Ann. § 15-253(B) (1991), the question next was referred to the Arizona Attorney General, who concurred in the County Attorney's opinion. Respondent accordingly declined to provide the requested interpreter.

Petitioners then instituted this action in the United States District Court for the District of Arizona under 20 U.S.C. § 1415(e)(4)(A), which grants the district courts jurisdiction over disputes regarding the services due disabled children under the IDEA. Petitioners asserted that the IDEA and the Free Exercise Clause of the First Amendment require respondent to provide James with an interpreter at Salpointe, and that the Establishment Clause does not bar such relief. The complaint sought a preliminary injunction and "such other and further relief as the Court deems just and proper." The District Court denied petitioners' request for a preliminary injunction, finding that the provision of an interpreter at Salpointe would likely offend the Establishment Clause. The court thereafter granted respondent summary judgment, on the ground that "[t]he interpreter would act as a conduit for the religious inculcation of James—thereby, promoting James' religious development at government expense." "That kind of entanglement of church and state," the District Court concluded, "is not allowed."

The Court of Appeals affirmed by a divided vote, applying the three-part test announced in *Lemon v. Kurtzman* (1971). It first found that the IDEA has a clear secular purpose: " 'to assist States and Localities to provide for the education of all handicapped children.' " Turning to the second prong of the *Lemon* inquiry, though, the Court of Appeals determined that the IDEA, if applied as petitioners proposed, would have the primary effect of advancing religion and thus would run afoul of the Establishment Clause. "By placing its employee in the sectarian school," the Court of Appeals reasoned, "the government would create the appearance that it was a 'joint sponsor' of the school's activities." This, the court held, would create the "symbolic union of government and religion" found impermissible in *School Dist. of Grand Rapids v. Ball* (1985). In contrast, the dissenting judge argued that "[g]eneral welfare programs neutrally available to all children," such as the IDEA, pass constitutional muster, "because their benefits diffuse over the entire population." We granted certiorari (1992), and now reverse.

Respondent has raised in its brief in opposition to certiorari and in isolated passages in its brief on the merits several issues unrelated to the Establishment Clause question. Respondent first argues that 34 CFR § 76.532(a)(1), a regulation promulgated under the IDEA, precludes it from using federal funds to provide an interpreter to James at Salpointe. In the alternative, respondent claims that even if there is no affirmative bar to the relief, it is not *required* by statute or regulation to furnish interpreters to students at sectarian schools. And respondent adds that providing such a service would offend Art. II, § 12, of the Arizona Constitution.

It is a familiar principle of our jurisprudence that federal courts will not pass on the constitutionality of an Act of Congress if a construction of the Act is fairly possible by which the constitutional question can be avoided....

Here ... only First Amendment questions were pressed in the Court of Appeals.... Respondent did not urge any statutory grounds for affirmance upon the Court of Appeals, and thus the Court of Appeals decided only the federal constitutional claims raised by petitioners. In the District Court, too, the parties chose to litigate the case on the federal constitutional issues alone.... Accordingly, the District Court's order granting respondent summary judgment addressed only the Establishment Clause question.

Given this posture of the case, we think the prudential rule of avoiding constitutional questions has no application.... We therefore turn to the merits of the constitutional claim.

We have never said that "religious institutions are disabled by the First Amendment from participating in publicly sponsored social welfare programs." *Bowen v. Kendrick* (1988). For if the Establishment Clause did bar religious groups from receiving general government benefits, then "a church could not be protected by the police and fire departments, or have its public sidewalk kept in repair." *Widmar v. Vincent* (1981). Given that a contrary rule would lead to such absurd results, we have consistently held that government programs that neutrally provide benefits to a broad class of citizens defined without reference to religion are not readily subject to an Establishment Clause challenge just because sectarian institutions may also receive an attenuated financial benefit. Nowhere have we stated this principle more clearly than in *Mueller v. Allen* (1983) and *Witters v. Washington Dept. of Services for Blind* (1986), two cases dealing specifically with government programs offering general educational assistance.

In *Mueller,* we rejected an Establishment Clause challenge to a Minnesota law allowing taxpayers to deduct certain educational expenses in computing their state income tax, even though the vast majority of those deductions (perhaps over 90%) went to parents whose children attended sectarian schools. Two factors, aside from States' traditionally broad taxing authority, informed our decision. We noted that the law "permits *all* parents—whether their children attend public school or private—to deduct their children's educational expenses." ... We also pointed out that under Minnesota's scheme, public funds become available to sectarian schools "only as a result of numerous private choices of individual parents of school-age children," thus distinguishing *Mueller* from our other cases involving "the direct transmission of assistance from the State to the schools themselves."

Witters was premised on virtually identical reasoning. In that case, we upheld against an Establishment Clause challenge the State of Washington's extension of vocational assistance, as part of a general state program, to a blind person studying at a private Christian college to become a pastor, missionary, or youth director.... [W]e held that Washington's program—even as applied to a student who sought state assistance so that he could become a pastor—would not advance religion in a manner inconsistent with the Establishment Clause.

That same reasoning applies with equal force here. The service at issue in this case is part of a general government program that distributes benefits neutrally to any child qualifying as "handicapped" under the IDEA, without regard to the "sectarian-nonsectarian, or public-nonpublic nature" of the school the child attends. By according parents freedom to select a school of their choice, the statute ensures that a government-paid interpreter will be present in a sectarian school only as a result of the private decision of individual parents. In other words, because the IDEA creates no financial incentive for parents to choose a sectarian school, an interpreter's presence there cannot be attributed to state decisionmaking. Viewed against the backdrop of *Mueller* and *Witters,* then, the Court of Appeals erred in its decision. When the government offers a neutral service on the premises of a sectarian school as part of a general program that "is in no way skewed towards religion," it follows under our prior decisions that provision of that service does not offend the Establishment Clause. Indeed, this is an even easier case than *Mueller* and *Witters* in the sense that, under the IDEA, no funds traceable to the government ever find their way into sectarian schools' coffers. The only indirect economic benefit a sectarian school might receive by client of the IDEA is the handicapped child's tuition—and that is, of course, assuming that the school makes a profit on each student; that, without an IDEA interpreter, the child would have gone to school elsewhere; and that the school, then, would have been unable to fill that child's spot.

Respondent contends, however, that this case differs from *Mueller* and *Witters,* in that petitioners seek to have a public employee physically present in a sectarian school to assist in James' religious education. In light of this distinction, respondent argues that this case more closely resembles *Meek v. Pittenger* (1975) and *School Dist. of Grand Rapids v. Ball* (1985). In *Meek,* we struck down a statute that, *inter alia,* provided "massive aid" to private schools—more than 75% of which were church related—through a direct loan of teaching material and equipment. The material and equipment covered by the statute included maps, charts, and tape recorders. According to respondent, if the government could not place a tape recorder in a sectarian school in *Meek,* then it surely cannot place an interpreter in Salpointe. The statute in *Meek* also authorized state-paid personnel to furnish "auxiliary services"—which included remedial and accelerated instruction and guidance counseling—on the premises of religious schools. We determined that this part of the statute offended the First Amendment as well. *Ball* similarly involved two public programs that provided services on private school premises; there, public employees taught classes to students in private school classrooms. We found that those programs likewise violated the Constitution, relying largely on *Meek.* According to respondent, if the government could not provide educational services on the premises of sectarian schools in *Meek* and *Ball,* then it surely cannot provide James with an interpreter on the premises of Salpointe.

Respondent's reliance on *Meek* and *Ball* is misplaced for two reasons. First, the programs in *Meek* and *Ball*—through direct grants of government aid—relieved sectarian schools of costs they otherwise would have borne in educating their students.... For example, the religious schools in *Meek* received teaching material and equipment from the State, relieving them of an otherwise necessary cost of performing their educational function. "Substantial aid to the educational function of such schools," we explained, "necessarily results in aid to the sectarian school enterprise as a whole," and therefore brings about "the direct and substantial advancement of religious activity." So, too, was the case in *Ball*: The programs challenged there, which provided teachers in addition to instructional equipment and material, "in effect subsidize[d] the religious functions of the parochial schools by taking over a substantial portion of their responsibility for teaching secular subjects." "This kind of direct aid," we determined, "is indistinguishable from the provision of a direct cash subsidy to the religious school." The extension of aid to petitioners, however, does not amount to "an impermissible 'direct subsidy' " of Salpointe. For Salpointe is not relieved of an expense that it otherwise would have assumed in educating its students. And, as we noted above, any attenuated financial benefit that parochial schools do ultimately receive from the IDEA is attributable to "the private choices of individual parents." Handicapped children, not sectarian schools, are the primary beneficiaries of the IDEA; to the extent sectarian schools benefit at all from the IDEA, they are only incidental beneficiaries. Thus, the function of the IDEA is hardly " 'to provide desired financial support for nonpublic, sectarian institutions.' "

Second, the task of a sign-language interpreter seems to us quite different from that of a teacher or guidance counselor. Notwithstanding the Court of Appeals' intimations to the contrary, the Establishment

Clause lays down no absolute bar to the placing of a public employee in a sectarian school. Such a flat rule, smacking of antiquated notions of "taint," would indeed exalt form over substance. Nothing in this record suggests that a sign-language interpreter would do more than accurately interpret whatever material is presented to the class as a whole. In fact, ethical guidelines require interpreters to "transmit everything that is said in exactly the same way it was intended." James' parents have chosen of their own free will to place him in a pervasively sectarian environment. The sign-language interpreter they have requested will neither add to nor subtract from that environment, and hence the provision of such assistance is not barred by the Establishment Clause.

The IDEA creates a neutral government program dispensing aid not to schools but to individual handicapped children. If a handicapped child chooses to enroll in a sectarian school, we hold that the Establishment Clause does not prevent the school district from furnishing him with a sign-language interpreter there in order to facilitate his education. The judgment of the Court of Appeals is therefore

Reversed.

JUSTICE BLACKMUN, with whom JUSTICE SOUTER joins, and with whom JUSTICE STEVENS and JUSTICE O'CONNOR join as to Part I, dissenting.

Today, the Court unnecessarily addresses an important constitutional issue, disregarding longstanding principles of constitutional adjudication. In so doing, the Court holds that placement in a parochial school classroom of a public employee whose duty consists of relaying religious messages does not violate the Establishment Clause of the First Amendment. I disagree both with the Court's decision to reach this question and with its disposition on the merits. I therefore dissent.

I

... Respondent School District makes two arguments that could provide grounds for affirmance, rendering consideration of the constitutional question unnecessary. First, respondent maintains that the Individuals with Disabilities Education Act (IDEA) does not require it to furnish petitioner with an interpreter at any private school so long as special education services are made available at a public school. The United States endorses this interpretation of the statute, explaining that "the IDEA itself does not establish an individual entitlement to services for students placed in private schools at their parents' option." And several courts have reached the same conclusion. ... Second, respondent contends that 34 CFR § 76.532(a)(1) (1992), a regulation promulgated under the

IDEA, which forbids the use of federal funds to pay for "[r]eligious worship, instruction, or proselytization," prohibits provision of a sign-language interpreter at a sectarian school. The United States asserts that this regulation does not preclude the relief petitioners seek, but at least one federal court has concluded otherwise. This Court could easily refrain from deciding the constitutional claim by vacating and remanding the case for consideration of the statutory and regulatory issues. Indeed, the majority's decision does not eliminate the need to resolve these remaining questions. For, regardless of the Court's views on the Establishment Clause, petitioners will not obtain what they seek if the federal statute does not require or the federal regulations prohibit provision of a sign-language interpreter in a sectarian school. . . .

II

Despite my disagreement with the majority's decision to reach the constitutional question, its arguments on the merits deserve a response. Until now, the Court never has authorized a public employee to participate directly in religious indoctrination. Yet that is the consequence of today's decision.

Let us be clear about exactly what is going on here. The parties have stipulated to the following facts. Petitioner requested the State to supply him with a sign-language interpreter at Salpointe High School, a private Roman Catholic school operated by the Carmelite Order of the Catholic Church. Salpointe is a "pervasively religious" institution where "[t]he two functions of secular education and advancement of religious values or beliefs are inextricably intertwined." . . .

At Salpointe, where the secular and the sectarian are "inextricably intertwined," governmental assistance to the educational function of the school necessarily entails governmental participation in the school's inculcation of religion. A state-employed sign-language interpreter would be required to communicate the material covered in religion class, the nominally secular subjects that are taught from a religious perspective, and the daily Masses at which Salpointe encourages attendance for Catholic students. In an environment so pervaded by discussions of the divine, the interpreter's every gesture would be infused with religious significance. Indeed, petitioners willingly concede this point: "That the interpreter conveys religious messages is a given in the case." By this concession, petitioners would seem to surrender their constitutional claim.

The majority attempts to elude the impact of the record by offering three reasons why this sort of aid to petitioners survives Establishment Clause scrutiny. First, the majority observes that provision of a sign-language interpreter occurs as "part of a general government program that distributes benefits neutrally to any child qualifying as 'handicapped' under the IDEA, without regard to the 'sectarian-nonsectarian, or public-nonpublic' nature of the school the child attends." Second, the majority finds significant the fact that aid is provided to pupils and their parents, rather than directly to sectarian schools. As a result, " '[a]ny aid . . . that ultimately flows to religious institutions does so only as a result of the genuinely independent and private choices of aid recipients.' " And, finally, the majority opines that "the task of a sign-language interpreter seems to us quite different from that of a teacher or guidance counselor."

But the majority's arguments are unavailing. As to the first two, even a general welfare program may have specific applications that are constitutionally forbidden under the Establishment Clause. . . . For example, a general program granting remedial assistance to disadvantaged schoolchildren attending public and private, secular and sectarian schools alike would clearly offend the Establishment Clause insofar as it authorized the provision of teachers. See *Aguilar v. Felton* (1985); *Grand Rapids School District v. Ball* (1985); *Meek v. Pittenger* (1975). Such a program would not be saved simply because it supplied teachers to secular as well as sectarian schools. Nor would the fact that teachers were furnished to pupils and their parents, rather than directly to sectarian schools, immunize such a program from Establishment Clause scrutiny. . . . The majority's decision must turn, then, upon the distinction between a teacher and a sign-language interpreter.

"Although Establishment Clause jurisprudence is characterized by few absolutes," at a minimum "the Clause does absolutely prohibit government-financed or government-sponsored indoctrination into the beliefs of a particular religious faith." *Grand Rapids.* . . . In keeping with this restriction, our cases consistently have rejected the provision by government of any resource capable of advancing a school's religious mission. Although the Court generally has permitted the provision of "secular and nonideological services unrelated to the primary, religion-oriented educational function of the sectarian school," *Meek,* it has always proscribed the provision of benefits that afford even "the opportunity for the transmission of sectarian views," *Wolman v. Walter* (1977).

Thus, the Court has upheld the use of public school buses to transport children to and from school, *Everson v. Board of Education* (1947), while striking down the employment of publicly funded buses for field trips controlled by parochial school teachers, *Wolman.* Similarly, the Court has permitted the provision of secular textbooks whose content is immutable and can be ascertained in advance, *Board of Education v. Allen* (1968), while prohibiting the provision of any instructional materials or equipment that could be used to convey a religious message, such as slide projectors, tape recorders, record players, and the like, *Wolman.* State-paid speech and hearing therapists have been allowed to administer diagnostic testing on the premises of parochial schools, *Wolman,* whereas state-paid remedial teachers and counselors have not been authorized to offer their services because of the risk that they may inculcate religious beliefs, *Meek.*

These distinctions perhaps are somewhat fine, but " 'lines must be drawn.' ".... And our cases make clear that government crosses the boundary when it furnishes the medium for communication of a religious message. If petitioners receive the relief they seek, it is beyond question that a state-employed sign-language interpreter would serve as the conduit for petitioner's religious education, thereby assisting Salpointe in its mission of religious indoctrination. But the Establishment Clause is violated when a sectarian school enlists "the machinery of the State to enforce a religious orthodoxy." *Lee v. Weisman* (1992).

Witters and *Mueller v. Allen* (1983) are not to the contrary. Those cases dealt with the payment of cash or a tax deduction, where governmental involvement ended with the disbursement of funds or lessening of tax. This case, on the other hand, involves ongoing, daily, and intimate governmental participation in the teaching and propagation of religious doctrine. When government dispenses public funds to individuals who employ them to finance private choices, it is difficult to argue that government is actually endorsing religion. But the graphic symbol of the concert of church and state that results when a public employee or instrumentality mouths a religious message is likely to "enlis[t]—at least in the eyes of impressionable youngsters—the powers of government to the support of the religious denomination operating the school." And the union of church and state in pursuit of a common enterprise is likely to place the imprimatur of governmental approval upon the favored religion, conveying a message of exclusion to all those who do not adhere to its tenets.

Moreover, this distinction between the provision of funds and the provision of a human being is not merely one of form. It goes to the heart of the principles animating the Establishment Clause. As *Amicus* Council on Religious Freedom points out, the provision of a state-paid sign-language interpreter may pose serious problems for the church as well as for the state. Many sectarian schools impose religiously based rules of conduct, as Salpointe has in this case. A traditional Hindu school would be likely to instruct its students and staff to dress modestly, avoiding any display of their bodies. And an orthodox Jewish yeshiva might well forbid all but kosher food upon its premises. To require public employees to obey such rules would impermissibly threaten individual liberty, but to fail to do so might endanger religious autonomy. For such reasons, it long has been feared that "a union of government and religion tends to destroy government and to degrade religion." *Engel v. Vitale* (1962). The Establishment Clause was designed to avert exactly this sort of conflict.

III

The Establishment Clause "rests upon the premise that both religion and government can best work to achieve their lofty aims if each is left free from the other within its respective sphere." *McCollum v. Board of Education* (1948). To this end, our cases have strived to "chart a course that preserve[s] the autonomy and freedom of religious bodies while avoiding any semblance of established religion." *Walz v. Tax Commission* (1970). I would not stray, as the Court does today, from the course set by nearly five decades of Establishment Clause jurisprudence. Accordingly, I dissent.

JUSTICE O'CONNOR, with whom JUSTICE STEVENS joins, dissenting.

I join Part I of JUSTICE BLACKMUN's dissent. In my view, the Court should vacate and remand this case for consideration of the various threshold problems, statutory and regulatory, that may moot the constitutional question urged upon us by the parties. "It is a fundamental rule of judicial restraint . . . that this Court will not reach constitutional questions in advance of the necessity of deciding them." . . . That "fundamental rule" suffices to dispose of the case before us, whatever the proper answer to the decidedly hypothetical issue addressed by the Court. I therefore refrain from addressing it myself. . . .

□□□

No. 92-344

Chris Sale, Acting Commissioner, Immigration and Naturalization Service, et al., Petitioners v. Haitian Centers Council, Inc., et al.

On writ of certiorari to the United States Court of Appeals for the Second Circuit

[June 21, 1993]

JUSTICE STEVENS delivered the opinion of the Court.

The President has directed the Coast Guard to intercept vessels illegally transporting passengers from Haiti to the United States and to return those passengers to Haiti without first determining whether they may qualify as refugees. The question presented in this case is whether such forced repatriation, "authorized to be undertaken only beyond the territorial sea of the United States," violates § 243(h)(1) of the Immigration and Nationality Act of 1952 (INA or Act). We hold that neither § 243(h) nor Article 33 of the United Nations Protocol Relating to the Status of Refugees applies to action taken by the Coast Guard on the high seas.

I

Aliens residing illegally in the United States are subject to deportation after a formal hearing. Aliens arriving at the border, or those who are temporarily paroled into the country, are subject to an exclusion hearing, the less formal process by which they, too, may eventually be removed from the United States. In either a deportation or exclusion proceeding the alien may seek asylum as a political refugee for whom removal to a particular country may threaten his life or freedom. Requests that the Attorney General grant asylum or withhold deportation to a particular country are typically, but not necessarily, advanced as parallel claims in either a deportation or an exclusion proceeding. When an alien proves that he is a "refugee," the Attorney General has discretion to grant him asylum pursuant to § 208 of the Act. If the proof shows that it is more likely than not that the alien's life or freedom would be threatened in a particular country because of his political or religious beliefs, under § 243(h) the Attorney General must not send him to that country. The INA offers these statutory protections only to aliens who reside in or have arrived at the border of the United States. For 12 years, in one form or another, the interdiction program challenged here has prevented Haitians such as respondents from reaching our shores and invoking those protections. . . .

On September 29, 1981, President Reagan issued a proclamation in which he characterized "the continuing illegal migration by sea of large numbers of undocumented aliens into the southeastern United States" as "a serious national problem detrimental to the interests of the United States." He therefore suspended the entry of undocumented aliens from the high seas and ordered the Coast Guard to intercept vessels carrying such aliens and to return them to their point of origin. His executive order expressly "provided, however, that no person who is a refugee will be returned without his consent."

In the ensuing decade, the Coast Guard interdicted approximately 25,000 Haitian migrants. After interviews conducted on board Coast Guard cutters, aliens who were identified as economic migrants were "screened out" and promptly repatriated. Those who made a credible showing of political refugee status were "screened in" and transported to the United States to file formal applications for asylum.

On September 30, 1991, a group of military leaders displaced the government of Jean Bertrand Aristide, the first democratically elected president in Haitian history. As the District Court stated in an uncontested finding of fact, since the military coup "hundreds of Haitians have been killed, tortured, detained without a warrant, or subjected to violence and the destruction of their property because of their political beliefs. Thousands have been forced into hiding." Following the coup the Coast Guard suspended repatriations for a period of several weeks, and the United States imposed economic sanctions on Haiti.

On November 18, 1991, the Coast Guard announced that it would resume the program of interdiction and forced repatriation. The following day, the Haitian Refugee Center, Inc., representing a class of interdicted Haitians, filed a complaint in the United States District Court for the Southern District of Florida alleging that the Government had failed to establish and implement adequate procedures to protect Haitians who qualified for asylum. The District Court granted temporary relief that precluded any repatriations until February 4, 1992, when a reversal on appeal in the Court of Appeals for the Eleventh Circuit and a denial of certiorari by this Court effectively terminated that litigation. . . .

In the meantime the Haitian exodus expanded dramatically. During the six months after October 1991, the Coast Guard interdicted over 34,000 Haitians. Because so many interdicted Haitians could not be safely processed on Coast Guard cutters, the Department of Defense established temporary facilities at the United States Naval Base in Guantanamo, Cuba, to accommodate them during the screening process. Those temporary facilities, however, had a capacity of only about 12,500 persons. In the first three weeks of May 1992, the Coast Guard intercepted 127 vessels (many of which were considered unseaworthy, overcrowded, and unsafe); those vessels carried 10,497 undocumented aliens. On May 22, 1992, the United States Navy determined that no additional migrants could safely be accommodated at Guantanamo.

With both the facilities at Guantanamo and available Coast Guard cutters saturated, and with the number of Haitian emigrants in unseaworthy craft increasing (many had drowned as they attempted the trip to Florida), the Government could no longer both protect our borders and offer the Haitians even a modified screening process. It had to choose between allowing Haitians into the United States for the screening process or repatriating them without giving them any opportunity to establish their qualifications as refugees. In the judgment of the President's advisors, the first choice not only would have defeated the original purpose of the program (controlling illegal immigration), but also would have impeded diplomatic efforts to restore democratic government in Haiti and would have posed a life-threatening danger to thousands of persons embarking on long voyages in dangerous craft. The second choice would have advanced those policies but deprived the fleeing Haitians of any screening process at a time when a significant minority of them were being screened in.

On May 23, 1992, President Bush adopted the second choice. After assuming office, President Clinton decided not to modify that order; it remains in effect today. The wisdom of the policy choices made by Presidents Reagan, Bush, and Clinton is not a matter for our consideration. We must decide only whether Executive Order No. 12807, which reflects and implements those choices, is consistent with § 243(h) of the INA.

II

Respondents filed this lawsuit in the United States District Court for the Eastern District of New York on March 18, 1992—before the promulgation of Executive Order No. 12807. The plaintiffs include organizations that represent interdicted Haitians as well as Haitians who were then being detained at Guantanamo. They sued the Commissioner of the Immigration and Naturalization Service, the Attorney General, the Secretary of State, the Commandant of the Coast Guard, and the Commander of the Guantanamo Naval Base, complaining that the screening procedures provided on Coast Guard cutters and at Guantanamo did not adequately protect their statutory and treaty rights to apply for refugee status and avoid repatriation to Haiti.

They alleged that the September 1991 coup had "triggered a continuing widely publicized reign of terror in Haiti"; that over 1,500 Haitians were believed to "have been killed or subjected to violence and destruction of their property because of their political beliefs and affiliations"; and that thousands of Haitian refugees "have set out in small boats that are often overloaded, unseaworthy, lacking basic safety equipment, and operated by inexperienced persons, braving the hazards of a prolonged journey over high seas in search of safety and freedom."

In April, the District Court granted the plaintiffs a preliminary injunction requiring defendants to give Haitians on Guantanamo access to counsel for the screening process. We stayed that order on April 22, 1992, and, while the defendants' appeal from it was pending, the President issued the Executive Order now under attack. Plaintiffs then applied for a temporary restraining order to enjoin implementation of the Executive Order. They contended that it violated § 243(h) of the Act and Article 33 of the United Nations Protocol Relating to the Status of Refugees. The District Court denied the application because it concluded that § 243(h) is "unavailable as a source of relief for Haitian aliens in international waters," and that such a statutory provision was necessary because the Protocol's provisions are not "self-executing."

The Court of Appeals reversed. . . . [T]he Court held that § 243(h)(1) does not apply only to aliens within the United States. The Court found its conclusion mandated by both the broad definition of the term "alien" and the plain language of § 243(h), from which the 1980 amendment had removed the words "within the United States." The Court reasoned that the text of the statute defeated . . . reliance on the placement of § 243(h)(1) in Part V of the INA (titled "Deportation; Adjustment of Status") as evidence that it applied only to aliens in the United States. Moreover, the Court of Appeals rejected the Government's suggestion that since § 243(h) restricted actions of the Attorney General only, it did not limit the President's power to order the Coast Guard to repatriate undocumented aliens intercepted on the high seas.

Nor did the Court of Appeals accept the Government's reliance on Article 33 of the United Nations Convention Relating to the Status of Refugees. It recognized that the 1980 amendment to the INA had been intended to conform our statutory law to the provisions of the Convention, but it read Article 33.1's prohibition against return, like the statute's, "plainly" to cover "*all* refugees, regardless of location." This reading was supported by the "object and purpose" not only of that Article but also of the Convention as a whole. . . .

The Second Circuit's decision conflicted with the Eleventh Circuit's decision in *Haitian Refugee Center v. Baker* (1992), and with the opinion expressed by Judge Edwards in *Haitian Refugee Center v. Gracey* (1987) (Edwards, J., concurring in part and dissenting in part). Because of the manifest importance of the issue, we granted certiorari (1992).

III

Both parties argue that the plain language of § 243(h)(1) is dispositive. It reads as follows:

> "The Attorney General shall not deport or return any alien (other than an alien described in section 1251(a)(4)(D) of this title) to a country if the Attorney General determines that such alien's life or freedom would be threatened in such country on account of race, religion, nationality, membership in a particular social group, or political opinion." 8 U.S.C. 1253(h)(1).

Respondents emphasize the words "any alien" and "return"; neither term is limited to aliens within the United States. Respondents also contend that the 1980 amendment deleting the words "within the United States" from the prior text of § 243(h) obviously gave the statute an extraterritorial effect. This change, they further argue, was required in order to conform the statute to the text of Article 33.1 of the Convention, which they find as unambiguous as the present statutory text.

Petitioners' response is that a fair reading of the INA as a whole demonstrates that § 243(h) does not apply to actions taken by the President or Coast Guard outside the United States; that the legislative history of the 1980 amendment supports their reading; and that both the text and the negotiating history of Article 33 of the Convention indicate that it was not intended to have any extraterritorial effect.

We shall first review the text and structure of the statute and its 1980 amendment, and then consider the text and negotiating history of the Convention.

A. The Text and Structure of the INA

Although § 243(h)(1) refers only to the Attorney General, the Court of Appeals found it "difficult to believe that the proscription of § 243(h)(l)—returning an alien to his persecutors—was forbidden if done by the attorney general but permitted if done by some other arm of the executive branch." Congress "understood" that the Attorney General is the "President's agent for dealing with immigration matters," and would intend any reference to her to restrict similar actions of any government official. . . .

Other provisions of the Act expressly confer certain responsibilities on the Secretary of State, the President, and, indeed, on certain other officers as well. . . . We cannot say that the interdiction program created by the President, which the Coast Guard was ordered to enforce, usurped authority that Congress had delegated to, or implicated responsibilities that it had imposed on, the Attorney General alone.

The reference to the Attorney General in the statutory text is significant not only because that term cannot reasonably be construed to describe either the President or the Coast Guard, but also because it suggests that it applies only to the Attorney General's normal responsibilities under the INA. The most relevant of those responsibilities for our purposes are her conduct of the deportation and exclusion hearings in which requests for asylum or for withholding of deportation under § 243(h) are ordinarily advanced. Since there is no provision in the statute for the conduct of such proceedings outside the United States, and since Part V and other provisions of the INA obviously contemplate that such proceedings would be held in the country, we cannot reasonably construe § 243(h) to limit the Attorney General's actions in geographic areas where she has not been authorized to conduct such proceedings. . . .

Even if Part V of the Act were not limited to strictly domestic procedures, the presumption that Acts of Congress do not ordinarily apply outside our borders would support an interpretation of § 243(h) as applying only within United States territory. . . . The Court of Appeals held that the presumption against extraterritoriality had "no relevance in the present context" because there was no risk that § 243(h), which can be enforced only in United States courts against the United States Attorney General, would conflict with the laws of other nations. We have recently held, however, that the presumption has a foundation broader than the desire to avoid conflict with the laws of other nations. *Smith v. United States* (1993).

Respondents' expansive interpretation of the word "return" raises another problem: it would make the word "deport" redundant. If "return" referred solely to the destination to which the alien is to be removed, it alone would have been sufficient to encompass aliens involved in both deportation and exclusion proceedings. And if Congress had meant to refer to all aliens who might be sent back to potential oppressors, regardless of their location, the word "deport" would have been unnecessary. By using both words, the statute implies an exclusively territorial application, in the context of both kinds of domestic immigration proceedings. The use of both words reflects the traditional division between the two kinds of aliens and the two kinds of hearings. We can reasonably conclude that Congress used the two words "deport or return" only to make § 243(h)'s protection available in both deportation and exclusion proceedings. Indeed, the history of the 1980 amendment confirms that conclusion.

B. The History of the Refugee Act of 1980

As enacted in 1952, § 243(h) authorized the Attorney General to withhold deportation of aliens "within the United States." Six years later we considered the question whether it applied to an alien who had been paroled into the country while her admissibility was being determined. We held that even though she was physically present within our borders, she was not "within the United States" as those words were used in § 243(h). *Leng May Ma v. Barber* (1958). . . . Under the INA, both then and now, those seeking "admission" and trying to avoid "exclusion" were already within our territory (or at its border), but the law treated them as though they had never entered the United States at all; they were within United States territory but not "within the United States." Those who had been admitted (or found their way in) but sought to avoid "expulsion" had the added benefit of "deportation proceedings"; they were both within United States territory *and* "within the United States." Although the phrase "within the United States" presumed the alien's actual presence in the United States, it had more to do with an alien's legal status than with his location.

The 1980 amendment erased the long-maintained distinction between deportable and excludable aliens for purposes of § 243(h). By adding the word "return" and removing the words "within the United States" from § 243(h), Congress extended the statute's protection to both types of aliens, but it did nothing to change the presumption that both types of aliens would continue to be found only within United States territory. The removal of the phrase "within the United States" cured the most obvious drawback of § 243(h): as interpreted in *Leng May Ma,* its protection was available only to aliens subject to deportation proceedings.

Of course, in addition to this most obvious purpose, it is possible that the 1980 amendment also removed any territorial limitation of the statute, and Congress might have intended a double-barreled result. That possibility, however, is not a substitute for the affirmative evidence of intended extraterritorial application that our cases require. Moreover, in our review of the history of the amendment, we have found no support whatsoever for that latter, alternative, purpose.

... There is no change in the 1980 amendment ... that could only be explained by an assumption that Congress also intended to provide for the statute's extraterritorial application. It would have been extraordinary for Congress to make such an important change in the law without any mention of that possible effect. Not a scintilla of evidence of such an intent can be found in the legislative history.

In sum, all available evidence about the meaning of § 243(h)—the government official at whom it is directed, its location in the Act, its failure to suggest any extraterritorial application, the 1980 amendment that gave it a dual reference to "deport or return," and the relevance of that dual structure to immigration law in general—leads unerringly to the conclusion that it applies in only one context: the domestic procedures by which the Attorney General determines whether deportable and excludable aliens may remain in the United States.

IV

... Like the text and the history of § 243(h), the text and negotiating history of Article 33 of the United Nations Convention are both completely silent with respect to the Article's possible application to actions taken by a country outside its own borders. Respondents argue that the Protocol's broad remedial goals require that a nation be prevented from repatriating refugees to their potential oppressors whether or not the refugees are within that nation's borders. In spite of the moral weight of that argument, both the text and negotiating history of Article 33 affirmatively indicate that it was not intended to have extraterritorial effect.

A. The Text of the Convention

... The full text of Article 33 reads as follows:

> *"Article 33.—Prohibition of expulsion or return ('refoulement')*
> "1. No Contracting State shall expel or return (*'refouler'*) a refugee in any manner whatsoever to the frontiers of territories where his life or freedom

would be threatened on account of his race, religion, nationality, membership of a particular social group or political opinion.

"2. The benefit of the present provision may not, however, be claimed by a refugee whom there are reasonable grounds for regarding as a danger to the security of *the country in which he is,* or who, having been convicted by a final judgment of a particularly serious crime, constitutes a danger to the community of that country." Convention Relating to the Status of Refugees, July 28, 1951 (emphasis added).

 . . . Article 33.1 uses the words "expel or return *('refouler')*" as an obvious parallel to the words "deport or return" in § 243(h)(1). There is no dispute that "expel" has the same meaning as "deport"; it refers to the deportation or expulsion of an alien who is already present in the host country. The dual reference identified and explained in our opinion in *Leng May Ma v. Barber,* suggests that the term "return ('refouler')" refers to the exclusion of aliens who are merely "on the threshold of initial entry.' " . . .

The text of Article 33 thus fits with Judge Edwards' understanding "that 'expulsion' would refer to a 'refugee already admitted into a country' and that 'return' would refer to a 'refugee already within the territory but not yet resident there.' Thus, the Protocol was not intended to govern parties' conduct outside of their national borders." *Haitian Refugee Center v. Gracey.* . . .

The drafters of the Convention and the parties to the Protocol—like the drafters of § 243(h)—may not have contemplated that any nation would gather fleeing refugees and return them to the one country they had desperately sought to escape; such actions may even violate the spirit of Article 33; but a treaty cannot impose uncontemplated extraterritorial obligations on those who ratify it through no more than its general humanitarian intent. Because the text of Article 33 cannot reasonably be read to say anything at all about a nation's actions toward aliens outside its own territory, it does not prohibit such actions. . . .

B. [Omitted]

V

Respondents contend that the dangers faced by Haitians who are unwillingly repatriated demonstrate that the judgment of the Court of Appeals fulfilled the central purpose of the Convention and the Refugee Act of 1980. While we must, of course, be guided by the high purpose of both the treaty and the statute, we are not persuaded that either one places any limit on the President's authority to repatriate aliens interdicted beyond the territorial seas of the United States.

It is perfectly clear that 8 U.S.C. § 1182(f) grants the President ample power to establish a naval blockade that would simply deny illegal Haitian migrants the ability to disembark on our shores. Whether the President's chosen method of preventing the "attempted mass migration" of thousands of Haitians ... poses a greater risk of harm to Haitians who might otherwise face a long and dangerous return voyage, is irrelevant to the scope of his authority to take action that neither the Convention nor the statute clearly prohibits. As we have already noted, Acts of Congress normally do not have extraterritorial application unless such an intent is clearly manifested. That presumption has special force when we are construing treaty and statutory provisions that may involve foreign and military affairs for which the President has unique responsibility. Cf. *United States v. Curtiss-Wright Export Corp.* (1936). We therefore find ourselves in agreement with the conclusion expressed in Judge Edwards' concurring opinion in *Gracey.*

> "This case presents a painfully common situation in which desperate people, convinced that they can no longer remain in their homeland, take desperate measures to escape. Although the human crisis is compelling, there is no solution to be found in a judicial remedy."

The judgment of the Court of Appeals is reversed.

It is so ordered.

JUSTICE BLACKMUN, dissenting.

When, in 1968, the United States acceded to the United Nations Protocol Relating to the Status of Refugees, it pledged not to "return (*'refouler'*) a refugee in any manner whatsoever" to a place where he would face political persecution. In 1980, Congress amended our immigration law to reflect the Protocol's directives. Refugee Act of 1980. ... Today's majority nevertheless decides that the forced re-patriation of the Haitian refugees is perfectly legal, because the word "return" does not mean return, because the opposite of "within the United States" is not outside the United States, and because the official charged with controlling immigration has no role in enforcing an order to control.

I believe that the duty of nonreturn expressed in both the Protocol and the statute is clear. The majority finds it "extraordinary" that Congress would have intended the ban on returning "any alien" to apply to aliens at sea. That Congress would have meant what it said is not remarkable. What is extraordinary in this case is that the Executive, in disregard of the law, would take to the seas to intercept fleeing refugees and force them back to their persecutors—and that the Court would strain to sanction that conduct.

I

I begin with the Convention, for it is undisputed that the Refugee Act of 1980 was passed to conform our law to Article 33, and that "the nondiscretionary duty imposed by § 243(h) parallels the United States' mandatory *nonrefoulement* obligations under Article 33.1...." *INS v. Doherty* (1992) (SCALIA, J., concurring in the judgment in part and dissenting in part).... The Convention thus constitutes the backdrop against which the statute must be understood.

A

Article 33.1 of the Convention states categorically and without geographical limitation:

> "No Contracting State shall expel or return (*'refouler'*) a refugee in any manner whatsoever to the frontiers of territories where his life or freedom would be threatened on account of his race, religion, nationality, membership of a particular social group or political opinion."

The terms are unambiguous. Vulnerable refugees shall not be returned. The language is clear, and the command is straightforward; that should be the end of the inquiry. Indeed, until litigation ensued, see *Haitian Refugee Center v. Gracey* (1987), the Government consistently acknowledged that the Convention applied on the high seas.

The majority, however, has difficulty with the Treaty's use of the term "return (*'refouler'*)." "Return," it claims, does not mean return, but instead has a distinctive legal meaning. For this proposition the Court relies almost entirely on the fact that *American* law makes a general distinction between *deportation* and *exclusion*. Without explanation, the majority asserts that in light of this distinction the word "return" as used in the Treaty somehow must refer only to "the exclusion of aliens who are ... 'on the threshold of initial entry.'"

... I find this tortured reading unsupported and unnecessary. The text of the Convention does not ban the "exclusion" of aliens who have reached some indeterminate "threshold"; it bans their "return." ... The ordinary meaning of "return" is "to bring, send, or put (a person or thing) back to or in a former position." That describes precisely what petitioners are doing to the Haitians. By dispensing with ordinary meaning at the outset, and by taking instead as its starting point the assumption that "return," as used in the Treaty, "has a legal meaning narrower than its common meaning," the majority leads itself astray....

Article 33.1 is clear not only in what it says, but also in what it does not say: it does not include any geographical limitation. It limits only where a refugee may be sent "to", not where he may be sent from. This is not surprising, given that the aim of the provision is to protect refugees against persecution. . . .

[B Omitted]

II

A

Like the Treaty whose dictates it embodies, § 243(h) is unambiguous. . . . The statement that "the Attorney General shall not deport or return any alien" obviously does not mean simply that the person who is the Attorney General at the moment is forbidden personally to deport or return any alien, but rather that her agents may not do so. In the present case the Coast Guard without question is acting as the agent of the Attorney General. . . .

Even the challenged Executive Order places the Attorney General "on the boat" with the Coast Guard. The Order purports to give the Attorney General "unreviewable discretion" to decide that an alien will not be returned. Discretion not to return an alien is of course discretion to return him. Such discretion cannot be given; Congress removed it in 1980 when it amended the Immigration Act to make mandatory (*"shall not deport or return"*) what had been a discretionary function ("The Attorney General is authorized to withhold deportation"). The Attorney General may not decline to follow the command of § 243(h). If she encounters a refugee, she must not return him to persecution.

The laws that the Coast Guard is engaged in enforcing when it takes to the seas under orders to prevent aliens from illegally crossing our borders are laws whose administration has been assigned to the Attorney General by Congress, which has plenary power over immigration matters. . . . Accordingly, there is no merit to the argument that the concomitant legal restrictions placed on the Attorney General by Congress do not apply with full force in this case.

B

Comparison with the pre-1980 version of § 243(h) confirms that the statute means what it says. Before 1980, § 243(h) provided:

"The Attorney General is authorized to *withhold deportation* of any alien . . . within the United States to any country in which in his opinion the alien would be subject to persecution on account of race, religion, or political opinion and for such period of time as he deems to be necessary for such reason" (emphasis added).

The Refugee Act of 1980 explicitly amended this provision in three critical respects. Congress (1) deleted the words "within the United States"; (2) barred the Government from "return[ing]," as well as "deport[ing]," alien refugees; and (3) made the prohibition against return mandatory, thereby eliminating the discretion of the Attorney General over such decisions.

The import of these changes is clear. Whether "within the United States" or not, a refugee may not be returned to his persecutors. To read into § 243(h)'s mandate a territorial restriction is to restore the very language that Congress removed. . . .

C

That the clarity of the text and the implausibility of its theories do not give the majority more pause is due, I think, to the majority's heavy reliance on the presumption against extraterritoriality. . . .

The judicially created canon of statutory construction against extraterritorial application of United States law has no role here, however. It applies only where congressional intent is "unexpressed." . . . Here there is no room for doubt: a territorial restriction has been deliberately deleted from the statute.

Even where congressional intent is unexpressed, however, a statute must be assessed according to its intended scope. The primary basis for the application of the presumption (besides the desire—not relevant here—to avoid conflict with the laws of other nations) is "the common-sense notion that Congress generally legislates with domestic concerns in mind." *Smith v. United States* (1993). Where that notion seems unjustified or unenlightening, however, generally-worded laws covering varying subject matters are routinely applied extraterritorially. See, *e.g.*, *Hellenic Lines Ltd. v. Rhoditis* (1970) (extraterritorial application of the Jones Act); *Steele v. Bulova Watch Co.* (1952) (Lanham Act applies extraterritorially); *Kawakita v. United States* (1952) (extraterritorial application of treason statute); *Ford v. United States* (1927) (applying National Prohibition Act to high seas despite its silence on issue of extraterritoriality).

In this case we deal with a statute that regulates a distinctively international subject matter: immigration, nationalities, and refugees. Whatever force the presumption may have with regard to a primarily domestic statute evaporates in this context. There is no danger that the Congress that enacted the Refugee Act was blind to the fact that the laws it was crafting had implications beyond this Nation's borders. The "common-sense notion" that Congress was looking inwards— perfectly valid in a case involving the Federal Tort Claims Act, such as *Smith*,—cannot be reasonably applied to the Refugee Act of 1980.

In this regard, the majority's dictum that the presumption has "special force" when we construe "statutory provisions that may involve foreign and military affairs for which the President has unique responsibility" is completely wrong. The presumption that Congress did not intend to legislate extraterritorially has less force—perhaps, indeed, no force at all—when a statute on its face relates to foreign affairs. What the majority appears to be getting at, as its citation to *United States v. Curtiss-Wright Export Corp.* (1936) suggests, is that in some areas, the President, and not Congress, has sole constitutional authority. Immigration is decidedly not one of those areas. . . . And the suggestion that the President somehow is acting in his capacity as Commander-in-Chief is thwarted by the fact that nowhere among Executive Order No. 12,807's numerous references to the immigration laws is that authority even once invoked.

If any canon of construction should be applied in this case, it is the well-settled rule that "an act of congress ought never to be construed to violate the law of nations if any other possible construction remains." *Murray v. The Charming Betsy* (1804). The majority's improbable construction of § 243(h), which flies in the face of the international obligations imposed by Article 33 of the Convention, violates that established principle.

III

The Convention that the Refugee Act embodies was enacted largely in response to the experience of Jewish refugees in Europe during the period of World War II. The tragic consequences of the world's indifference at that time are well known. The resulting ban on *refoulement*, as broad as the humanitarian purpose that inspired it, is easily applicable here, the Court's protestations of impotence and regret notwithstanding.

The refugees attempting to escape from Haiti do not claim a right of admission to this country. They do not even argue that the Government has no right to intercept their boats. They demand only that the United States, land of refugees and guardian of freedom, cease forcibly driving them back to detention, abuse, and death. That is a modest plea, vindicated by the Treaty and the statute. We should not close our ears to it.

I dissent.

□□□

No. 92-602

St. Mary's Honor Center, et al., Petitioners v. Melvin Hicks

On writ of certiorari to the United States Court of Appeals
for the Eighth Circuit

[June 25, 1993]

JUSTICE SCALIA delivered the opinion of the Court.

We granted certiorari to determine whether, in a suit against an employer alleging intentional racial discrimination in violation of § 703(a)(1) of Title VII of the Civil Rights Act of 1964, 78 Stat. 255, 42 U.S.C. § 2000e-2(a)(1), the trier of fact's rejection of the employer's asserted reasons for its actions mandates a finding for the plaintiff.

I

Petitioner St. Mary's Honor Center (St. Mary's) is a halfway house operated by the Missouri Department of Corrections and Human Resources (MDCHR). Respondent Melvin Hicks, a black man, was hired as a correctional officer at St. Mary's in August 1978 and was promoted to shift commander, one of six supervisory positions, in February 1980.

In 1983 MDCHR conducted an investigation of the administration of St. Mary's, which resulted in extensive supervisory changes in January 1984. Respondent retained his position, but John Powell became the new chief of custody (respondent's immediate supervisor) and petitioner Steve Long the new superintendent. Prior to these personnel changes respondent had enjoyed a satisfactory employment record, but soon thereafter became the subject of repeated, and increasingly severe, disciplinary actions. He was suspended for five days for violations of institutional rules by his subordinates on March 3, 1984. He received a letter of reprimand for alleged failure to conduct an adequate investigation of a brawl between inmates that occurred during his shift on March 21. He was later demoted from shift commander to correctional officer for his failure to ensure that his subordinates entered their use of a St. Mary's vehicle into the official log book on March 19, 1984. Finally, on June 7, 1984, he was discharged for threatening Powell during an exchange of heated words on April 19.

Respondent brought this suit in the United States District Court for the Eastern District of Missouri, alleging that petitioner St. Mary's violated § 703(a)(1) of Title VII of the Civil Rights Act of 1964, 42 U.S.C. § 2000e-2(a)(1), and that petitioner Long violated Rev. Stat. § 1979, 42 U.S.C. § 1983, by demoting and then discharging him because of his race. After a full bench trial, the District Court found for petitioners. (ED Mo. 1991.) The United States Court of Appeals for the Eighth Circuit reversed and remanded, (1992), and we granted certiorari (1993).

II

Section 703(a)(1) of Title VII of the Civil Rights Act of 1964 provides in relevant part:

> "It shall be an unlawful employment practice for an employer— "(1) . . . to discharge any individual, or otherwise to discriminate against any individual with respect to his compensation, terms, conditions, or privileges of employment, because of such individual's race. . . ." 42 U.S.C. § 2000e-2(a).

With the goal of "progressively . . . sharpen[ing] the inquiry into the elusive factual question of intentional discrimination," *Texas Dept. of Community Affairs v. Burdine* (1981), our opinion in *McDonnell Douglas Corp. v. Green* (1973) established an allocation of the burden of production and an order for the presentation of proof in Title VII discriminatory-treatment cases. The plaintiff in such a case, we said, must first establish, by a preponderance of the evidence, a "prima facie" case of racial discrimination. . . . Petitioners do not challenge the District Court's finding that respondent satisfied the minimal requirements of such a prima facie case (set out in *McDonnell Douglas*) by proving (1) that he is black, (2) that he was qualified for the position of shift commander, (3) that he was demoted from that position and ultimately discharged, and (4) that the position remained open and was ultimately filled by a white man.

Under the *McDonnell Douglas* scheme, "[e]stablishment of the prima facie case in effect creates a presumption that the employer unlawfully discriminated against the employee.". . . To establish a "presumption" is to say that a finding of the predicate fact (here, the prima facie case) produces "a required conclusion in the absence of explanation" (here, the finding of unlawful discrimination). Thus, the *McDonnell Douglas* presumption places upon the defendant the burden of producing an explanation to rebut the prima facie case—*i.e.*, the burden of "producing evidence" that the adverse employment actions were taken "for a legitimate, nondiscriminatory reason.". . . "[T]he defendant must clearly set forth, through the introduction of admissible evidence," reasons for its actions which, *if believed by the trier of fact,* would support a finding that unlawful discrimination was not the cause of the employment action. It is important to note, however, that although the *McDonnell Douglas* presumption shifts the burden of *production* to the defendant, "[t]he ultimate burden of persuading the trier of fact that the defendant intentionally discriminated against the plaintiff remains at all times with the plaintiff." In this regard it operates like all presumptions, as described in Rule 301 of the Federal Rules of Evidence:

> "In all civil actions and proceedings not otherwise provided for by Act of Congress or by these rules, a presumption imposes on the party against whom it is directed the burden of going forward with evidence to rebut or meet the presumption, but does not shift to such party the burden of proof in the sense of the risk of nonpersuasion, which remains throughout the trial upon the party on whom it was originally cast."

Respondent does not challenge the District Court's finding that petitioners sustained their burden of production by introducing evidence of two legitimate, nondiscriminatory reasons for their actions: the severity and the accumulation of rules violations committed by respondent. Our cases make clear that at that point the shifted burden of production became irrelevant. . . .

The District Court, acting as trier of fact in this bench trial, found that the reasons petitioners gave were not the real reasons for respondent's demotion and discharge. It found that respondent was the only supervisor disciplined for violations committed by his subordinates; that similar and even more serious violations committed by respondent's coworkers were either disregarded or treated more leniently; and that Powell manufactured the final verbal confrontation in order to provoke respondent into threatening him. It nonetheless held that respondent had failed to carry his ultimate burden of proving that his race was the determining factor in petitioners' decision first to demote and then to dismiss him. In short, the District Court concluded that "although [respondent] has proven the existence of a crusade to terminate him, he has not proven that the crusade was racially rather than personally motivated."

The Court of Appeals set this determination aside on the ground that "[o]nce [respondent] proved all of [petitioners'] proffered reasons for the adverse employment actions to be pretextual, [respondent] was entitled to judgment as a matter of law." The Court of Appeals reasoned:

> "Because all of defendants' proffered reasons were discredited, defendants were in a position of having offered no legitimate reason for their actions. In other words, defendants were in no better position than if they had remained silent, offering no rebuttal to an established inference that they had unlawfully discriminated against plaintiff on the basis of his race."

That is not so. By producing *evidence* (whether ultimately persuasive or not) of nondiscriminatory reasons, petitioners sustained their burden of production, and thus placed themselves in a "better position than if they had remained silent." . . .

If . . . the defendant has succeeded in carrying its burden of production, the *McDonnell Douglas* framework—with its presumptions and burdens—is no longer relevant. To resurrect it later, after the trier of fact has determined that what was "produced" to meet the burden of production is not credible, flies in the face of our holding in *Burdine* that to rebut the presumption "[t]he defendant need not persuade the court that it was actually motivated by the proffered reasons." The presumption, having fulfilled its role of forcing the defendant to come forward with some response, simply drops out of the picture. The defendant's "production" (whatever its persuasive effect) having been made, the trier of fact proceeds to decide the ultimate question: whether plaintiff has proven "that the defendant intentionally discriminated against [him]" because of his race. The factfinder's disbelief of the reasons put forward by the defendant (particularly if disbelief is accompanied by a suspicion of mendacity) may, together with the elements of the prima facie case, suffice to show intentional discrimination. Thus, rejection of the defendant's proffered reasons, will *permit* the trier of fact to infer the ultimate fact of intentional discrimination, and the Court of Appeals was correct when it noted that, upon such rejection, "[n]o additional proof of discrimination is *required*," (emphasis added). But the Court of Appeals' holding that rejection of the defendant's proffered reasons *compels* judgment for the plaintiff disregards the fundamental principle of Rule 301 that a presumption does not shift the burden of proof, and ignores our repeated admonition that the Title VII plaintiff at all times bears the "ultimate burden of persuasion.". . .

[III Omitted]

IV

We turn, finally, to the dire practical consequences that the respondents and the dissent claim our decision today will produce. What appears to trouble the dissent more than anything is that, in its view, our rule is adopted "for the benefit of employers who have been found to have given false evidence in a court of law," whom we "favo[r]" by "exempting them from responsibility for lies." As we shall explain, our rule in no way gives special favor to those employers whose evidence is disbelieved. But initially we must point out that there is no justification for assuming (as the dissent repeatedly does) that those employers whose evidence is disbelieved are perjurers and liars. . . .

Undoubtedly some employers (or at least their employees) will be lying. But even if we could readily identify these perjurers, what an extraordinary notion, that we "exempt them from responsibility for their lies" unless we enter Title VII judgments for the plaintiffs! Title VII is not a cause of action for perjury; we have other civil and criminal remedies for that. The dissent's notion of judgment-for-lying is seen to be not even a fair and evenhanded punishment for vice, when one realizes how strangely selective it is: the employer is free to lie to its heart's content about whether the plaintiff ever applied for a job, about how long he worked, how much he made—indeed, about anything and everything *except* the reason for the adverse employment action. And the plaintiff is permitted to lie about absolutely *everything* without losing a verdict he otherwise deserves. This is not a major, or even a sensible, blow against fibbery. . . .

Respondent contends that "[t]he litigation decision of the employer to place in controversy only . . . particular explanations eliminates from further consideration the alternative explanations that the employer chose not to advance." The employer should bear, he contends, "the responsibility for its choices and the risk that plaintiff will disprove any pretextual reasons *and therefore prevail.*" ([E]mphasis added.) It is the "therefore" that is problematic. Title VII does not award damages against employers who cannot prove a nondiscriminatory reason for adverse employment action, but only against employers who are proven to have taken adverse employment action by reason of (in the context of the present case) race. That the employer's proffered reason is unpersuasive, or even obviously contrived, does not necessarily establish that the plaintiff's proffered reason of race is correct. That remains a question for the factfinder to answer, subject, of course, to appellate review—which should be conducted on remand in this case under the "clearly erroneous" standard of Federal Rule of Civil Procedure 52(a). . . .

Finally, respondent argues that it "would be particularly ill-advised" for us to come forth with the holding we pronounce today "just as Congress has provided a right to jury trials in Title VII" cases. . . . We think quite the opposite is true. Clarity regarding the requisite elements of proof becomes all the more important when a jury must be instructed concerning them, and when detailed factual findings by the trial court will not be available upon review. . . .

The judgment of the Court of Appeals is reversed, and the case is remanded for further proceedings consistent with this opinion.

It is so ordered.

JUSTICE SOUTER, with whom JUSTICE WHITE, JUSTICE BLACKMUN, and JUSTICE STEVENS join, dissenting.

Twenty years ago, in *McDonnell Douglas Corp. v. Green* (1973), this Court unanimously prescribed a "sensible, orderly way to evaluate the evidence" in a Title VII disparate-treatment case, giving both plaintiff and defendant fair opportunities to litigate "in light of common experience as it bears on the critical question of discrimination." *Furnco Construction Corp. v. Waters* (1978). We have repeatedly reaffirmed and refined the *McDonnell Douglas* framework, most notably in *Texas Dept. of Commu-*

nity Affairs v. Burdine (1981), another unanimous opinion. . . . But today, after two decades of stable law in this Court and only relatively recent disruption in some of the Circuits, the Court abandons this practical framework together with its central purpose, which is "to sharpen the inquiry into the elusive factual question of intentional discrimination.". . . Ignoring language to the contrary in both *McDonnell Douglas* and *Burdine,* the Court holds that, once a Title VII plaintiff succeeds in showing at trial that the defendant has come forward with pretextual reasons for its actions in response to a prima facie showing of discrimination, the factfinder still may proceed to roam the record, searching for some nondiscriminatory explanation that the defendant has not raised and that the plaintiff has had no fair opportunity to disprove. Because the majority departs from settled precedent in substituting a scheme of proof for disparate-treatment actions that promises to be unfair and unworkable, I respectfully dissent. . . .

At the outset, under the *McDonnell Douglas* framework, a plaintiff alleging disparate treatment in the workplace in violation of Title VII must provide the basis for an inference of discrimination. In this case, as all agree, Melvin Hicks met this initial burden by proving by a preponderance of the evidence that he was black and therefore a member of a protected class; he was qualified to be a shift commander; he was demoted and then terminated; and his position remained available and was later filled by a qualified applicant. Hicks thus proved what we have called a "prima facie case" of discrimination, and it is important to note that in this context a prima facie case is indeed a proven case. Although, in other contexts, a prima facie case only requires production of enough evidence to raise an issue for the trier of fact, here it means that the plaintiff has actually established the elements of the prima facie case to the satisfaction of the factfinder by a preponderance of the evidence. . . .

Under *McDonnell Douglas* and *Burdine,* however, proof of a prima facie case not only raises an inference of discrimination; in the absence of further evidence, it also creates a mandatory presumption in favor of the plaintiff. Although the employer bears no trial burden at all until the plaintiff proves his prima facie case, once the plaintiff does so the employer must either respond or lose. . . .

The Court emphasizes that the employer's obligation at this stage is only a burden of production and that, if the employer meets the burden, the presumption entitling the plaintiff to judgment "drops from the case." This much is certainly true, but the obligation also serves an important function neglected by the majority, in requiring the employer "to frame the factual issue with sufficient clarity so that the plaintiff will have a full and fair opportunity to demonstrate pretext." The employer, in other words, has a "burden of production" that gives it the right to choose the scope of the factual issues to be resolved by the factfinder. . . .

Once the employer chooses the battleground in this manner, "the factual inquiry proceeds to a new level of specificity." During this final, more specific enquiry, the employer has no burden to prove that its proffered reasons are true; rather, the plaintiff must prove by a preponderance of the evidence that the proffered reasons are pretextual. *McDonnell Douglas* makes it clear that if the plaintiff fails to show "pretext," the challenged employment action "must stand." If, on the other hand, the plaintiff carries his burden of showing "pretext," the court "must order a prompt and appropriate remedy." . . .

The Court today decides to abandon the settled law that sets out this structure for trying disparate-treatment Title VII cases, only to adopt a scheme that will be unfair to plaintiffs, unworkable in practice, and inexplicable in forgiving employers who present false evidence in court. Under the majority's scheme, once the employer succeeds in meeting its burden of production, "the *McDonnell Douglas* framework . . . is no longer relevant." Whereas we said in *Burdine* that if the employer carries its burden of production, "the factual inquiry proceeds to a new level of specificity," the Court now holds that the further enquiry is wide open, not limited at all by the scope of the employer's proffered explanation. . . . The Court thus transforms the employer's burden of production from a device used to provide notice and promote fairness into a misleading and potentially useless ritual.

The majority's scheme greatly disfavors Title VII plaintiffs without the good luck to have direct evidence of discriminatory intent. The Court repeats the truism that the plaintiff has the "ultimate burden" of proving discrimination, without ever facing the practical question of how the plaintiff without such direct evidence can meet this burden. *Burdine* provides the answer, telling us that such a plaintiff may succeed in meeting his ultimate burden of proving discrimination "indirectly by showing that the employer's proffered explanation is unworthy of credence." The possibility of some practical procedure for addressing what *Burdine* calls indirect proof is crucial to the success of most Title VII claims, for the simple reason that employers who discriminate are not likely to announce their discriminatory motive. And yet, under the majority's scheme, a victim of discrimination lacking direct evidence will now be saddled with the tremendous disadvantage of having to confront, not the defined task of proving the employer's stated reasons to be false, but the amorphous requirement of disproving all possible nondiscriminatory reasons that a factfinder might find lurking in the record. In the Court's own words, the plaintiff must "disprove *all* other reasons suggested, no matter how vaguely, in the record." ([E]mphasis in original.) . . .

The enhancement of a Title VII plaintiff's burden wrought by the Court's opinion is exemplified in this case. Melvin Hicks was denied any opportunity, much less a full and fair one, to demonstrate that the supposedly nondiscriminatory explanation for his demotion and termination, the personal animosity of his immediate supervisor, was unworthy of credence. In fact, the District Court did not find that personal animosity (which it failed to recognize might be racially motivated) was the true reason for the actions St. Mary's took; it adduced this reason simply as a possibility in explaining that Hicks had failed to prove "that the crusade [to terminate him] was racially rather than personally motivated." It is hardly surprising that Hicks failed to prove anything about this supposed personal crusade, since St. Mary's never articulated such an explanation for Hicks's discharge, and since the person who allegedly conducted this crusade denied at trial any personal difficulties between himself and Hicks. While the majority may well be troubled about the unfair treatment of Hicks in this instance and thus remands for review of whether the District Court's factual conclusions were clearly erroneous, the majority provides Hicks with no opportunity to produce evidence showing that the District Court's hypothesized explanation, first articulated six months after trial, is unworthy of credence. Whether Melvin Hicks wins or loses on remand, many plaintiffs in a like position will surely lose under the scheme adopted by the Court today, unless they possess both prescience and resources beyond what this Court has previously required Title VII litigants to employ.

Because I see no reason why Title VII interpretation should be driven by concern for employers who are too ashamed to be honest in court, at the expense of victims of discrimination who do not happen to have direct evidence of discriminatory intent, I respectfully dissent.

□□□

No. 92-357

Ruth O. Shaw, et al., Appellants v. Janet Reno, Attorney General, et al.

On appeal from the United States District Court
for the Eastern District of North Carolina

[June 28, 1993]

JUSTICE O'CONNOR delivered the opinion of the Court.

This case involves two of the most complex and sensitive issues this Court has faced in recent years: the meaning of the constitutional "right" to vote, and the propriety of race-based state legislation designed to benefit members of historically disadvantaged racial minority groups. As a result of the 1990 census, North Carolina became entitled to a twelfth seat in the United States House of Representatives. The General Assembly enacted a reapportionment plan that included one majority-black congressional district. After the Attorney General of the United States objected to the plan pursuant to § 5 of the Voting Rights Act of 1965, 79 Stat. 439, as amended, 42 U.S.C. § 1973c, the General Assembly passed new legislation creating a second majority-black district. Appellants allege that the revised plan, which contains district boundary lines of dramatically irregular shape, constitutes an unconstitutional racial gerrymander. The question before us is whether appellants have stated a cognizable claim.

I

The voting age population of North Carolina is approximately 78% white, 20% black, and 1% Native American; the remaining 1% is predominantly Asian. The black population is relatively dispersed; blacks constitute a majority of the general population in only 5 of the State's 100 counties. Geographically, the State divides into three regions: the eastern Coastal Plain, the central Piedmont Plateau, and the western mountains. The largest concentrations of black citizens live in the Coastal Plain, primarily in the northern part. The General Assembly's first redistricting plan contained one majority-black district centered in that area of the State.

Forty of North Carolina's one hundred counties are covered by § 5 of the Voting Rights Act of 1965, which prohibits a jurisdiction subject to its provisions from implementing changes in a "standard, practice, or procedure with respect to voting" without federal authorization. The jurisdiction must obtain either a judgment from the United States District Court for the District of Columbia declaring that the proposed change "does not have the purpose and will not have the effect of denying or abridging the right to vote on account of race or color" or administrative preclearance from the Attorney General. Because the General Assembly's reapportionment plan affected the covered counties, the parties agree that § 5 applied. The State chose to submit its plan to the Attorney General for preclearance.

The Attorney General, acting through the Assistant Attorney General for the Civil Rights Division, interposed a formal objection to the General Assembly's plan. The Attorney General specifically objected to the configuration of boundary lines drawn in the south-central to southeastern region of the State. In the Attorney General's view, the General Assembly could have created a second majority-minority district "to give effect to black and Native American voting strength in this area" by using boundary lines "no more irregular than [those] found elsewhere in the proposed plan," but failed to do so for "pretextual reasons."

Under § 5, the State remained free to seek a declaratory judgment from the District Court for the District of Columbia notwithstanding the Attorney General's objection. It did not do so. Instead, the General Assembly enacted a revised redistricting plan, 1991 N.C. Extra Sess. Laws, ch. 7, that included a second majority-black district. The General Assembly located the second district not in the south-central to southeastern part of the State, but in the north-central region along Interstate 85.

The first of the two majority-black districts contained in the revised plan, District 1, is somewhat hook shaped. Centered in the northeast portion of the State, it moves southward until it tapers to a narrow band; then, with finger-like extensions, it reaches far into the southernmost part of the State near the South Carolina border. District 1 has been compared to a "Rorschach ink-blot test," *Shaw v. Barr* (EDNC 1992) (Voorhees, C. J., concurring in part and dissenting in part) and a "bug splattered on a windshield," Wall Street Journal, Feb. 4, 1992, p. A14.

The second majority-black district, District 12, is even more unusually shaped. It is approximately 160 miles long and, for much of its length, no wider than the I-85 corridor. It winds in snake-like fashion through tobacco country, financial centers, and manufacturing areas "until it gobbles in enough enclaves of black neighborhoods." *Shaw v. Barr*. Northbound and southbound drivers on I-85 sometimes find themselves in separate districts in one county, only to "trade" districts when they enter the next county. Of the 10 counties through which District 12 passes, five are cut into three different districts; even towns are divided. At one point the district remains contiguous only because it intersects at a single point with two other districts before crossing over them. . . .

The Attorney General did not object to the General Assembly's revised plan. But numerous North Carolinians did. The North Carolina Republican Party and individual voters brought suit in Federal District Court alleging that the plan constituted an unconstitutional political gerrymander under *Davis v. Bandemer* (1986). That claim was dismissed, see *Pope v. Blue* (WDNC 1992), and this Court summarily affirmed, (1992).

Shortly after the complaint in *Pope v. Blue* was filed, appellants instituted the present action in the United States District Court for the Eastern District of North Carolina. Appellants alleged not that the revised plan constituted a political gerrymander, nor that it violated the "one person, one vote" principle, see *Reynolds v. Sims* (1964), but that the State had created an unconstitutional *racial* gerrymander. Appellants are five residents of Durham County, North Carolina, all registered to vote in that county. Under the General Assembly's plan, two will vote for congressional representatives in District 12 and three will vote in neighboring District 2. Appellants sued the Governor of North Carolina, the Lieutenant Governor, the Secretary of State, the Speaker of the North Carolina House of Representatives, and members of the North Carolina State Board of Elections (state appellees), together with two federal officials, the Attorney General and the Assistant Attorney General for the Civil Rights Division (federal appellees).

Appellants contended that the General Assembly's revised reapportionment plan violated several provisions of the United States Constitution, including the Fourteenth Amendment. They alleged that the General Assembly deliberately "create[d] two Congressional Districts in which a majority of black voters was concentrated arbitrarily—without regard to any other considerations, such as compactness, contiguousness, geographical boundaries, or political subdivisions" with the purpose "to create Congressional Districts along racial lines" and to assure the election of two black representatives to Congress. Appellants sought declaratory and injunctive relief against the state appellees. They sought similar relief against the federal appellees, arguing, alternatively, that the federal appellees had misconstrued the Voting Rights Act or that the Act itself was unconstitutional.

The three-judge District Court granted the federal appellees' motion to dismiss. The court agreed unanimously that it lacked subject matter jurisdiction by reason of § 14(b) of the Voting Rights Act, which vests the District Court for the District of Columbia with exclusive jurisdiction to issue injunctions against the execution of the Act and to enjoin actions taken by federal officers pursuant thereto.

By a 2-to-1 vote, the District Court also dismissed the complaint against the state appellees. The majority found no support for appellants' contentions that race-based districting is prohibited by Article I, § 4, or Article I, § 2, of the Constitution, or by the Privileges and Immunities Clause of the Fourteenth Amendment. It deemed appellants' claim under the Fifteenth Amendment essentially subsumed within their related claim under the Equal Protection Clause. That claim, the majority concluded, was barred by *United Jewish Organizations of Williamsburgh, Inc. v. Carey* (1977) (*UJO*).

The majority first took judicial notice of a fact omitted from appellants' complaint: that appellants are white. It rejected the argument that race-conscious redistricting to benefit minority voters is *per se* unconstitutional. The majority also rejected appellants' claim that North Carolina's reapportionment plan was impermissible. The majority read *UJO* to stand for the proposition that a redistricting scheme violates white voters' rights only if it is "adopted with the purpose and effect of discriminating against white voters ... on account of their race." The purposes of favoring minority voters and complying with the Voting Rights Act are not discriminatory in the constitutional sense, the court reasoned, and majority-minority districts have an impermissibly discriminatory effect only when they unfairly dilute or cancel out white voting strength. Because the State's purpose here was to comply with the Voting Rights Act, and because the General Assembly's plan did not lead to proportional underrepresentation of white voters statewide, the majority concluded that appellants had failed to state an equal protection claim.

Chief Judge Voorhees agreed that race-conscious redistricting is not per se unconstitutional but dissented from the rest of the majority's equal protection analysis. He read JUSTICE WHITE's opinion in *UJO* to authorize race-based reapportionment only when the State employs traditional districting principles such as compactness and contiguity. North Carolina's failure to respect these principles, in Judge Voorhees' view, "augur[ed] a constitutionally suspect, and potentially unlawful, intent" sufficient to defeat the state appellees' motion to dismiss.

We noted probable jurisdiction.

II

A

"The right to vote freely for the candidate of one's choice is of the essence of a democratic society. . . ." *Reynolds v. Sims.* For much of our Nation's history, that right sadly has been denied to many because of race. The Fifteenth Amendment, ratified in 1870 after a bloody Civil War, promised unequivocally that "[t]he right of citizens of the United States to vote" no longer would be "denied or abridged . . . by any State on account of race, color, or previous condition of servitude."

But "[a] number of states . . . refused to take no for an answer and continued to circumvent the fifteenth amendment's prohibition through the use of both subtle and blunt instruments, perpetuating ugly patterns of pervasive racial discrimination." Ostensibly race-neutral devices such as literacy tests with "grandfather" clauses and "good character" provisos were devised to deprive black voters of the franchise. Another of the weapons in the States' arsenal was the racial gerrymander—"the deliberate and arbitrary distortion of district boundaries . . . for [racial] purposes." *Bandemer* (Powell, J., concurring in part and dissenting in part). In the 1870's, for example, opponents of Reconstruction in Mississippi "concentrated the bulk of the black population in a 'shoestring' Congressional district running the length of the Mississippi River, leaving five others with white majorities." Some 90 years later, Alabama redefined the boundaries of the city of Tuskegee "from a square to an uncouth twenty-eight-sided figure" in a manner that was alleged to exclude black voters, and only black voters, from the city limits. *Gomillion v. Lightfoot* (1960).

Alabama's exercise in geometry was but one example of the racial discrimination in voting that persisted in parts of this country nearly a century after ratification of the Fifteenth Amendment. In some States, registration of eligible black voters ran 50% behind that of whites. Congress enacted the Voting Rights Act of 1965 as a dramatic and severe response to the situation. The Act proved immediately successful in ensuring racial minorities access to the voting booth; by the early 1970's, the spread between black and white registration in several of the targeted Southern States had fallen to well below 10%

But it soon became apparent that guaranteeing equal access to the polls would not suffice to root out other racially discriminatory voting practices. Drawing on the "one person, one vote" principle, this Court recognized that "[t]he right to vote can be affected by a *dilution* of voting power as well as by an absolute prohibition on casting a ballot." *Allen v. State Board of Elections* (1969) (emphasis added). Where members of a racial minority group vote as a cohesive unit, practices such as multimember or at-large electoral systems can reduce or nullify minority voters' ability, as a group, "to elect the candidate of their choice." Accordingly, the Court held that such schemes violate the Fourteenth Amendment when they are adopted with a discriminatory purpose and have the effect of diluting minority voting strength. See, *e.g., Rogers v. Lodge* (1982); *White v. Regester* (1973). Congress, too, responded to the problem of vote dilution. In 1982, it amended § 2 of the Voting Rights Act to prohibit legislation that *results* in the dilution of a minority group's voting strength, regardless of the legislature's intent. 42 U.S.C. § 1973; see *Thornburg v. Gingles* (1986) (applying amended § 2 to vote-dilution claim involving multimember districts); see also *Voinovich v. Quilter* (1993) (single-member districts).

B

It is against this background that we confront the questions presented here. In our view, the District Court properly dismissed appellants' claims against the federal appellees. Our focus is on appellants' claim that the State engaged in unconstitutional racial gerrymandering. That argument strikes a powerful historical chord: It is unsettling how closely the North Carolina plan resembles the most egregious racial gerrymanders of the past.

An understanding of the nature of appellants' claim is critical to our resolution of the case. In their complaint, appellants did not claim that the General Assembly's reapportionment plan unconstitutionally "diluted" white voting strength. They did not even claim to be white. Rather, appellants' complaint alleged that the deliberate segregation of voters into separate districts on the basis of race violated their constitutional right to participate in a "color-blind" electoral process.

Despite their invocation of the ideal of a "color-blind" Constitution, see *Plessy v. Ferguson* (1896) (Harlan, J., dissenting), appellants appear to concede that race-conscious redistricting is not always unconstitutional. That concession is wise: This Court never has held that race-conscious state decisionmaking is impermissible in *all* circumstances. What appellants object to is redistricting legislation that is so extremely irregular on its face that it rationally can be viewed only as an effort to segregate the races for purposes of voting, without regard for traditional districting principles and without sufficiently compelling justification. For the reasons that follow, we conclude that appellants have stated a claim upon which relief can be granted under the Equal Protection Clause.

III

A

The Equal Protection Clause provides that "[n]o State shall . . . deny to any person within its jurisdiction the equal protection of the laws." Its central purpose is to prevent the States from purposefully discriminating between individuals on the basis of race. *Washington v. Davis* (1976). Laws that explicitly distinguish between individuals on racial grounds fall within the core of that prohibition.

No inquiry into legislative purpose is necessary when the racial classification appears on the face of the statute. . . . Express racial classifications are immediately suspect because, "[a]bsent searching judicial inquiry . . . , there is simply no way of determining what classifications are 'benign' or 'remedial' and what classifications are in fact motivated by illegitimate notions of racial inferiority or simple racial politics." *Richmond v. J. A. Croson* (1989); see also *UJO* ("[A] purportedly preferential race assignment may in fact disguise a policy that perpetuates disadvantageous treatment of the plan's supposed beneficiaries").

Classifications of citizens solely on the basis of race "are by their very nature odious to a free people whose institutions are founded upon the doctrine of equality." . . . They threaten to stigmatize individuals by reason of their membership in a racial group and to incite racial hostility. . . . Accordingly, we have held that the Fourteenth Amendment requires state legislation that expressly distinguishes among citizens because of their race to be narrowly tailored to further a compelling governmental interest. See, *e.g., Wygant v. Jackson Bd. of Ed.* (1986).

These principles apply not only to legislation that contains explicit racial distinctions, but also to those "rare" statutes that, although race-neutral, are, on their face, "unexplainable on grounds other than race." *Arlington Heights v. Metropolitan Housing Development Corp.* (1977). . . .

B

Appellants contend that redistricting legislation that is so bizarre on its face that it is "unexplainable on grounds other than race" . . . demands the same close scrutiny that we give other state laws that classify citizens by race. Our voting rights precedents support that conclusion.

In *Guinn v. United States* (1915), the Court invalidated under the Fifteenth Amendment a statute that imposed a literacy requirement on voters but contained a "grandfather clause" applicable to individuals and their lineal descendants entitled to vote "on [or prior to] January 1, 1866." The determinative consideration for the Court was that the law, though ostensibly race-neutral, on its face "embod[ied] no exercise of judgment and rest[ed] upon no discernible reason" other than to circumvent the prohibitions of the Fifteenth Amendment. In other words, the statute was invalid because, on its face, it could not be explained on grounds other than race.

The Court applied the same reasoning to the "uncouth twenty-eight-sided" municipal boundary line at issue in *Gomillion*. Although the statute that redrew the city limits of Tuskegee was race-neutral on its face, plaintiffs alleged that its effect was impermissibly to remove from the city virtually all black voters and no white voters. The Court reasoned:

> "If these allegations upon a trial remained uncontradicted or unqualified, the conclusion would be irresistible, tantamount for all practical purposes to a mathematical demonstration, that the legislation is solely concerned with segregating white and colored voters by fencing Negro citizens out of town so as to deprive them of their pre-existing municipal vote."

The majority resolved the case under the Fifteenth Amendment. Justice Whittaker, however, concluded that the "unlawful segregation of races of citizens" into different voting districts was cognizable under the Equal Protection Clause. This Court's subsequent reliance on *Gomillion* in other Fourteenth Amendment cases suggests the correctness of Justice Whittaker's view. . . . *Gomillion* thus supports appellants' contention that district lines obviously drawn for the purpose of separating voters by race require careful scrutiny under the Equal Protection Clause regardless of the motivations underlying their adoption.

The Court extended the reasoning of *Gomillion* to congressional districting in *Wright v. Rockefeller* (1964). At issue in *Wright* were four districts contained in a New York apportionment statute. The plaintiffs alleged that the statute excluded nonwhites from one district and concentrated them in the other three. Every member of the Court assumed that the plaintiffs' allegation that the statute "segregate[d] eligible voters by race and place of origin" stated a constitutional claim. The Justices disagreed only as to whether the plaintiffs had carried their burden of proof at trial. The dissenters thought the unusual shape of the district lines could "be explained only in racial terms." The majority, however, accepted the District Court's finding that the plaintiffs had failed to establish that the districts were in fact drawn on racial lines. . . .

Wright illustrates the difficulty of determining from the face of a single-member districting plan that it purposefully distinguishes between voters on the basis of race. A reapportionment statute typically does not classify persons at all; it classifies tracts of land, or addresses. Moreover, redistricting differs from other kinds of state decisionmaking in that the legislature always is *aware* of race when it draws district lines, just as it is aware of age, economic status, religious and political persuasion, and a variety of other demographic factors. That sort of race consciousness does not lead inevitably to impermissible race discrimination. As *Wright* demonstrates, when members of a racial group live together in one community, a reapportionment plan that concentrates members of the group in one district and excludes them from others may reflect wholly legitimate purposes. The district lines may be drawn, for example, to provide for compact districts of contiguous territory, or to maintain the integrity of political subdivisions. . . .

The difficulty of proof, of course, does not mean that a racial gerrymander, once established, should receive less scrutiny under the Equal Protection Clause than other state legislation classifying citizens by race. Moreover, it seems clear to us that proof sometimes will not be difficult at all. In some exceptional cases, a reapportionment plan may be so highly irregular that, on its face, it rationally cannot be understood as anything other than an effort to "segregat[e] . . . voters" on the basis of race. . . . *Gomillion,* in which a tortured municipal boundary line was drawn to exclude black voters, was such a case. So, too, would be a case in which a State concentrated a dispersed minority population in a single district by disregarding traditional districting principles such as compactness, contiguity, and respect for political subdivisions. We emphasize that these criteria are important not because they are constitutionally required—they are not . . . —but because they are objective factors that may serve to defeat a claim that a district has been gerrymandered on racial lines. . . .

Put differently, we believe that reapportionment is one area in which appearances do matter. A reapportionment plan that includes in one district individuals who belong to the same race, but who are otherwise widely separated by geographical and political boundaries, and who may have little in common with one another but the color of their skin, bears an uncomfortable resemblance to political apartheid. It reinforces the perception that members of the same racial group—regardless of their age, education, economic status, or the community in which they live— think alike, share the same political interests, and will prefer the same candidates at the polls. We have rejected such perceptions elsewhere as impermissible racial stereotypes. . . . By perpetuating such notions, a racial gerrymander may exacerbate the very patterns of racial bloc voting that majority-minority districting is sometimes said to counteract.

The message that such districting sends to elected representatives is equally pernicious. When a district obviously is created solely to effectuate the perceived common interests of one racial group, elected officials are more likely to believe that their primary obligation is to represent only the members of that group, rather than their constituency as a whole. This is altogether antithetical to our system of representative democracy. . . .

For these reasons, we conclude that a plaintiff challenging a reapportionment statute under the Equal Protection Clause may state a claim by alleging that the legislation, though race-neutral on its face, rationally cannot be understood as anything other than an effort to separate voters into different districts on the basis of race, and that the separation lacks sufficient justification. It is unnecessary for us to decide whether or how a reapportionment plan that, on its face, can be explained in nonracial terms successfully could be challenged. Thus, we express no view as to whether "the intentional creation of majority-minority districts, without more" always gives rise to an equal protection claim. We hold only that, on the facts of this case, plaintiffs have stated a claim sufficient to defeat the state appellees' motion to dismiss.

C

The dissenters consider the circumstances of this case "functionally indistinguishable" from multimember districting and at-large voting systems, which are loosely described as "other varieties of gerrymandering." We have considered the constitutionality of these practices in other Fourteenth Amendment cases and have required plaintiffs to demonstrate that the challenged practice has the purpose and effect of diluting a racial group's voting strength. . . . At-large and multimember schemes, however, do not classify voters on the basis of race. Classifying citizens by race, as we have said, threatens special harms that are not present in our vote-dilution cases. It therefore warrants different analysis.

JUSTICE SOUTER apparently believes that racial gerrymandering is harmless unless it dilutes a racial group's voting strength. As we have explained, however, reapportionment legislation that cannot be understood as anything other than an effort to classify and separate voters by race injures voters in other ways. It reinforces racial stereotypes and threatens to undermine our system of representative democracy by signaling to elected officials that they represent a particular racial group rather than their constituency as a whole. JUSTICE SOUTER does not adequately explain why these harms are not cognizable under the Fourteenth Amendment.

The dissenters make two other arguments that cannot be reconciled with our precedents. First, they suggest that a racial gerrymander of the sort alleged here is functionally equivalent to gerrymanders for nonracial purposes, such as political gerrymanders. This Court has held political gerrymanders to be justiciable under the Equal Protection Clause. See *Davis v. Bandemer.* But nothing in our case law compels the conclusion that racial and political gerrymanders are subject to precisely the same constitutional scrutiny. In fact, our country's long and persistent history of racial discrimination in voting—as well as our Fourteenth Amendment jurisprudence, which always has reserved the strictest scrutiny for discrimination on the basis of race—would seem to compel the opposite conclusion.

Second, JUSTICE STEVENS argues that racial gerrymandering poses no constitutional difficulties when district lines are drawn to favor the minority, rather than the majority. We have made clear, however, that equal protection analysis "is not dependent on the race of those burdened or benefited by a particular classification." ... Indeed, racial classifications receive close scrutiny even when they may be said to burden or benefit the races equally....

Finally, nothing in the Court's highly fractured decision in *UJO* ... forecloses the claim we recognize today. *UJO* concerned New York's revision of a reapportionment plan to include additional majority-minority districts in response to the Attorney General's denial of administrative preclearance under § 5. In that regard, it closely resembles the present case. But the cases are critically different in another way. The plaintiffs in *UJO*—members of a Hasidic community split between two districts under New York's revised redistricting plan—did not allege that the plan, on its face, was so highly irregular that it rationally could be understood only as an effort to segregate voters by race. Indeed, the facts of the case would not have supported such a claim. Three Justices approved the New York statute, in part, precisely because it adhered to traditional districting principles....

IV

JUSTICE SOUTER contends that exacting scrutiny of racial gerrymanders under the Fourteenth Amendment is inappropriate because reapportionment "nearly always require[s] some consideration of race for legitimate reasons." . . . JUSTICE SOUTER's reasoning is flawed.

Earlier this Term, we unanimously reaffirmed that racial bloc voting and minority-group political cohesion never can be assumed, but specifically must be proved in each case in order to establish that a redistricting plan dilutes minority voting strength in violation of § 2. See *Growe v. Emison* (1993). That racial bloc voting or minority political cohesion may be found to exist in *some* cases, of course, is no reason to treat *all* racial gerrymanders differently from other kinds of racial classification. JUSTICE SOUTER apparently views racial gerrymandering of the type presented here as a special category of "benign" racial discrimination that should be subject to relaxed judicial review. As we have said, however, the very reason that the Equal Protection Clause demands strict scrutiny of all racial classifications is because without it, a court cannot determine whether or not the discrimination truly is "benign." Thus, if appellants' allegations of a racial gerrymander are not contradicted on remand, the District Court must determine whether the General Assembly's reapportionment plan satisfies strict scrutiny. We therefore consider what that level of scrutiny requires in the reapportionment context.

The state appellees suggest that a covered jurisdiction may have a compelling interest in creating majority-minority districts in order to comply with the Voting Rights Act. The States certainly have a very strong interest in complying with federal antidiscrimination laws that are constitutionally valid as interpreted and as applied. But in the context of a Fourteenth Amendment challenge, courts must bear in mind the difference between what the law permits, and what it requires.

For example, on remand North Carolina might claim that it adopted the revised plan in order to comply with the § 5 "nonretrogression" principle. Under that principle, a proposed voting change cannot be precleared if it will lead to "a retrogression in the position of racial minorities with respect to their effective exercise of the electoral franchise." *Beer v. United States* (1976). In *Beer,* we held that a reapportionment plan that created one majority-minority district where none existed before passed muster under § 5 because it improved the position of racial minorities. . . .

Although the Court concluded that the redistricting scheme at issue in *Beer* was nonretrogressive, it did not hold that the plan, for that reason, was immune from constitutional challenge. The Court expressly declined to reach that question. . . . Thus, we do not read *Beer* or any of our other § 5 cases to give covered jurisdictions *carte blanche* to engage in racial gerrymandering in the name of nonretrogression. A reapportionment plan would not be narrowly tailored to the goal of avoiding retrogression if the State went beyond what was reasonably necessary to avoid retrogression. . . .

Before us, the state appellees contend that the General Assembly's revised plan was necessary not to prevent retrogression, but to avoid dilution of black voting strength in violation of § 2, as construed in *Thornburg v. Gingles* (1986). In *Gingles* the Court considered a multimember redistricting plan for the North Carolina State Legislature. The Court held that members of a racial minority group claiming § 2 vote dilution through the use of multimember districts must prove three threshold conditions: that the minority group "is sufficiently large and geographically compact to constitute a majority in a single-member district," that the minority group is "politically cohesive," and that "the white majority votes sufficiently as a bloc to enable it . . . usually to defeat the minority's preferred candidate." We have indicated that similar preconditions apply in challenges to single-member districts. . . .

Appellants maintain that the General Assembly's revised plan could not have been required by § 2. They contend that the State's black population is too dispersed to support two geographically compact majority-black districts, as the bizarre shape of District 12 demonstrates, and that there is no evidence of black political cohesion. They also contend that recent black electoral successes demonstrate the willingness of white voters in North Carolina to vote for black candidates. Appellants point out that blacks currently hold the positions of State Auditor, Speaker of the North Carolina House of Representatives, and chair of the North Carolina State Board of Elections. They also point out that in 1990 a black candidate defeated a white opponent in the Democratic Party run-off for a United States Senate seat before being defeated narrowly by the Republican incumbent in the general election. Appellants further argue that if § 2 did require adoption of North Carolina's revised plan, § 2 is to that extent unconstitutional. These arguments were not developed below, and the issues remain open for consideration on remand.

The state appellees alternatively argue that the General Assembly's plan advanced a compelling interest entirely distinct from the Voting Rights Act. We previously have recognized a significant state interest in eradicating the effects of past racial discrimination. . . . But the State must have a " 'strong basis in evidence for [concluding] that remedial action [is] necessary.' " . . .

The state appellees submit that two pieces of evidence gave the General Assembly a strong basis for believing that remedial action was warranted here: the Attorney General's imposition of the § 5 preclearance requirement on 40 North Carolina counties, and the *Gingles* District Court's findings of a long history of official racial discrimination in North Carolina's political system and of pervasive racial bloc voting. The state appellees assert that the deliberate creation of majority-minority districts is the most precise way—indeed the only effective way—to overcome the effects of racially polarized voting. This question also need not be decided at this stage of the litigation. We note, however, that only three Justices in *UJO* were prepared to say that States have a significant interest in minimizing the consequences of racial bloc voting apart from the requirements of the Voting Rights Act. And those three Justices specifically concluded that race-based districting, as a response to racially polarized voting, is constitutionally permissible only when the State "employ[s] sound districting principles," and only when the affected racial group's "residential patterns afford the opportunity of creating districts in which they will be in the majority."

V

Racial classifications of any sort pose the risk of lasting harm to our society. They reinforce the belief, held by too many for too much of our history, that individuals should be judged by the color of their skin. Racial classifications with respect to voting carry particular dangers. Racial gerrymandering, even for remedial purposes, may balkanize us into competing racial factions; it threatens to carry us further from the goal of a political system in which race no longer matters—a goal that the Fourteenth and Fifteenth Amendments embody, and to which the Nation continues to aspire. It is for these reasons that race-based districting by our state legislatures demands close judicial scrutiny.

In this case, the Attorney General suggested that North Carolina could have created a reasonably compact second majority-minority district in the south-central to southeastern part of the State. We express no view as to whether appellants successfully could have challenged such a district under the Fourteenth Amendment. We also do not decide whether appellants' complaint stated a claim under constitutional provisions other than the Fourteenth Amendment. Today we hold only that appellants have stated a claim under the Equal Protection Clause by alleging that the North Carolina General Assembly adopted a reapportionment scheme so irrational on its face that it can be understood only as an effort to segregate voters into separate voting districts because of their race, and that the separation lacks sufficient justification. If the allegation of racial gerrymandering remains uncontradicted, the District Court further must determine whether the North Carolina plan is narrowly tailored to further a compelling governmental interest. Accordingly, we reverse the judgment of the District Court and remand the case for further proceedings consistent with this opinion.

It is so ordered.

JUSTICE WHITE, with whom JUSTICE BLACKMUN and JUSTICE STEVENS join, dissenting.

The facts of this case mirror those presented in *United Jewish Organizations of Williamsburgh, Inc. v. Carey* (1977) (*UJO*), where the Court rejected a claim that creation of a majority-minority district violated the Constitution, either as a *per se* matter or in light of the circumstances leading to the creation of such a district. Of particular relevance, five of the Justices reasoned that members of the white majority could not plausibly argue that their influence over the political process had been unfairly cancelled or that such had been the State's intent. Accordingly, they held that plaintiffs were not entitled to relief under the Constitution's Equal Protection Clause. On the same reasoning, I would affirm the district court's dismissal of appellants' claim in this instance.

The Court today chooses not to overrule, but rather to sidestep, *UJO*. It does so by glossing over the striking similarities, focusing on surface differences, most notably the (admittedly unusual) shape of the newly created district, and imagining an entirely new cause of action. Because the holding is limited to such anomalous circumstances, it perhaps will not substantially hamper a State's legitimate efforts to redistrict in favor of racial minorities. Nonetheless, the notion that North Carolina's plan, under which whites remain a voting majority in a disproportionate number of congressional districts, and pursuant to which the State has sent its first black representatives since Reconstruction to the United States Congress, might have violated appellants' constitutional rights is both a fiction and a departure from settled equal protection principles. Seeing no good reason to engage in either, I dissent.

I

A

The grounds for my disagreement with the majority are simply stated: Appellants have not presented a cognizable claim, because they have not alleged a cognizable injury. To date, we have held that only two types of state voting practices could give rise to a constitutional claim. The first involves direct and outright deprivation of the right to vote, for example by means of a poll tax or literacy test. . . . Plainly, this variety is not implicated by appellants' allegations and need not detain us further. The second type of unconstitutional practice is that which "affects the political strength of various groups," . . . in violation of the Equal Protection Clause. As for this latter category, we have insisted that members of the political or racial group demonstrate that the challenged action have the intent and effect of unduly diminishing their influence on the political process. Although this severe burden has limited the number of successful suits, it was adopted for sound reasons.

The central explanation has to do with the nature of the redistricting process. As the majority recognizes, "redistricting differs from other kinds of state decisionmaking in that the legislature always is *aware* of race when it draws district lines, just as it is aware of age, economic status, religious and political persuasion, and a variety of other demographic factors." "Being aware," in this context, is shorthand for "taking into account," and it hardly can be doubted that legislators routinely engage in the business of making electoral predictions based on group characteristics—racial, ethnic, and the like. . . . Because extirpating such considerations from the redistricting process is unrealistic, the Court has not invalidated all plans that consciously use race, but rather has looked at their impact.

Redistricting plans also reflect group interests and inevitably are conceived with partisan aims in mind. To allow judicial interference whenever this occurs would be to invite constant and unmanageable intrusion. Moreover, a group's power to affect the political process does not automatically dissipate by virtue of an electoral loss. Accordingly, we have asked that an identifiable group demonstrate more than mere lack of success at the polls to make out a successful gerrymandering claim. . . .

With these considerations in mind, we have limited such claims by insisting upon a showing that "the political processes . . . were not equally open to participation by the group in question—that its members had less opportunity than did other residents in the district to participate in the political processes and to elect legislators of their choice." . . . Indeed, as a brief survey of decisions illustrates, the Court's gerrymandering cases all carry this theme—that it is not mere suffering at the polls but discrimination in the polity with which the Constitution is concerned. . . .

To distinguish a claim that alleges that the redistricting scheme has discriminatory intent and effect from one that does not has nothing to do with dividing racial classifications between the "benign" and the malicious—an enterprise which, as the majority notes, the Court has treated with skepticism. Rather, the issue is whether the classification based on race discriminates against *anyone* by denying equal access to the political process. . . .

B

The most compelling evidence of the Court's position prior to this day, for it is most directly on point, is *UJO* (1977). The Court characterizes the decision as "highly fractured," but that should not detract attention from the rejection by a majority in *UJO* of the claim that the State's intentional creation of majority-minority districts transgressed constitutional norms. As stated above, five Justices were of the view that, absent any contention that the proposed plan was adopted with the intent, *or* had the effect, of unduly minimizing the white majority's voting strength, the Fourteenth Amendment was not implicated. . . .

. . . As was the case in New York, a number of North Carolina's political subdivisions have interfered with black citizens' meaningful exercise of the franchise, and are therefore subject to §§ 4 and 5 of the Voting Rights Act. . . .

Like New York, North Carolina failed to prove to the Attorney General's satisfaction that its proposed redistricting had neither the purpose nor the effect of abridging the right to vote on account of race or color. The Attorney General's interposition of a § 5 objection "properly is viewed" as "an administrative finding of discrimination" against a racial minority. . . . Finally, like New York, North Carolina reacted by modifying its plan and creating additional majority-minority districts.

In light of this background, it strains credulity to suggest that North Carolina's purpose in creating a second majority-minority district was to discriminate against members of the majority group by "impair[ing] or burden[ing their] opportunity . . . to participate in the political process." The State has made no mystery of its intent, which was to respond to the Attorney General's objections by improving the minority group's prospects of electing a candidate of its choice. I doubt that this constitutes a discriminatory purpose as defined in the Court's equal protection cases—*i.e.,* an intent to aggravate "the unequal distribution of electoral power." But even assuming that it does, there is no question that appellants have not alleged the requisite discriminatory effects. Whites constitute roughly 76 percent of the total population and 79 percent of the voting age population in North Carolina. Yet, under the State's plan, they still constitute a voting majority in 10 (or 83 percent) of the 12 congressional districts. Though they might be dissatisfied at the prospect of casting a vote for a losing candidate—a lot shared by many, including a disproportionate number of minority voters—surely they cannot complain of discriminatory treatment.

II

The majority attempts to distinguish *UJO* by imagining a heretofore unknown type of constitutional claim. . . . The logic of its theory appears to be that race-conscious redistricting that "segregates" by drawing odd-shaped lines is qualitatively different from race-conscious redistricting that affects groups in some other way. The distinction is without foundation.

A

The essence of the majority's argument is that *UJO* dealt with a claim of vote dilution—which required a specific showing of harm—and that cases such as *Gomillion v. Lightfoot* (1960), and *Wright v. Rockefeller* (1964), dealt with claims of racial segregation—which did not. I read these decisions quite differently. Petitioners' claim in *UJO* was that the State had "violated the Fourteenth and Fifteenth Amendments by *deliberately revising its reapportionment plan along racial lines.*" ([P]lurality opinion)(emphasis added.) They also stated: " 'Our argument is . . . that the history of the area demonstrates that there could be—and in fact was—*no reason other than race to divide the community at this time.*' " Nor was it ever in doubt that "the State deliberately used race in a purposeful manner." In other words, the "analytically distinct claim" the majority discovers today was in plain view and did not carry the day for petitioners. The fact that a demonstration of discriminatory effect was required in that case was not a function of the kind of claim that was made. It was a function of the type of injury upon which the Court insisted.

Gomillion is consistent with this view. . . . In *Gomillion*, . . . the group that formed the majority at the state level purportedly set out to manipulate city boundaries in order to remove members of the minority, thereby denying them valuable municipal services. No analogous purpose or effect has been alleged in this case.

The only other case invoked by the majority is *Wright v. Rockefeller*. *Wright* involved a challenge to a legislative plan that created four districts. In the Seventeenth, Nineteenth, and Twentieth Districts, Whites constituted respectively 94.9%, 71.5%, and 72.5% of the population. 86.3% percent of the population in the Eighteenth District was classified as nonwhite or Puerto Rican. . . . The plaintiffs alleged that the plan was drawn with the intent to segregate voters on the basis of race, in violation of the Fourteenth and Fifteenth Amendments. The Court affirmed the District Court's dismissal of the complaint on the ground that plaintiffs had not met their burden of proving discriminatory intent. I fail to see how a decision based on a failure to establish discriminatory *intent* can support the inference that it is unnecessary to prove discriminatory *effect*.

Wright is relevant only to the extent that it illustrates a proposition with which I have no problem: That a complaint stating that a plan has carved out districts on the basis of race *can*, under certain circumstances, state a claim under the Fourteenth Amendment. To that end, however, there must be an allegation of discriminatory purpose and effect, for the constitutionality of a race-conscious redistricting plan depends on these twin elements. In *Wright*, for example, the facts might have supported the contention that the districts were intended to, and did in fact, shield the Seventeenth District from any minority influence and "pack" black and Puerto Rican voters in the Eighteenth, thereby invidiously minimizing their voting strength. In other words, the purposeful creation of a majority-minority district could have discriminatory effect if it is achieved by means of "packing"—*i.e.*, over-concentration of minority voters. In the present case, the facts could sustain no such allegation.

B

Lacking support in any of the Court's precedents, the majority's novel type of claim also makes no sense. As I understand the theory that is put forth, a redistricting plan that uses race to "segregate" voters by drawing "uncouth" lines is harmful in a way that a plan that uses race to distribute voters differently is not, for the former "bears an uncomfortable resemblance to political apartheid." The distinction is untenable.

Racial gerrymanders come in various shades: At-large voting schemes ... ; the fragmentation of a minority group among various districts "so that it is a majority in none" ... otherwise known as "cracking" ... ; the "stacking" of "a large minority population concentration ... with a larger white population"; and, finally, the "concentration of [minority voters] into districts where they constitute an excessive majority" ... also called "packing." In each instance, race is consciously utilized by the legislature for electoral purposes; in each instance, we have put the plaintiff challenging the district lines to the burden of demonstrating that the plan was meant to, and did in fact, exclude an identifiable racial group from participation in the political process.

Not so, apparently, when the districting "segregates" by drawing odd-shaped lines. In that case, we are told, such proof no longer is needed. Instead, it is the *State* that must rebut the allegation that race was taken into account, a fact that, together with the legislators' consideration of ethnic, religious, and other group characteristics, I had thought we practically took for granted. Part of the explanation for the majority's approach has to do, perhaps, with the emotions stirred by words such as "segregation" and "political apartheid." But their loose and imprecise use by today's majority has, I fear, led it astray. The consideration of race in "segregation" cases is no different than in other race-conscious districting; from the standpoint of the affected groups, moreover, the line-drawings all act in similar fashion. A plan that "segregates" being functionally indistinguishable from any of the other varieties of gerrymandering, we should be consistent in what we require from a claimant: Proof of discriminatory purpose and effect.

The other part of the majority's explanation of its holding is related to its simultaneous discomfort and fascination with irregularly shaped districts. Lack of compactness or contiguity, like uncouth district lines, certainly is a helpful indicator that some form of gerrymandering (racial or other) might have taken place and that "something may be amiss." . . . Disregard for geographic divisions and compactness often goes hand in hand with partisan gerrymandering. . . .

But while district irregularities may provide strong indicia of a potential gerrymander, they do no more than that. In particular, they have no bearing on whether the plan ultimately is found to violate the Constitution. Given two districts drawn on similar, race-based grounds, the one does not become more injurious than the other simply by virtue of being snake-like, at least so far as the Constitution is concerned and absent any evidence of differential racial impact. The majority's contrary view is perplexing in light of its concession that "compactness or attractiveness has never been held to constitute an independent federal constitutional requirement for state legislative districts." . . . It is shortsighted as well, for a regularly shaped district can just as effectively effectuate racially discriminatory gerrymandering as an odd-shaped one. By focusing on looks rather than impact, the majority "immediately casts attention in the wrong direction—toward superficialities of shape and size, rather than toward the political realities of district composition."

Limited by its own terms to cases involving unusually-shaped districts, the Court's approach nonetheless will unnecessarily hinder to some extent a State's voluntary effort to ensure a modicum of minority representation. This will be true in areas where the minority population is geographically dispersed. It also will be true where the minority population is not scattered but, for reasons unrelated to race—for example incumbency protection—the State would rather not create the majority-minority district in its most "obvious" location. When, as is the case here, the creation of a majority-minority district does not unfairly minimize the voting power of any other group, the Constitution does not justify, much less mandate, such obstruction. . . .

III

Although I disagree with the holding that appellants' claim is cognizable, the Court's discussion of the level of scrutiny it requires warrants a few comments. I have no doubt that a State's compliance with the Voting Rights Act clearly constitutes a compelling interest. . . . Here, the Attorney General objected to the State's plan on the ground that it failed to draw a second majority-minority district for what appeared to be pretextual reasons. Rather than challenge this conclusion, North Carolina chose to draw the second district. As *UJO* held, a State is entitled to take such action. . . .

The Court, while seemingly agreeing with this position, warns that the State's redistricting effort must be "narrowly tailored" to further its interest in complying with the law. It is evident to me, however, that what North Carolina did was precisely tailored to meet the objection of the Attorney General to its prior plan. Hence, I see no need for a remand at all, even accepting the majority's basic approach to this case.

Furthermore, how it intends to manage this standard, I do not know. Is it more "narrowly tailored" to create an irregular majority-minority district as opposed to one that is compact but harms other State interests such as incumbency protection or the representation of rural interests? Of the following two options—creation of two minority influence districts or of a single majority-minority district—is one "narrowly tailored" and the other not? Once the Attorney General has found that a proposed redistricting change violates § 5's nonretrogression principle in that it will abridge a racial minority's right to vote, does "narrow tailoring" mean that the most the State can do is preserve the *status quo*? Or can it maintain that change, while attempting to enhance minority voting power in some other manner? This small sample only begins to scratch the surface of the problems raised by the majority's test. But it suffices to illustrate the unworkability of a standard that is divorced from any measure of constitutional harm. In that, State efforts to remedy minority vote dilution are wholly unlike what typically has been labeled "affirmative action." To the extent that no other racial group is injured, remedying a Voting Rights Act violation does not involve preferential treatment.... It involves, instead, an attempt to *equalize* treatment, and to provide minority voters with an effective voice in the political process. The Equal Protection Clause of the Constitution, surely, does not stand in the way.

IV

Since I do not agree that petitioners alleged an Equal Protection violation and because the Court of Appeals faithfully followed the Court's prior cases, I dissent and would affirm the judgment below.

JUSTICE BLACKMUN, dissenting.

I join JUSTICE WHITE's dissenting opinion.... I ... agree that the conscious use of race in redistricting does not violate the Equal Protection Clause unless the effect of the redstricting plan is to deny a particular group equal access to the political process or to minimize its voting strength unduly.... It is particularly ironic that the case in which today's majority chooses to abandon settled law and to recognize for the first time this "analytically distinct" constitutional claim is a challenge by white voters to the plan under which North Carolina has sent black representatives to Congress for the first time since Reconstruction. I dissent.

JUSTICE STEVENS, dissenting.

For the reasons stated by JUSTICE WHITE, the decision of the District Court should be affirmed. . . .

. . . [W]e must ask whether otherwise permissible redistricting to benefit an underrepresented minority group becomes impermissible when the minority group is defined by its race. The Court today answers this question in the affirmative, and its answer is wrong. If it is permissible to draw boundaries to provide adequate representation for rural voters, for union members, for Hasidic Jews, for Polish Americans, or for Republicans, it necessarily follows that it is permissible to do the same thing for members of the very minority group whose history in the United States gave birth to the Equal Protection Clause. A contrary conclusion could only be described as perverse.

Accordingly, I respectfully dissent.

JUSTICE SOUTER, dissenting.

Today, the Court recognizes a new cause of action under which a State's electoral redistricting plan that includes a configuration "so bizarre" that it "rationally cannot be understood as anything other than an effort to separate voters into different districts on the basis of race [without] sufficient justification" will be subjected to strict scrutiny. In my view there is no justification for the Court's determination to depart from our prior decisions by carving out this narrow group of cases for strict scrutiny in place of the review customarily applied in cases dealing with discrimination in electoral districting on the basis of race.

[I and II Omitted]

III

. . . [T]he Court creates a new "analytically distinct" cause of action, the principal element of which is that a districting plan be "so bizarre on its face" or "irrational on its face" or "extremely irregular on its face" that it "rationally cannot be understood as anything other than an effort to segregate citizens into separate voting districts on the basis of race without sufficient justification." Pleading such an element, the Court holds, suffices without a further allegation of harm, to state a claim upon which relief can be granted under the Fourteenth Amendment.

It may be that the terms for pleading this cause of action will be met so rarely that this case will wind up an aberration. The shape of the district at issue in this case is indeed so bizarre that few other examples are ever likely to carry the unequivocal implication of impermissible use of race that the Court finds here. It may therefore be that few electoral districting cases are ever likely to employ the strict scrutiny the Court holds to be applicable on remand if appellants' allegations are "not contradicted."

Nonetheless, in those cases where this cause of action is sufficiently pleaded, the State will have to justify its decision to consider race as being required by a compelling state interest, and its use of race as narrowly tailored to that interest. Meanwhile, in other districting cases, specific consequential harm will still need to be pleaded and proven, in the absence of which the use of race may be invalidated only if it is shown to serve no legitimate state purpose. . . .

The Court offers no adequate justification for treating the narrow category of bizarrely shaped district claims differently from other districting claims. The only justification I can imagine would be the preservation of "sound districting principles," such as compactness and contiguity. But as JUSTICE WHITE points out, and as the Court acknowledges, we have held that such principles are not constitutionally required, with the consequence that their absence cannot justify the distinct constitutional regime put in place by the Court today. Since there is no justification for the departure here from the principles that continue to govern electoral districting cases generally in accordance with our prior decisions, I would not respond to the seeming egregiousness of the redistricting now before us by untethering the concept of racial gerrymander in such a case from the concept of harm exemplified by dilution. In the absence of an allegation of such harm, I would affirm the judgment of the District Court. I respectfully dissent.

□□□

No. 92-6073

Richard Lyle Austin, Petitioner v. United States

On writ of certiorari to the United States Court of Appeals
for the Eighth Circuit

[June 28, 1993]

JUSTICE BLACKMUN delivered the opinion of the Court.

In this case, we are asked to decide whether the Excessive Fines Clause of the Eighth Amendment applies to forfeitures of property under 21 U.S.C. §§ 881(a)(4) and (a)(7). We hold that it does and therefore remand the case for consideration of the question whether the forfeiture at issue here was excessive.

I

On August 2, 1990, petitioner Richard Lyle Austin was indicted on four counts of violating South Dakota's drug laws. Austin ultimately pleaded guilty to one count of possessing cocaine with intent to distribute and was sentenced by the state court to seven years' imprisonment. On September 7, the United States filed an *in rem* action in the United States District Court for the District of South Dakota seeking forfeiture of Austin's mobile home and auto body shop under 21 U.S.C. §§ 881(a)(4) and (a)(7). Austin filed a claim and an answer to the complaint.

On February 4, 1991, the United States made a motion, supported by an affidavit from Sioux Falls Police Officer Donald Satterlee, for summary judgment. According to Satterlee's affidavit, Austin met Keith Engebretson at Austin's body shop on June 13, 1990, and agreed to sell cocaine to Engebretson. Austin left the shop, went to his mobile home, and returned to the shop with two grams of cocaine which he sold to Engebretson. State authorities executed a search warrant on the body shop and mobile home the following day. They discovered small amounts of marijuana and cocaine, a .22 caliber revolver, drug paraphernalia, and approximately $4,700 in cash. In opposing summary judgment, Austin argued that forfeiture of the properties would violate the Eighth Amendment. The District Court rejected this argument and entered summary judgment for the United States.

The United States Court of Appeals for the Eighth Circuit "reluctantly agree[d] with the government" and affirmed. *United States v. One Parcel of Property* (1992). Although it thought that "the principle of proportionality should be applied in civil actions that result in harsh penalties" and that the Government was "exacting too high a penalty in relation to the offense committed," the court felt constrained from holding the forfeiture unconstitutional. It cited this Court's decision in *Calero-Toledo v. Pearson Yacht Leasing Co.* (1974), for the proposition that, when the Government is proceeding against property *in rem,* the guilt or innocence of the property's owner "is constitutionally irrelevant." It then reasoned: "We are constrained to agree with the Ninth Circuit that '[i]f the constitution allows *in rem* forfeiture to be visited upon innocent owners ... the constitution hardly requires proportionality review of forfeitures.' " ...

We granted certiorari (1993) to resolve an apparent conflict with the Court of Appeals for the Second Circuit over the applicability of the Eighth Amendment to *in rem* civil forfeitures....

II

Austin contends that the Eighth Amendment's Excessive Fines Clause applies to *in rem* civil forfeiture proceedings. We have had occasion to consider this Clause only once before. In *Browning-Ferris Industries v. Kelco Disposal, Inc.* (1989), we held that the Excessive Fines Clause does not limit the award of punitive damages to a private party in a civil suit when the government neither has prosecuted the action nor has any right to receive a share of the damages. The Court's opinion and JUSTICE O'CONNOR's opinion, concurring in part and dissenting in part, reviewed in some detail the history of the Excessive Fines Clause. The Court concluded that both the Eighth Amendment and § 10 of the English Bill of Rights of 1689, from which it derives, were intended to prevent *the government* from abusing its power to punish and therefore "that the Excessive Fines Clause was intended to limit only those fines directly imposed by, and payable to, the government."

We found it unnecessary to decide in *Browning-Ferris* whether the Excessive Fines Clause applies only to criminal cases. The United States now argues that

> "any claim that the government's conduct in a civil proceeding is limited by the Eighth Amendment generally, or by the Excessive Fines Clause in particular, must fail unless the challenged governmental action, despite its label, would have been recognized as a criminal punishment at the time the Eighth Amendment was adopted." ([E]mphasis added.)

It further suggests that the Eighth Amendment cannot apply to a civil proceeding unless that proceeding is so punitive that it must be considered criminal under *Kennedy v. Mendoza-Martinez* (1963) and *United States v. Ward* (1980). We disagree.

Some provisions of the Bill of Rights are expressly limited to criminal cases. The Fifth Amendment's Self-Incrimination Clause, for example, provides: "No person . . . shall be compelled in any criminal case to be a witness against himself." The protections provided by the Sixth Amendment are explicitly confined to "criminal prosecutions.". . . The text of the Eighth Amendment includes no similar limitation.

Nor does the history of the Eighth Amendment require such a limitation. JUSTICE O'CONNOR noted in *Browning-Ferris:* "Consideration of the Eighth Amendment immediately followed consideration of the Fifth Amendment. After deciding to confine the benefits of the Self-Incrimination Clause of the Fifth Amendment to criminal proceedings, the Framers turned their attention to the Eighth Amendment. There were no proposals to limit that Amendment to criminal proceedings. . . ." Section 10 of the English Bill of Rights of 1689 is not expressly limited to criminal cases either. . . .

The purpose of the Eighth Amendment ... was to limit the governments power to punish. ... The Cruel and Unusual Punishments Clause is self-evidently concerned with punishment. The Excessive Fines Clause limits the Government's power to extract payments, whether in cash or in kind, "as *punishment* for some offense.". ... Thus, the question is not, as the United States would have it, whether forfeiture under §§ 881(a)(4) and (a)(7) is civil or criminal, but rather whether it is punishment.

In considering this question, we are mindful of the fact that sanctions frequently serve more than one purpose. We need not exclude the possibility that a forfeiture serves remedial purposes to conclude that it is subject to the limitations of the Excessive Fines Clause. We, however, must determine that it can only be explained as serving in part to punish. We said in [*United States v.*] *Halper* [1989] that "a civil sanction that cannot fairly be said solely to serve a remedial purpose, but rather can only be explained as also serving either retributive or deterrent purposes, is punishment, as we have come to understand the term." We turn, then, to consider whether, at the time the Eighth Amendment was ratified, forfeiture was understood at least in part as punishment and whether forfeiture under §§ 881(a)(4) and (a)(7) should be so understood today.

III

[A Omitted]

B

... The First Congress passed laws subjecting ships and cargos involved in customs offenses to forfeiture. It does not follow from that fact, however, that the First Congress thought such forfeitures to be beyond the purview of the Eighth Amendment. Indeed, examination of those laws suggests that the First Congress viewed forfeiture as punishment. ...

C

... The same understanding of forfeiture as punishment runs through our cases rejecting the "innocence" of the owner as a common-law defense to forfeiture. See, *e.g.*, *Calero-Toledo; Goldsmith-Grant Co. v. United States* (1921); *Dobbins's Distillery v. United States* (1878); *United States v. Brig Malek Adhe* (1844); *The Palmyra* (1827). In these cases, forfeiture has been justified on two theories—that the property itself is "guilty" of the offense, and that the owner may be held accountable for the wrongs of others to whom he entrusts his property. Both theories rest, at bottom, on the notion that the owner has been negligent in allowing his property to be misused and that he is properly punished for that negligence. . . .

. . . [E]ven though this Court has rejected the "innocence" of the owner as a common-law defense to forfeiture, it consistently has recognized that forfeiture serves, at least in part, to punish the owner. See *Peisch v. Ware* [1808] ("the act punishes the owner with a forfeiture of the goods"); *Dobbins's Distillery* ("the acts of violation as to the penal consequences to the property are to be considered just the same as if they were the acts of the owner"); *Goldsmith-Grant Co.* (" 'such misfortunes are in part owing to the negligence of the owner, and therefore he is properly punished by the forfeiture' "). More recently, we have noted that forfeiture serves "punitive and deterrent purposes," *Calero-Toledo,* and "impos[es] an economic penalty." We conclude, therefore, that forfeiture generally and statutory *in rem* forfeiture in particular historically have been understood, at least in part, as punishment.

IV

We turn next to consider whether forfeitures under 21 U.S.C. §§ 881(a)(4) and (a)(7) are properly considered punishment today. We find nothing in these provisions or their legislative history to contradict the historical understanding of forfeiture as punishment. Unlike traditional forfeiture statutes, §§ 881(a)(4) and (a)(7) expressly provide an "innocent owner" defense. . . . These exemptions serve to focus the provisions on the culpability of the owner in a way that makes them look more like punishment, not less. . . .

Furthermore, Congress has chosen to tie forfeiture directly to the commission of drug offenses. Thus, under § 881(a)(4), a conveyance is forfeitable if it is used or intended for use to facilitate the transportation of controlled substances, their raw materials, or the equipment used to manufacture or distribute them. Under § 881(a)(7), real property is forfeitable if it is used or intended for use to facilitate the commission of a drug-related crime punishable by more than one year's imprisonment.

The legislative history of § 881 confirms the punitive nature of these provisions. When it added subsection (a)(7) to § 881 in 1984, Congress recognized "that the traditional criminal sanctions of fine and imprisonment are inadequate to deter or punish the enormously profitable trade in dangerous drugs." (1983). It characterized the forfeiture of real property as "a powerful deterrent." . . .

The Government argues that §§ 881(a)(4) and (a)(7) are not punitive but, rather, should be considered remedial in two respects. First, they remove the "instruments" of the drug trade "thereby protecting the community from the threat of continued drug dealing." Second, the forfeited assets serve to compensate the Government for the expense of law enforcement activity and for its expenditure on societal problems such as urban blight, drug addiction, and other health concerns resulting from the drug trade.

In our view, neither argument withstands scrutiny. Concededly, we have recognized that the forfeiture of contraband itself may be characterized as remedial because it removes dangerous or illegal items from society. See *United States v. One Assortment of 89 Firearms* (1984). The Court, however, previously has rejected government's attempt to extend that reasoning to conveyances used to transport illegal liquor. See *One 1958 Plymouth Sedan v. Pennsylvania* (1965). In that case it noted: "There is nothing even remotely criminal in possessing an automobile." The same, without question, is true of the properties involved here, and the Government's attempt to characterize these properties as "instruments" of the drug trade must meet the same fate as Pennsylvania's effort to characterize the 1958 Plymouth Sedan as "contraband."

The Government's second argument about the remedial nature of this forfeiture is no more persuasive. We previously have upheld the forfeiture of goods involved in customs violations as "a reasonable form of liquidated damages." *One Lot Emerald Cut Stones v. United States* (1972). But the dramatic variations in the value of conveyances and real property forfeitable under §§ 881(a)(4) and (a)(7) undercut any similar argument with respect to those provisions. The Court made this very point in *Ward:* the "forfeiture of property . . . [is] a penalty that ha[s] absolutely no correlation to any damages sustained by society or to the cost of enforcing the law."

Fundamentally, even assuming that §§ 881(a)(4) and (a)(7) serve some remedial purpose, the Government's argument must fail. "[A] civil sanction that cannot fairly be said *solely* to serve a remedial purpose, but rather can only be explained as also serving either retributive or deterrent purposes, is punishment, as we have come to understand the term." *Halper* (emphasis added). In light of the historical understanding of forfeiture as punishment, the clear focus of §§ 881(a)(4) and (a)(7) on the culpability of the owner, and the evidence that Congress understood those provisions as serving to deter and to punish, we cannot conclude that forfeiture under §§ 881(a)(4) and (a)(7) serves solely a remedial purpose. We therefore conclude that forfeiture under these provisions constitutes "payment to a sovereign as punishment for some offense," *Browning-Ferris,* and, as such, is subject to the limitations of the Eighth Amendment's Excessive Fines Clause.

V

Austin asks that we establish a multifactor test for determining whether a forfeiture is constitutionally "excessive." We decline that invitation. Although the Court of Appeals opined "that the government is exacting too high a penalty in relation to the offense committed," it had no occasion to consider what factors should inform such a decision because it thought it was foreclosed from engaging in the inquiry. Prudence dictates that we allow the lower courts to consider that question in the first instance. . . .

The judgment of the Court of Appeals is reversed and the case is remanded to that court for further proceedings consistent with this opinion.

It is so ordered.

JUSTICE SCALIA, concurring in part and concurring in the judgment.

We recently stated that, at the time the Eighth Amendment was drafted, the term "fine" was "understood to mean a payment to a sovereign as punishment for some offense." *Browning-Ferris Industries of Vermont, Inc. v. Kelco Disposal, Inc.* (1989). It seems to me that the Court's opinion obscures this clear statement, and needlessly attempts to derive from our sparse caselaw on the subject of *in rem* forfeiture the questionable proposition that the owner of property taken pursuant to such forfeiture is always blameworthy. I write separately to explain why I consider this forfeiture a fine, and to point out that the excessiveness inquiry for statutory *in rem* forfeitures is different from the usual excessiveness inquiry.

I

. . . In order to constitute a fine under the Eighth Amendment . . . the forfeiture must constitute "punishment," and it is a much closer question whether statutory *in rem* forfeitures, as opposed to *in personam* forfeitures, meet this requirement. The latter are assessments, whether monetary or in-kind, to punish the property owner's criminal conduct, while the former are confiscations of property rights based on improper use of the property, regardless of whether the owner has violated the law. Statutory *in rem* forfeitures have a long history. . . . The property to which they apply is not contraband, see the forfeiture passed by the First Congress, nor is necessarily property that can only be used for illegal purposes. The theory of *in rem* forfeiture is said to be that the lawful property has committed an offense. . . .

However the theory may be expressed, it seems to me that this taking of lawful property must be considered, in whole or in part, see *United States v. Halper* (1989), punitive. Its purpose is not compensatory, to make someone whole for injury caused by unlawful use of the property. Punishment is being imposed, whether one quaintly considers its object to be the property itself, or more realistically regards its object to be the property's owner. . . .

The Court apparently believes, however, that only actual culpability of the affected property owner can establish that a forfeiture provision is punitive, and sets out to establish (in Part III) that such culpability exists in the case of *in rem* forfeitures. In my view, however, the caselaw is far more ambiguous than the Court acknowledges. We have never held that the Constitution requires negligence, or any other degree of culpability, to support such forfeitures. . . . If the Court is correct that culpability of the owner is essential, then there is no difference (except perhaps the burden of proof) between the traditional *in rem* forfeiture and the traditional *in personam* forfeiture. Well-established common-law distinctions should not be swept away by reliance on bits of dicta. Moreover, if some degree of personal culpability on the part of the property owner always exists for *in rem* forfeitures, then it is hard to understand why this Court has kept reserving the (therefore academic) question whether personal culpability is constitutionally required, as the Court does again today.

I would have reserved the question without engaging in the misleading discussion of culpability. *Even if* punishment of personal culpability is necessary for a forfeiture to be a fine; and *even if in rem* forfeitures in general do not punish personal culpability; the *in rem* forfeiture in *this* case is a fine. As the Court discusses in Part IV, this statute, in contrast to the traditional *in rem* forfeiture, requires that the owner not be innocent—that he have some degree of culpability for the "guilty" property. See also *United States v. 92 Buena Vista Ave., Rumson* (1993) (contrasting drug forfeiture statute with traditional statutory *in rem* forfeitures). Here, the property must "offend" *and* the owner must not be completely without fault. Nor is there any consideration of compensating for loss, since the value of the property is irrelevant to whether it is forfeited. That is enough to satisfy the *Browning-Ferris* standard, and to make the entire discussion in Part III dictum. Statutory forfeitures under § 881(a) are certainly payment (in kind), *to a sovereign* as *punishment* for an *offense.*

II

That this forfeiture works as a fine raises the excessiveness issue, on which the Court remands. I agree that a remand is in order, but think it worth pointing out that on remand the excessiveness analysis must be different from that applicable to monetary fines and, perhaps, to *in personam* forfeitures. In the case of a monetary fine, the Eighth Amendment's origins in the English Bill of Rights, intended to limit the abusive penalties assessed against the king's opponents, see *Browning-Ferris,* demonstrate that the touchstone is value of the fine in relation to the offense. And in *Alexander v. United States* [1993], we indicated that the same is true for *in personam* forfeiture.

Here, however, the offense of which petitioner has been convicted is not relevant to the forfeiture. Section 881 requires only that the Government show probable cause that the subject property was used for the prohibited purpose. The burden then shifts to the property owner to show, by a preponderance of the evidence, that the use was made without his "knowledge, consent, or willful blindness," 21 U.S.C. §§ 881(a)(4)(C), see also (a)(7), or that the property was not so used. See § 881(d) (incorporating 19 U.S.C. § 1615). Unlike monetary fines, statutory *in rem* forfeitures have traditionally been fixed, not by determining the appropriate value of the penalty in relation to the committed offense, but by determining what property has been "tainted" by unlawful use, to which issue the value of the property is irrelevant. Scales used to measure out unlawful drug sales, for example, are confiscable whether made of the purest gold or the basest metal. But an *in rem* forfeiture goes beyond the traditional limits that the Eighth Amendment permits if it applies to property that cannot properly be regarded as an instrumentality of the offense—the building, for example, in which an isolated drug sale happens to occur. Such a confiscation would be an excessive fine. The question is not *how much* the confiscated property is worth, but *whether* the confiscated property has a close enough relationship to the offense.

. . . The relevant inquiry for an excessive forfeiture under § 881 is the relationship of the property to the offense: Was it close enough to render the property, under traditional standards, "guilty" and hence forfeitable?

I join the Court's opinion in part, and concur in the judgment.

JUSTICE KENNEDY, with whom THE CHIEF JUSTICE and JUSTICE THOMAS join, concurring in part and concurring in the judgment.

I am in substantial agreement with Part I of JUSTICE SCALIA's opinion concurring in part and concurring in the judgment. I share JUSTICE SCALIA's belief that Part III of the Court's opinion is quite unnecessary for the decision of the case, fails to support the Court's argument, and seems rather doubtful as well. . . .

At some point, we may have to confront the constitutional question whether forfeiture is permitted when the owner has committed no wrong of any sort, intentional or negligent. That for me would raise a serious question. Though the history of forfeiture laws might not be determinative of that issue, it would have an important bearing on the outcome. I would reserve for that or some other necessary occasion the inquiry the Court undertakes here. Unlike JUSTICE SCALIA, I would also reserve the question whether *in rem* forfeitures always amount to an intended punishment of the owner of forfeited property.

With these observations, I concur in part and concur in the judgment.

□□□

No. 92-102

William Daubert, et ux., etc., et al., Petitioners v. Merrell Dow Pharmaceuticals, Inc.

On writ of certiorari to the United States Court of Appeals for the Ninth Circuit

[June 28, 1993]

JUSTICE BLACKMUN delivered the opinion of the Court.

In this case we are called upon to determine the standard for admitting expert scientific testimony in a federal trial.

I

Petitioners Jason Daubert and Eric Schuller are minor children born with serious birth defects. They and their parents sued respondent in California state court, alleging that the birth defects had been caused by the mothers' ingestion of Bendectin, a prescription anti-nausea drug marketed by respondent. Respondent removed the suits to federal court on diversity grounds.

After extensive discovery, respondent moved for summary judgment, contending that Bendectin does not cause birth defects in humans and that petitioners would be unable to come forward with any admissible evidence that it does. In support of its motion, respondent submitted an affidavit of Steven H. Lamm, physician and epidemiologist, who is a well-credentialed expert on the risks from exposure to various chemical substances. Doctor Lamm stated that he had reviewed all the literature on Bendectin and human birth defects—more than 30 published studies involving over 130,000 patients. No study had found Bendectin to be a human teratogen (*i.e.*, a substance capable of causing malformations in fetuses). On the basis of this review, Doctor Lamm concluded that maternal use of Bendectin during the first trimester of pregnancy has not been shown to be a risk factor for human birth defects.

Petitioners did not (and do not) contest this characterization of the published record regarding Bendectin. Instead, they responded to respondent's motion with the testimony of eight experts of their own, each of whom also possessed impressive credentials. These experts had concluded that Bendectin can cause birth defects. Their conclusions were based upon "in vitro" (test tube) and "in vivo" (live) animal studies that found a link between Bendectin and malformations; pharmacological studies of the chemical structure of Bendectin that purported to show similarities between the structure of the drug and that of other substances known to cause birth defects; and the "reanalysis" of previously published epidemiological (human statistical) studies.

The District Court granted respondent's motion for summary judgment. The court stated that scientific evidence is admissible only if the principle upon which it is based is " 'sufficiently established to have general acceptance in the field to which it belongs.' " The court concluded that petitioners' evidence did not meet this standard. Given the vast body of epidemiological data concerning Bendectin, the court held, expert opinion which is not based on epidemiological evidence is not admissible to establish causation. Thus, the animal-cell studies, live-animal studies, and chemical-structure analyses on which petitioners had relied could not raise by themselves a reasonably disputable jury issue regarding causation. Petitioners' epidemiological analyses, based as they were on recalculations of data in previously published studies that had found no causal link between the drug and birth defects, were ruled to be inadmissible because they had not been published or subjected to peer review.

The United States Court of Appeals for the Ninth Circuit affirmed. (1991). Citing *Frye v. United States* (1923), the court stated that expert opinion based on a scientific technique is inadmissible unless the technique is "generally accepted" as reliable in the relevant scientific community. The court declared that expert opinion based on a methodology that diverges "significantly from the procedures accepted by recognized authorities in the field . . . cannot be shown to be 'generally accepted as a reliable technique.' "

The court emphasized that other Courts of Appeals considering the risks of Bendectin had refused to admit reanalyses of epidemiological studies that had been neither published nor subjected to peer review. Those courts had found unpublished reanalyses "particularly problematic in light of the massive weight of the original published studies supporting [respondent's] position, all of which had undergone full scrutiny from the scientific community." Contending that reanalysis is generally accepted by the scientific community only when it is subjected to verification and scrutiny by others in the field, the Court of Appeals rejected petitioners' reanalyses as "unpublished, not subjected to the normal peer review process and generated solely for use in litigation." The court concluded that petitioners' evidence provided an insufficient foundation to allow admission of expert testimony that Bendectin caused their injuries and, accordingly, that petitioners could not satisfy their burden of proving causation at trial.

We granted certiorari (1992) in light of sharp divisions among the courts regarding the proper standard for the admission of expert testimony. . . .

II

A

In the 70 years since its formulation in the *Frye* case, the "general acceptance" test has been the dominant standard for determining the admissibility of novel scientific evidence at trial. Although under increasing attack of late, the rule continues to be followed by a majority of courts, including the Ninth Circuit.

The *Frye* test has its origin in a short and citation-free 1923 decision concerning the admissibility of evidence derived from a systolic blood pressure deception test, a crude precursor to the polygraph machine. In what has become a famous (perhaps infamous) passage, the then Court of Appeals for the District of Columbia described the device and its operation and declared:

> "Just when a scientific principle or discovery crosses the line between the experimental and demonstrable stages is difficult to define. Somewhere in this twilight zone the evidential force of the principle must be recognized, and while courts will go a long way in admitting expert testimony deduced from a well-recognized scientific principle or discovery, *the thing from which the deduction is made must be sufficiently established to have gained general acceptance in the particular field in which it belongs.*" ([E]mphasis added.)

Because the deception test had "not yet gained such standing and scientific recognition among physiological and psychological authorities as would justify the courts in admitting expert testimony deduced from the discovery, development, and experiments thus far made," evidence of its results was ruled inadmissible.

The merits of the *Frye* test have been much debated, and scholarship on its proper scope and application is legion. Petitioners' primary attack, however, is not on the content but on the continuing authority of the rule. They contend that the *Frye* test was superseded by the adoption of the Federal Rules of Evidence. We agree.

We interpret the legislatively-enacted Federal Rules of Evidence as we would any statute. *Beech Aircraft Corp. v. Rainey* (1988). Rule 402 provides the baseline:

> "All relevant evidence is admissible, except as otherwise provided by the Constitution of the United States, by Act of Congress, by these rules, or by other rules prescribed by the Supreme Court pursuant to statutory authority. Evidence which is not relevant is not admissible."

"Relevant evidence" is defined as that which has "any tendency to make the existence of any fact that is of consequence to the determination of the action more probable or less probable than it would be without the evidence." The Rule's basic standard of relevance thus is a liberal one.

Frye, of course, predated the Rules by half a century. In *United States v. Abel* (1984), we considered the pertinence of background common law in interpreting the Rules of Evidence. We noted that the Rules occupy the field, but ... explained that the common law nevertheless could serve as an aid to their application....

Here there is a specific Rule that speaks to the contested issue. Rule 702, governing testimony, provides:

> "If scientific, technical, or other specialized knowledge will assist the trier of fact to understand the evidence or to determine a fact in issue, a witness qualified as an expert by knowledge, skill, experience, training, or education, may testify thereto in the form of an opinion or otherwise."

Nothing in the text of this Rule establishes "general acceptance" as an absolute prerequisite to admissibility. Nor does respondent present any clear indication that Rule 702 or the Rules as a whole were intended to incorporate a "general acceptance" standard. The drafting history makes no mention of *Frye,* and a rigid "general acceptance" requirement would be at odds with the "liberal thrust" of the Federal Rules and their "general approach of relaxing the traditional barriers to 'opinion' testimony." *Beech Aircraft Corp. v. Rainey* (citing Rules 701 to 705).... Given the Rules' permissive backdrop and their inclusion of a specific rule on expert testimony that does not mention "general acceptance," the assertion that the Rules somehow assimilated *Frye* is unconvincing. *Frye* made "general acceptance" the exclusive test for admitting expert scientific testimony. That austere standard, absent from and incompatible with the Federal Rules of Evidence, should not be applied in federal trials.

B

That the *Frye* test was displaced by the Rules of Evidence does not mean, however, that the Rules themselves place no limits on the admissibility of purportedly scientific evidence. Nor is the trial judge disabled from screening such evidence. To the contrary, under the Rules the trial judge must ensure that any and all scientific testimony or evidence admitted is not only relevant, but reliable.

The primary locus of this obligation is Rule 702, which clearly contemplates some degree of regulation of the subjects and theories about which an expert may testify. "*If scientific,* technical, or other specialized *knowledge will assist the trier of fact* to understand the evidence or to determine a fact in issue" an expert "may testify *thereto.*" The subject of an expert's testimony must be "scientific . . . knowledge." The adjective "scientific" implies a grounding in the methods and procedures of science. Similarly, the word "knowledge" connotes more than subjective belief or unsupported speculation. The term "applies to any body of known facts or to any body of ideas inferred from such facts or accepted as truths on good grounds." Webster's Third New International Dictionary 1252 (1986). Of course, it would be unreasonable to conclude that the subject of scientific testimony must be "known" to a certainty; arguably, there are no certainties in science. . . . But, in order to qualify as "scientific knowledge," an inference or assertion must be derived by the scientific method. Proposed testimony must be supported by appropriate validation—*i.e.,* "good grounds," based on what is known. In short, the requirement that an expert's testimony pertain to "scientific knowledge" establishes a standard of evidentiary reliability.

Rule 702 further requires that the evidence or testimony "assist the trier of fact to understand the evidence or to determine a fact in issue." This condition goes primarily to relevance. . . . The consideration has been aptly described by Judge Becker as one of "fit." "Fit" is not always obvious, and scientific validity for one purpose is not necessarily scientific validity for other, unrelated purposes. The study of the phases of the moon, for example, may provide valid scientific "knowledge" about whether a certain night was dark, and if darkness is a fact in issue, the knowledge will assist the trier of fact. However (absent creditable grounds supporting such a link), evidence that the moon was full on a certain night will not assist the trier of fact in determining whether an individual was unusually likely to have behaved irrationally on that night. Rule 702's "helpfulness" standard requires a valid scientific connection to the pertinent inquiry as a precondition to admissibility.

That these requirements are embodied in Rule 702 is not surprising. Unlike an ordinary witness, see Rule 701, an expert is permitted wide latitude to offer opinions, including those that are not based on first-hand knowledge or observation. See Rules 702 and 703. Presumably, this relaxation of the usual requirement of first-hand knowledge . . . is premised on an assumption that the expert's opinion will have a reliable basis in the knowledge and experience of his discipline.

C

Faced with a proffer of expert scientific testimony, then, the trial judge must determine at the outset, pursuant to Rule 104(a), whether the expert is proposing to testify to (1) scientific knowledge that (2) will assist the trier of fact to understand or determine a fact in issue. This entails a preliminary assessment of whether the reasoning or methodology underlying the testimony is scientifically valid and of whether that reasoning or methodology properly can be applied to the facts in issue. We are confident that federal judges possess the capacity to undertake this review. Many factors will bear on the inquiry, and we do not presume to set out a definitive checklist or test. But some general observations are appropriate.

Ordinarily, a key question to be answered in determining whether a theory or technique is scientific knowledge that will assist the trier of fact will be whether it can be (and has been) tested. "Scientific methodology today is based on generating hypotheses and testing them to see if they can be falsified; indeed, this methodology is what distinguishes science from other fields of human inquiry." . . .

Another pertinent consideration is whether the theory or technique has been subjected to peer review and publication. Publication (which is but one element of peer review) is not a *sine qua non* of admissibility; it does not necessarily correlate with reliability, and in some instances well-grounded but innovative theories will not have been published. Some propositions, moreover, are too particular, too new, or of too limited interest to be published. But submission to the scrutiny of the scientific community is a component of "good science," in part because it increases the likelihood that substantive flaws in methodology will be detected. The fact of publication (or lack thereof) in a peer-reviewed journal thus will be a relevant, though not dispositive, consideration in assessing the scientific validity of a particular technique or methodology on which an opinion is premised.

Additionally, in the case of a particular scientific technique, the court ordinarily should consider the known or potential rate of error . . . and the existence and maintenance of standards controlling the technique's operation. . . .

Finally, "general acceptance" can yet have a bearing on the inquiry. A "reliability assessment does not require, although it does permit, explicit identification of a relevant scientific community and an express determination of a particular degree of acceptance within that community." . . . Widespread acceptance can be an important factor in ruling particular evidence admissible, and "a known technique that has been able to attract only minimal support within the community," may properly be viewed with skepticism.

The inquiry envisioned by Rule 702 is, we emphasize, a flexible one. Its overarching subject is the scientific validity—and thus the evidentiary relevance and reliability—of the principles that underlie a proposed submission. The focus, of course, must be solely on principles and methodology, not on the conclusions that they generate.

Throughout, a judge assessing a proffer of expert scientific testimony under Rule 702 should also be mindful of other applicable rules. Rule 703 provides that expert opinions based on otherwise inadmissible hearsay are to be admitted only if the facts or data are "of a type reasonably relied upon by experts in the particular field in forming opinions or inferences upon the subject." Rule 706 allows the court at its discretion to procure the assistance of an expert of its own choosing. Finally, Rule 403 permits the exclusion of relevant evidence "if its probative value is substantially outweighed by the danger of unfair prejudice, confusion of the issues, or misleading the jury...." Judge Weinstein has explained: "Expert evidence can be both powerful and quite misleading because of the difficulty in evaluating it. Because of this risk, the judge in weighing possible prejudice against probative force under Rule 403 of the present rules exercises more control over experts than over lay witnesses."

III

We conclude by briefly addressing what appear to be two underlying concerns of the parties and *amici* in this case. Respondent expresses apprehension that abandonment of "general acceptance" as the exclusive requirement for admission will result in a "free-for-all" in which befuddled juries are confounded by absurd and irrational pseudoscientific assertions. In this regard respondent seems to us to be overly pessimistic about the capabilities of the jury, and of the adversary system generally. Vigorous cross-examination, presentation of contrary evidence, and careful instruction on the burden of proof are the traditional and appropriate means of attacking shaky but admissible evidence. See *Rock v. Arkansas* (1987). Additionally, in the event the trial court concludes that the scintilla of evidence presented supporting a position is insufficient to allow a reasonable juror to conclude that the position more likely than not is true, the court remains free to direct a judgment, Fed. Rule Civ. Proc. 50 (a), and likewise to grant summary judgment, Fed. Rule Civ. Proc. 56.... These conventional devices, rather than wholesale exclusion under an uncompromising "general acceptance" test, are the appropriate safeguards where the basis of scientific testimony meets the standards of Rule 702.

Petitioners and, to a greater extent, their *amici* exhibit a different concern. They suggest that recognition of a screening role for the judge that allows for the exclusion of "invalid" evidence will sanction a stifling and repressive scientific orthodoxy and will be inimical to the search for truth. It is true that open debate is an essential part of both legal and scientific analyses. Yet there are important differences between the quest for truth in the courtroom and the quest for truth in the laboratory. Scientific conclusions are subject to perpetual revision. Law, on the other hand, must resolve disputes finally and quickly. The scientific project is advanced by broad and wide-ranging consideration of a multitude of hypotheses, for those that are incorrect will eventually be shown to be so, and that in itself is an advance. Conjectures that are probably wrong are of little use, however, in the project of reaching a quick, final, and binding legal judgment—often of great consequence—about a particular set of events in the past. We recognize that in practice, a gatekeeping role for the judge, no matter how flexible, inevitably on occasion will prevent the jury from learning of authentic insights and innovations. That, nevertheless, is the balance that is struck by Rules of Evidence designed not for the exhaustive search for cosmic understanding but for the particularized resolution of legal disputes.

IV

To summarize: "general acceptance" is not a necessary precondition to the admissibility of scientific evidence under the Federal Rules of Evidence, but the Rules of Evidence—especially Rule 702—do assign to the trial judge the task of ensuring that an expert's testimony both rests on a reliable foundation and is relevant to the task at hand. Pertinent evidence based on scientifically valid principles will satisfy those demands.

The inquiries of the District Court and the Court of Appeals focused almost exclusively on "general acceptance," as gauged by publication and the decisions of other courts. Accordingly, the judgment of the Court of Appeals is vacated and the case is remanded for further proceedings consistent with this opinion.

It is so ordered.

CHIEF JUSTICE REHNQUIST, with whom JUSTICE STEVENS joins, concurring in part and dissenting in part.

The petition for certiorari in this case presents two questions: first, whether the rule of *Frye v. United States* (1923), remains good law after the enactment of the Federal Rules of Evidence; and second, if *Frye* remains valid, whether it requires expert scientific testimony to have been subjected to a peer-review process in order to be admissible. The Court concludes, correctly in my view, that the *Frye* rule did not survive the enactment of the Federal Rules of Evidence, and I therefore join Parts I and II-A of its opinion. The second question presented in the petition for certiorari necessarily is mooted by this holding, but the Court nonetheless proceeds to construe Rules 702 and 703 very much in the abstract, and then offers some "general observations."

"General observations" by this Court customarily carry great weight with lower federal courts, but the ones offered here suffer from the flaw common to most such observations—they are not applied to deciding whether or not particular testimony was or was not admissible, and therefore they tend to be not only general, but vague and abstract....

But even if it were desirable to make "general observations" not necessary to decide the questions presented, I cannot subscribe to some of the observations made by the Court. In Part II-B, the Court concludes that reliability and relevancy are the touchstones of the admissibility of expert testimony. Federal Rule of Evidence 402 provides, as the Court points out, that "[e]vidence which is not relevant is not admissible." But there is no similar reference in the Rule to "reliability." The Court constructs its argument by parsing the language "[i]f scientific, technical, or other specialized knowledge will assist the trier of fact to understand the evidence or to determine a fact in issue ... an expert ... may testify thereto...." Fed. Rule Evid. 702. It stresses that the subject of the expert's testimony must be "scientific ... knowledge," and points out that "scientific" "implies a grounding in the methods and procedures of science," and that the word "knowledge" "connotes more than subjective belief or unsupported speculation." From this it concludes that "scientific knowledge" must be "derived by the scientific method." Proposed testimony, we are told, must be supported by "appropriate validation." Indeed, in footnote 9, the Court decides that "[i]n a case involving scientific evidence, *evidentiary reliability* will be based upon *scientific validity*." ([E]mphasis in original.)

Questions arise simply from reading this part of the Court's opinion, and countless more questions will surely arise when hundreds of district judges try to apply its teaching to particular offer of expert testimony.... The Court speaks of its confidence that federal judges can make a "preliminary assessment of whether the reasoning or methodology underlying the testimony is scientifically valid and of whether that reasoning or methodology properly can be applied to the facts in issue." The Court then states that a "key question" to be answered in deciding whether something is "scientific knowledge" "will be whether it can be (and has been) tested." Following this sentence are three quotations from treatises, which speak not only of empirical testing, but one of which states that "the criterion of the scientific status of a theory is its falsifiability, or refutability, or testability."

I defer to no one in my confidence in federal judges; but I am at a loss to know what is meant when it is said that the scientific status of a theory depends on its "falsifiability," and I suspect some of them will be, too.

I do not doubt that Rule 702 confides to the judge some gatekeeping responsibility in deciding questions of the admissibility of proffered expert testimony. But I do not think it imposes on them either the obligation or the authority to become amateur scientists in order to perform that role. I think the Court would be far better advised in this case to decide only the questions presented, and to leave the further development of this important area of the law to future cases.

5 | *Preview of the 1993–1994 Term*

The rap music group known as 2 Live Crew made its reputation, and its living, by going beyond the limits of mainstream sensibilities. So the performers probably gave little thought to the likelihood of giving offense when they created a raunchy parody of a country music classic from the 1960s, "Oh, Pretty Woman," by the late Roy Orbison.

Acuff-Rose Music, the song's copyright holder, also thought little of the idea. When the group's manager wrote for permission to use the song and offered to pay the customary fees, the reply was curt. "I must inform you," an Acuff-Rose executive wrote, "that we cannot permit the use of a parody of 'Oh, Pretty Woman.' "

The reply did not derail 2 Live Crew's plans for "Pretty Woman." The group included the parody in a 1989 album that sold a quarter-million copies. Acuff-Rose sued for copyright infringement.

The legal issue in *Campbell v. Acuff-Rose Music, Inc.* pitted against each other two constitutionally protected interests: freedom of expression and the right of authors and composers to profit from their creations. The rap group won an early round, but a federal appeals court in 1992 ordered the case to go to trial. Then the U.S. Supreme Court decided to take up the issue.

The dispute, one of forty-six cases the justices carried over for the start of their 1993-1994 term, attracted a star-studded cast of "friends of the Court." Weighing in for Acuff-Rose were superstars Michael Jackson and Dolly Parton and the estates of thirteen of the nation's greatest twentieth century composers from Irving Berlin to Leonard Bernstein. For 2 Live Crew, the supporting cast included political satirist Mark Russell, a Washington satirical troupe known as the Capitol Steps, and the irrepressible Harvard Lampoon.

The Court's calendar also included many cases of perhaps greater weight. The Court once again faced emotionally charged issues such as abortion and racial redistricting. The abortion case involved the effort to use the powerful federal antiracketeering law against antiabortion groups engaged in blockades of abortion clinics. The redistricting case came from ethnically diverse Dade County (Miami), Florida, where two "minority" groups—African Americans and Hispanics—staked rival claims for new legislative seats.

The Court was also to consider a flurry of important civil rights issues, such as how to define sexual harassment in the workplace. A new challenge to forfeiture laws posed the question whether the government

The controversial 2 Live Crew rap group included a parody of a Roy Orbison classic in one of their albums and was sued for copyright infringement. The Supreme Court will rule on this case during the 1993-1994 term.

must give advance notice before seizing property from drug offenders. Other cases raised questions being closely watched by business interests, organized labor, environmental groups, advocacy groups for the disabled, and state and local governments.

The number of cases carried over from the previous term was unusually low. The justices had calendared sixty-six cases at the beginning of the 1991-1992 term and seventy cases at the start of the 1990-1991 term. When argument schedules for October and November were released, observers were surprised to see that instead of the customary four cases per day, the justices were to hear arguments in only two or three cases each day.

To fill out their argument schedule, the justices took the unprecedented step of adding eight cases on September 28, six days before the term was to begin. The accelerated action was apparently aimed at permitting the Court to schedule the cases for argument in what had been shaping up as an almost empty two-week session in January.

The new cases included an important dispute between the broadcasting and cable industries over a new law requiring most cable systems to carry local broadcast stations. Broadcasters contended that the "must-carry" provisions of the Cable Television Consumer Protection and Competition Act of 1992 were needed to offset cable's "monopoly" over access to television viewers. Cable operators argued that the requirements violated their First Amendment rights. *(Turner Broadcasting System, Inc. v. Federal Communications Commission)*

None of the cases matched the "Pretty Woman" dispute for entertainment value, however. Entered as an exhibit in the Supreme Court clerk's office was an audiotape containing excerpts of musical parodies dating from the first days of the Republic and reaching up to recent compositions such as "Hello, Lyndon" and "Ol' Man Gipper." In their amicus brief, the Capitol Steps reminded the justices of their recent musical parody of the Clinton-Gore campaign: "Why Not Take Al and Me."

To composers and songwriters, however, the case was no laughing matter, but a serious dispute that threatened their economic and creative

rights. "If the Court were to unleash a sweeping privilege to use copyrighted musical works in favor of parodists," the songwriters argued, "customary practices in the songwriting and music publishing industries would be totally disrupted and songwriters and music publishers would suffer severe economic harm."

Despite the First Amendment implications of the case, the legal issue actually was how to define a judicially created copyright law doctrine called "fair use." Courts had developed the doctrine in an effort to balance copyright protections with freedom of expres-

The late Roy Orbison.

sion. Some uses of copyrighted material, the courts reasoned, did little harm to the copyright owner while encouraging public use of their works. Over time, the doctrine evolved into a four-part test that Congress finally wrote into law in 1976. Fair use was to be defined by looking at the purpose of the use, including whether it was of "a commercial nature," the nature of the copyrighted work, the amount of the copyrighted work to be used, and the effect of the use on the market for the copyrighted work.

Those tests made sense for traditional plagiarism-type disputes, but they were harder to apply to parodies—where the very idea was to imitate the copyrighted work in order to make fun of it. Courts were all over the ballpark on the issue, and they had special difficulty with sexually laced parodies. One federal court permitted *Screw* magazine to use the Pillsbury Doughboy, but another court turned thumbs down on a blue version of "The Boogie Woogie Bugler Boy of Company B."

Defending its parody, 2 Live Crew insisted that its recording did not compete with the original song and therefore posed no economic threat under the fair-use doctrine. The federal appeals court, however, posed the issue more simply. Since the parody was a "commercial use," the court held, it was presumptively an infringement of the copyright.

Satirists, joined by the American Civil Liberties Union, argued that the ruling gave scant regard to the country's "rich tradition of social and political satire." A broader reading of the fair-use defense was necessary, they added, because copyright owners typically turn down requests to use their works for satirical purposes. And too much judicial discretion in such disputes ran the risk of "regulation of parody based on the popularity and political acceptability of the parodist."

The music industry countered by opposing what it called "special treatment" for parody. Instead, Acuff-Rose said in its brief, "A cautious application" of fair-use doctrine was "essential if owners of musical copyrights are not to be deprived of revenues . . . and parody is not to be permitted to serve as a disguise for piracy."

Predicting the outcome of the case was problematic. The Court in 1988 had strengthened the constitutional protection for parody in rejecting a damage suit by the evangelist Jerry Falwell against *Hustler* magazine. But in other decisions the Court had also been solicitous of copyright protections. "One of the areas where First Amendment values have been trumped in recent years is in intellectual property," observed Rodney Smolla, a First Amendment expert at the College of William and Mary's Marshall-Blythe School of Law.

Following are some of the other major cases on the Supreme Court calendar as it began its 1993-1994 term:

Business Law

Airport user fees. The nation's financially troubled airlines won the justices' attention with a challenge to escalating airport user fees. The dispute reached the Court in a challenge by seven U.S. airlines to fees imposed by the Kent County (Michigan) International Airport near Grand Rapids.

The airlines contended that the levies violated federal laws requiring user fees to be spent only for airport purposes and limiting any direct tax on air passengers. The airlines said the Kent County airport's fees generated "huge surpluses" totaling $9 million at the end of 1989. Nationwide, the Air Transport Association said in a supporting brief, airport user fees rose 83 percent from 1982 to 1992 and totaled more than $3.4 billion in 1991.

A federal appeals court upheld the airport's fees, however. In defense of the ruling, the airport argued that its rate-making procedures were reasonable and the funds were needed to pay for future capital improvements. The government, partly siding with the airport, said the airlines should have taken their dispute over the fees to the secretary of transportation instead of to court. *(Northwest Airlines, Inc. v. Kent County, Mich.)*

Securities fraud. The Central Bank of Denver was ordered to stand trial for allegedly aiding and abetting securities fraud in connection with bonds issued to pay for a real estate development. In contesting the suit, the bank argued that federal securities law did not recognize liability for aiding and abetting fraud. It also urged that a defendant could be found liable only on the basis of intentional wrongdoing. Supporting the plaintiffs, the government urged the justices to permit liability on proof of recklessness. *(Central Bank of Denver N.A. v. First Interstate Bank of Denver N.A.)*

Courts and Procedure

Jury selection. The jury chosen to try a civil paternity action against an Alabama man, identified in court papers as J. E. B., consisted of twelve women and no men. The state's attorney in the case used "peremptory challenges" to remove nine potential male jurors without stating any reason for disqualifying them.

After the jury determined he was the father of the child in question, J. E. B. challenged the exclusion of men from the jury as a violation of the Equal Protection Clause. He cited U.S. Supreme Court decisions that have barred removal of jurors because of race in criminal and civil cases. The Alabama Supreme Court rejected the argument.

In urging a reversal of that decision, J. E. B. gained the support of the Clinton administration and women's rights groups. The government's brief argued that the use of gender-based peremptory challenges "impairs public confidence in the fairness of the judicial system." *(J. E. B. v. T. B.)*

Military justice. Two former servicemen convicted of crimes in courts martial challenged the system of appointing military judges. Under existing procedure, the judge advocate general of each of the services had unlimited power to appoint—and remove—military judges. The former servicemen contended that the arrangement violated the Constitution's Appointments Clause and the lack of fixed terms violated the Due Process Clause. The government defended the present system. *(Weiss v. United States)*

Criminal Law

Forfeiture laws. James Daniel Good was convicted of possessing eighty-nine pounds of marijuana in Hawaii in 1985 and placed on probation for five years. Four years later, U.S. agents invoked federal drug forfeiture laws to seize Good's house and four-acre parcel of land. Good, working for a charitable organization in Central America at the time, had no prior warning of the forfeiture.

A federal appeals court ruled the seizure violated Good's due process rights because he had not been given notice and an opportunity for a hearing. The government asked the justices to overturn the decision, arguing that it would require "costly and burdensome new procedures." But Good, supported by the American Civil Liberties Union and the National Association of Criminal Defense Attorneys, argued the safeguards were needed to prevent abuses. *(United States v. James Daniel Good Real Property)*

Capital punishment. Three cases raised relatively narrow issues about state death penalty laws. The state of Tennessee sought to reinstate a provision that listed murder committed during the course of a felony as an aggravating factor to be used to impose the death penalty. The state supreme court said the law violated constitutional guidelines by failing to narrow imposition of the death penalty in felony-murder cases. *(Tennessee v. Middlebrooks)*

In an Indiana case, a death row inmate asked the Court to overturn a death sentence a judge imposed after the jury refused to convict him of intentional murder and recommended a life sentence. *(Schiro v. Clark)*

In an Illinois case, a condemned prisoner argued that the state's highest court should have reevaluated the death sentence after one of three aggravating factors was thrown out on appeal. *(Pasch v. Illinois)*

Child pornography. A graduate student in Pennsylvania was convicted under the federal child pornography law for possessing three videotapes that showed young girls in provocative poses wearing bathing suits or underpants. In urging a reversal, he argued that the law applied only to materials showing children with their genitals exposed. The Bush administration defended the appeals court's expansive interpretation of the act, but the Clinton administration endorsed a narrower reading and urged the justices to send the case back to the appeals court for reconsideration. *(Knox v. United States)*

Elections

Reapportionment and redistricting. The issue of racial redistricting in the United States moved from North Carolina to Florida for the 1993-1994 term. As the Florida legislature worked to redraw district lines, Hispanics and African Americans said they were entitled to additional seats in surrounding Dade County under the federal Voting Rights Act. A three-judge federal court left both sides unhappy, and the dispute landed in the Supreme Court.

With the Hispanic population in Miami and the rest of the state rapidly increasing, the Democratic-controlled legislature drew up a districting plan for the Dade County area that gave Hispanics a majority in nine of eighteen House districts and created four black majority districts. For the Senate, the legislature's plan put Hispanic majorities in three districts, black majorities in two.

A group of Hispanic plaintiffs, led by a Republican state House member, Miguel de Grandy, challenged the plans. Given the statewide underrepresentation of Hispanics, they argued, additional Hispanic-majority districts had to be created in south Florida. The suits had a partisan tinge: Miami's Cuban-American population votes predominantly Republican, while African Americans mostly vote Democratic. The Bush administration, filing a separate legal action, sided with the Hispanics.

The three-judge federal court that heard the cases agreed that Hispanics were entitled under the Voting Rights Act to more seats in both chambers to remedy previous "dilution" of their voting strength. It ordered a new plan drawn up for the House to give Hispanics two more seats. But it left the Senate plan in place, saying that creating an additional seat for Hispanics would have a "retrogressive" effect on blacks.

The Supreme Court stayed the ruling, allowing the 1992 elections to be conducted under the legislature's plan, and then agreed to put the multisided dispute on its docket. For the justices, the legal issues were as complex as the demographics of the case: how to apply principles developed in the context of black-white politics to a multiethnic population. *(Johnson v. De Grandy; De Grandy v. Johnson; United States v. Florida)*

Single-commissioner government. Bleckley County, Georgia, with a population of 10,767, has a single commissioner who holds all executive and legislative power. A group of African American residents argued that the structure, used by sixteen other counties in the state, violated the federal Voting Rights Act by "diluting" minority voting strength. A federal appeals court agreed. The county asked the justices to overturn the decision, saying the Voting Rights Act "does not empower courts to alter local governments to ensure proportional minority representation." *(Holder v. Hall)*

Environmental Law

Hazardous waste disposal. Municipal waste-to-energy plants, which burn garbage to produce electricity, seemed to offer an ideal solution to the nation's environmental and energy problems. But the trash incinerators also produce ash that environmental groups say contains concentrated levels of highly toxic chemicals. Municipalities wanted to dispose of the ash in sanitary landfills, but environmentalists argued that federal law imposed stricter requirements for disposing of the ash.

The two federal appeals courts that had ruled on the question came to different conclusions. The Second U.S. Circuit Court of Appeals in New York ruled that the Resource Conservation and Recovery Act exempted waste plants from regulations that applied to other hazardous waste generators. But in 1991 the Seventh U.S. Circuit Court of Appeals, ruling in a case involving a plant owned by the city of Chicago, said the hazardous waste regulations did apply. The Seventh Circuit reaffirmed that decision in 1992 even though the Environmental Protection Agency, reversing its previous position, argued in favor of an exemption.

In its brief, Chicago argued that Congress intended to encourage solid waste recovery plants, but that compliance with the hazardous waste regulations would cost ten times as much as disposing of ash in landfills. The Environmental Defense Fund countered by saying that Congress did not intend to permit "the dumping of massive amounts of hazardous waste in the form of ash into ordinary landfills." *(City of Chicago v. Environmental Defense Fund)*

"Flow-control laws." The Court also agreed to resolve a second important issue for waste-to-energy plants: the constitutionality of local "flow-control laws" that require solid waste processed within a municipality to be handled at such facilities. The town of Clarkstown, New York, passed such an ordinance to ensure a steady supply of trash for its plant, but a private waste hauling company that previously handled trash from the town, at a lower cost, said the law unconstitutionally interfered with interstate commerce. Two trade associations supporting the challenge argued in their brief that flow-control laws "jeopardize the industries . . . by denying to them the very materials they need to survive." *(C & A Carbone, Inc. v. Clarkstown, N.Y.)*

Federal Government

Labor relations. Two unions trying to organize civilian workers at military post exchanges have fought a legal battle to get the home addresses of the employees. The Defense Department turned down the request, saying disclosure would violate the employees' rights under the federal Privacy Act. But the Federal Labor Relations Authority (FLRA), the agency that administers the federal labor-management statute, ordered the department to provide the addresses to the unions.

In challenging the order, the Defense Department's brief stated that disclosure "infringes substantial privacy interests." But the FLRA argued that the invasion of privacy would be "relatively minimal." In a supporting brief, the American Federation of Government Employees argued that refusal to produce the address list would hamper "the strong public policy of promoting an efficient and effective system of federal sector collective bargaining." *(United States Department of Defense v. FLRA)*

Individual Rights

Abortion. To combat militant tactics by antiabortion groups, the National Organization for Women (NOW) turned to a powerful federal law, the Racketeer Influenced and Corrupt Organizations Act (RICO). In an amended complaint filed in 1989 in behalf of abortion clinics in Delaware and Wisconsin, NOW argued that Operation Rescue and other groups had engaged in an illegal campaign of vandalism, intimidation, and extortion aimed at closing the clinics. They asked for triple damages under the RICO law.

Two federal courts, however, rejected the RICO claims. In its ruling, the federal appeals court in Chicago agreed that the antiabortion groups' tactics were "otherwise criminal," but said that RICO did not cover "non-economic crimes committed in furtherance of non-economic motives."

Defending the ruling, Operation Rescue said, "Civil disobedience and social and political pressure are as American as apple pie." But NOW insisted that the suit was not aimed at lawful speech, but only at "the independently illegal and tortious conduct of the extremists." The Clinton administration, supporting the suit, argued that the lower courts had interpreted the RICO statute in a "narrow and grudging" way. *(National Organization for Women v. Scheidler)*

Job discrimination. The justices agreed to decide in a pair of cases whether the Civil Rights Act of 1991, which broadened remedies in job discrimination suits, applies to cases pending when the law went into effect.

The law, signed by President George Bush November 16, 1991, after a two-year battle with the Democratic-controlled Congress, was silent on the issue. Bush in 1990 vetoed an earlier version of the bill that contained an explicit retroactivity provision. All but one of the federal appeals courts that ruled on the issue said the law applied only to cases filed after the law took effect. To settle the question, the justices took up two cases: a Texas woman's sexual harassment suit and a racial harassment complaint by two black mechanics from Ohio.

In the first case, the woman claimed that she had been subjected to sexual harassment by a co-worker for nearly two years and finally had to resign. In a nonjury trial, a federal judge agreed the plaintiff had been harassed, but barred any relief because the harassment did not amount to "constructive discharge." On appeal, the woman unsuccessfully argued for a new trial under the newly enacted 1991 law, which would have allowed her a jury trial and compensatory or punitive damages. *(Landgraf v. USI Film Products)*

In the second case, the Ohio mechanics argued that racially motivated disciplinary proceedings against them had violated their rights under a Reconstruction-era law guaranteeing blacks equal rights in making contracts. The Supreme Court in 1989 ruled the law did not apply to racial harassment in the workplace, but Congress intended the 1991 law to overturn that decision. A federal appeals court refused, however, to give the mechanics the benefit of the new law. *(Rivers v. Roadway Express, Inc.)*

The Bush administration had urged the justices to rule the 1991 act did not apply retroactively. In a new brief filed after the justices decided to review the two cases, however, the Clinton administration argued that the law's "procedural and remedial provisions" should apply to cases pending at the time of enactment.

Sexual harassment. A Tennessee woman who worked for a heavy equipment sales and rental company accused the company's president of sexual harassment, citing a long history of vulgar and suggestive comments he had made to her. A federal magistrate agreed that the president "demeans the female employees in his work place," but rejected the suit after finding that the woman had not suffered "serious psychological injury."

Supporting her effort to overturn that decision, the government and a number of civil rights groups contended the "serious psychological injury" standard was stricter than the rule announced by the Supreme Court in a 1986 case. "This Court should strike down any test which ignores the inherent harm of discrimination," the National Organization for Women Legal Defense Fund argued.

Defending the ruling, an employers group, the Equal Employment Advisory Council, argued that a plaintiff should be required to prove that sexual harassment had a "detrimental effect on the terms and conditions of her employment." *(Harris v. Forklift Systems, Inc.)*

Disability rights. A South Carolina couple enrolled their learning-disabled daughter in a private school after a dispute about the local school district's education plan for her. A federal court agreed the plan did not satisfy a federal law requiring appropriate education for the disabled and ordered the school district to reimburse the parents for the private school tuition.

Supporting the parents, advocacy groups for the disabled told the justices that reimbursement was needed to ensure "meaningful enforcement" of the federal law. But associations representing local governments and school boards said the ruling "hinders the ability of state and local governments to devote their limited resources to high quality, cost-effective educational services." *(Florence County School District Four v. Carter)*

Malicious prosecution. An Illinois man filed a federal civil rights suit against a local police detective for malicious prosecution after dismissal of a drug charge against him. But a federal appeals court rejected the suit, saying the federal suit could be maintained only if he suffered incarceration, loss of employment, or "some other palpable consequences."

Supporting the plaintiff, the American Civil Liberties Union said the federal civil rights law should protect against "the deliberate bringing of false charges against an individual." But local government groups told the justices that such suits "would seriously disrupt the functioning of the criminal process." *(Albright v. Oliver)*

Labor

False testimony. The National Labor Relations Board (NLRB) ordered a union dockworker at a truck terminal in Albuquerque, New Mexico, reinstated with back pay after concluding he had been fired in retaliation for filing a complaint with the board. A federal appeals court upheld the ruling even though the employee lied about one of several instances of lateness that the company cited as the reason for firing him.

On appeal, the company contended that the court's ruling "condoned manipulation of the NLRB process" and conflicted with other court decisions barring relief to workers who lied during administrative hearings. But the government responded that the board had discretion to order reinstatement despite the false testimony, which it called "an isolated lapse." *(ABF Freight Systems, Inc. v. NLRB)*

Contempt fines. In the midst of a bitter and protracted coal-mine strike, a state judge in Virginia imposed fines totaling $64 million against the United Mine Workers for contempt of court for violating an injunction against violence. After the strike was settled, the judge reduced the fines to $52 million but refused a joint request by the company and the union to lift them altogether. The union contended the judge used improper summary power to impose the fines. But the state defended the fines, saying they were necessary to end a "reign of terror." *(United Mine Workers v. Bagwell)*

Appendix

Appendix

How the Court Works

The Constitution makes the Supreme Court the final arbiter in "cases" and "controversies" arising under the Constitution or the laws of the United States. As the interpreter of the law, the Court often is viewed as the least mutable and most tradition-bound of the three branches of the federal government. But the Court has undergone innumerable changes in its history, some of which have been mandated by law. Some of these changes are embodied in Court rules; others are informal adaptations to needs and circumstances.

The Schedule of the Term

Annual Terms

By law, the Supreme Court begins its regular annual term on the first Monday in October, and the term lasts approximately nine months. This session is known as the October term. The summer recess, which is not determined by statute or Court rules, generally begins in late June or early July of the following year. This system—staying in continuous session throughout the year, with periodic recesses—makes it unnecessary to convene a special term to deal with matters arising in the summer.

The justices actually begin work before the official opening of the term. They hold their initial conference during the last week in September. When the justices formally convene on the first Monday in October, oral arguments begin.

Arguments and Conferences

At least four justices must request that a case be argued before it can be accepted. Arguments are heard on Monday, Tuesday, and Wednesday for seven two-week sessions, beginning in the first week in October and ending in mid-April. Recesses of two weeks or longer recesses occur between the sessions of oral arguments so that justices can consider the cases and deal with other Court business.

The schedule for oral arguments is 10:00 a.m. to noon and 1 p.m. to 3 p.m. Because most cases receive one hour apiece for argument, the Court can hear twelve cases a week.

The Court holds conferences on the Friday just before the two-week oral argument periods and on Wednesday and Friday during the weeks when oral arguments are scheduled. The conferences are designed for consideration of cases already heard in oral argument.

Before each of the Friday conferences, the chief justice circulates a "discuss" list—a list of cases deemed important enough for discussion and a vote. Appeals are placed on the discuss list almost automatically, but as many as three-quarters of the petitions for certiorari are dismissed. No case is denied review during conference, however, without an initial examination by the justices and their law clerks. Any justice can have a case placed on the Court's conference agenda for review. Most of the cases scheduled for the discuss list also are denied review in the end, but only after discussion by the justices during the conference.

Although the last oral arguments have been heard by mid-April each year, the conferences of the justices continue until the end of the term to consider cases remaining on the Court's agenda. All conferences are held in secret, with no legal assistants or other staff present. The attendance of six justices constitutes a quorum. Conferences begin with handshakes all around. In discussing a case, the chief justice speaks first, followed by each justice in order of seniority.

Decision Days

Opinions are released on Tuesdays and Wednesdays during the weeks that the Court is hearing oral arguments; during other weeks, they are released on Mondays. In addition to opinions, the Court also releases an "orders" list—the summary of the Court's action granting or denying review. The orders list is posted at the beginning of the Monday session. It is not announced orally but can be obtained from the clerk and the public information officer. When urgent or important matters arise, the Court's summary orders may be made available on a day other than Monday.

Unlike its orders, decisions of the Court are announced orally in open Court. The justice who wrote the opinion announces the Court's decision, and justices writing concurring or dissenting opinions may state their views as well. When more than one decision is to be rendered, the justices who wrote the opinion make their announcements in reverse order of seniority. Occasionally, all or a large portion of the opinion is read aloud. More often, the author summarizes the opinion or simply announces the result and states that a written opinion has been filed.

Reviewing Cases

In determining whether to accept a case for review, the Court has considerable discretion, subject only to the restraints imposed by the

Visiting the Supreme Court

The Supreme Court building has six levels, two of which—the ground and main floors—are accessible to the public. The basement contains a parking garage, a printing press, and offices for security guards and maintenance personnel. On the ground floor are the John Marshall statue, the exhibition area, the public information office, and a cafeteria. The main corridor, known as the Great Hall, the courtroom, and justices' offices are on the main floor. The second floor contains dining rooms, the justices' reading room, and other offices; the third floor, the Court library; and the fourth floor, the gym and storage areas.

From October to mid-April, the Court hears oral arguments Monday through Wednesday for about two weeks a month. These sessions begin at 10 a.m. and continue until 3 p.m., with a one-hour recess starting at noon. They are open to the public on a first-come, first-served basis.

Visitors may inspect the Supreme Court chamber any time the Court is not in session. Historical exhibits and a free motion picture on how the Court works also are available throughout the year. The Supreme Court building is open from 9 a.m. to 4:30 p.m. Monday through Friday, except for legal holidays. When the Court is not in session, lectures are given in the courtroom every hour on the half hour between 9:30 a.m. and 3:30 p.m.

Constitution and Congress. Article III, section 2, of the Constitution provides that "In all Cases affecting Ambassadors, other public Ministers and Consuls, and those in which a State shall be Party, the supreme Court shall have original Jurisdiction. In all the other Cases . . . the supreme Court shall have appellate Jurisdiction, both as to Law and Fact, with such Exceptions, and under such Regulations as the Congress shall make."

Original jurisdiction refers to the right of the Supreme Court to hear a case before any other court does. Appellate jurisdiction is the right to review the decision of a lower court. The vast majority of cases reaching the Supreme Court are appeals from rulings of the lower courts; generally only a handful of original jurisdiction cases are filed each term.

After enactment of the Judiciary Act of 1925, the Supreme Court had broad discretion to decide for itself what cases it would hear. Since Congress in 1988 virtually eliminated the Court's mandatory jurisdiction through which it was obliged to hear most appeals, that discretion has been virtually unlimited.

Methods of Appeal

Cases come to the Supreme Court in several ways: through petitions for writs of certiorari, appeals, and requests for certification.

In petitioning for a writ of certiorari, a litigant who has lost a case in a lower court sets out the reasons why the Supreme Court should review the case. If a writ is granted, the Court requests a certified record of the case from the lower court.

The main difference between the certiorari and appeal routes is that the Court has complete discretion to grant a request for a writ of certiorari but is under more obligation to accept and decide a case that comes to it on appeal.

Most cases reach the Supreme Court by means of the writ of certiorari. In the relatively few cases to reach the Court by means of appeal, the appellant must file a jurisdictional statement explaining why the case qualifies for review and why the Court should grant it a hearing. Often the justices dispose of these cases by deciding them summarily, without oral argument or formal opinion.

Those whose petitions for certiorari have been granted must pay the Court's standard $300 fee for docketing the case. The U.S. government does not have to pay these fees, nor do persons too poor to afford them. The latter may file in forma pauperis (in the character or manner of a pauper) petitions. Another, seldom used, method of appeal is certification, the request by a lower court—usually a court of appeals—for a final answer to questions of law in a particular case. The Court, after examining the certificate, may order the case argued before it.

Process of Review

In the 1992-1993 term the Court was asked to review about 7,000 cases. All petitions are examined by the staff of the clerk of the Court; those found to be in reasonably proper form are placed on the docket and given a number. All cases, except those falling within the Court's original jurisdiction, are placed on a single docket, known simply as "the docket." Only in the numbering of the cases is a distinction made between prepaid and in forma pauperis cases on the docket. The first case filed in the 1993-1994 term, for example, would be designated 93-1. In forma pauperis cases contain the year and begin with the number 5001. The second in forma pauperis case filed in the 1993-1994 term would thus be number 93-5002.

Each justice, aided by law clerks, is responsible for reviewing all cases on the docket. In recent years a number of justices have used a "cert pool" system in this review. Their clerks work together to examine cases, writing a pool memo on several petitions. The memo then is given to the justices who determine if more research is needed. Other justices may prefer to review each petition themselves or have their clerks do it.

Petitions on the docket vary from elegantly printed and bound documents, of which multiple copies are submitted to the Court, to single sheets of prison stationery scribbled in pencil. The decisions to grant or deny review of cases are made in conferences, which are held in the conference room adjacent to the chief justice's chambers. Justices are summoned to the conference room by a buzzer, usually between 9:30 and 10:00 a.m. They shake hands with each other and take their appointed seats, and the chief justice then begins the discussion.

Discuss and Orders Lists

A few days before the conference convenes, the chief justice compiles the discuss list of cases deemed important enough for discussion and a vote. As many as three-quarters of the petitions for certiorari are denied a place on the list and thus rejected without further consideration. Any justice can have a case placed on the discuss list simply by requesting that it be placed there.

Only the justices attend conferences; no legal assistants or staff are present. The junior associate justice acts as doorkeeper and messenger, sending for reference material and receiving messages and data. Unlike with other parts of the federal government, few leaks have occurred about what transpires during the conferences.

At the start of the conference, the chief justice makes a brief statement outlining the facts of each case. Then each justice, beginning with the senior associate justice, comments on the case, usually indicating in the course of the comments how he or she intends to vote. A traditional but unwritten rule is that four affirmative votes puts a case on the schedule for oral argument.

Petitions for certiorari, appeals, and in forma pauperis motions that are approved for review or denied review during conference are placed on a certified orders list to be released the next Monday in open court.

Arguments

Once the Court announces it will hear a case, the clerk of the Court arranges the schedule for oral argument. Cases are argued roughly in the order in which they were granted review, subject to modification if more time is needed to acquire all the necessary documents. Cases generally are heard not sooner than three months after the Court has agreed to review them. Under special circumstances, the date scheduled for oral argument can be advanced or postponed.

Well before oral argument takes place, the justices receive the briefs and records from counsel in the case. The measure of attention the brief receives—from a thorough and exhaustive study to a cursory glance—depends both on the nature of the case and the work habits of the justice.

As one of the two public functions of the Court, oral arguments are viewed by some as very important. Others dispute the significance of oral arguments, contending that by the time a case is heard most of the justices already have made up their minds.

Time Limits

The time allowed each side for oral argument is thirty minutes. Because the time allotted must accommodate any questions the justices may wish to ask, the actual time for presentation may be considerably shorter than thirty minutes. Under the current rules of the Court, one counsel only will be heard for each side, except by special permission.

An exception is made for an amicus curiae, a "friend of the court," a person who volunteers or is invited to take part in matters before a court but is not a party in the case. Counsel for an amicus curiae may participate in oral argument if the party supported by the amicus allows use of part of its argument time or the Court grants a motion permitting argument by this counsel. The motion must show, the rules state, that the amicus's argument "is thought to provide assistance to the Court not otherwise available." The Court is generally unreceptive to such motions.

Court rules provide advice to counsel presenting oral arguments before the Court: "Oral argument should emphasize and clarify the written arguments appearing in the briefs on the merits." That same rule warns—with italicized emphasis—that the Court "looks with disfavor on oral argument read from a prepared text." Most attorneys appearing before the Court use an outline or notes to make sure they cover the important points.

Circulating the Argument

The Supreme Court has tape-recorded oral arguments since 1955. In 1968 the Court, in addition to its own recording, began contracting with private firms to tape and transcribe all oral arguments. The contract stipulates that the transcript "shall include everything spoken in argument, by Court, counsel, or others, and nothing shall be omitted from the transcript unless the Chief Justice or Presiding Justice so directs." But "the names of Justices asking questions shall not be recorded or transcribed; questions shall be indicated by the letter 'Q.' "

The marshal of the Court keeps the tapes during the term, and their use usually is limited to the justices and their law clerks. At the end of the term, the tapes are sent to the National Archives. Persons wishing to listen to the tapes or buy a copy of a transcript can apply to the Archives for permission to do so.

Transcripts made by a private firm can be acquired more quickly. These transcripts usually are available a week after arguments are heard. Those who purchase the transcripts must agree that they will not be photographically reproduced. Transcripts usually run from forty to fifty pages for one hour of oral argument.

Proposals have been made to tape arguments for television and radio use or to permit live broadcast coverage of arguments. The Court has rejected these proposals.

Use of Briefs

The brief of the petitioner or appellant must be filed within forty-five days of the Court's announced decision to hear the case. Except for in forma pauperis cases, forty copies of the brief must be filed with the Court. For in forma pauperis proceedings, the Court requires only that documents be legible. The opposing brief from the respondent or appellee is to be filed within thirty days of receipt of the brief of the petitioner or appellant. Either party may appeal to the clerk for an extension of time in filing the brief.

Court Rule 24 sets forth the elements that a brief should contain. These are: the questions presented for review; a list of all parties to the proceeding; a table of contents and table of authorities; citations of the opinions and judgments delivered in the lower courts; "a concise statement of the grounds on which the jurisdiction of this Court is invoked"; constitutional provisions, treaties, statutes, ordinances, and regulations involved; "a concise statement of the case containing all that is material to the consideration of the questions presented"; a summary of argument; the argument, which exhibits "clearly the points of fact and of law being presented and citing the authorities and statutes relied upon"; and a conclusion "specifying with particularity the relief which the party seeks."

The form and organization of the brief are covered by rules 33 and 34. The rules limit the number of pages in various types of briefs. The rules also set out a color code for the covers of different kinds of briefs. Petitions are white; motions opposing them are orange. Petitioner's briefs on the merits are light blue, while those of respondents are red. Reply briefs are yellow; amicus curiae, green; and documents filed by the United States, gray.

Questioning

During oral argument the justices may interrupt with questions or remarks as often as they wish. Unless counsel has been granted special permission extending the thirty-minute limit, he or she can continue talking after the time has expired only to complete a sentence.

The frequency of questioning, as well as the manner in which questions are asked, depends on the style of the justices and their interest in a particular case. Questions from the justices may upset and unnerve counsel by interrupting a well-rehearsed argument and introducing an unexpected element. Nevertheless, questioning has several advantages. It serves to alert counsel about what aspects of the case need further elaboration or more information. For the Court, questions can bring out weak points in an argument—and sometimes strengthen it.

Conferences

Cases for which oral arguments have been heard are then dealt with in conference. During the Wednesday afternoon conference, the cases that were argued the previous Monday are discussed and decided. At the all-day Friday conference, the cases argued on the preceding Tuesday and Wednesday are discussed and decided. Justices also consider new motions, appeals, and petitions while in conference.

Conferences are conducted in complete secrecy. No secretaries, clerks, stenographers, or messengers are allowed into the room. This practice began many years ago when the justices became convinced that decisions were being disclosed prematurely.

The justices meet in an oak-paneled, book-lined conference room adjacent to the chief justice's suite. Nine chairs surround the large rectangular table, each chair bearing the nameplate of the justice who sits there. The chief justice sits at the east end of the table, and the senior associate justice at the west end. The other justices take their places in order of seniority. The junior justice is charged with sending for and receiving documents or other information the Court needs.

On entering the conference room the justices shake hands with each other, a symbol of harmony that began in the 1880s. The chief justice begins the conference by calling the first case to be decided and discussing it. When the chief justice is finished, the senior associate justice speaks, followed by the other justices in order of seniority.

The justices can speak for as long as they wish, but they practice restraint because of the amount of business to be completed. By custom each justice speaks without interruption. Other than these procedural arrangements, little is known about what transpires in conference. Although discussions generally are said to be polite and orderly, occasionally they can be acrimonious. Likewise, consideration of the issues in a particular case may be full and probing, or perfunctory, leaving the real debate on the question for the written drafts of opinions circulating up and down the Court's corridors between chambers.

Generally the discussion of the case clearly indicates how a justice plans to vote on it. A majority vote is needed to decide a case—five votes if all nine justices are participating.

Opinions

After the justices have voted on a case, the writing of the opinion or opinions begins. An opinion is a reasoned argument explaining the legal issues in the case and the precedents on which the opinion is based. Soon after a case is decided in conference, the task of writing the majority opinion is assigned. When in the majority, the chief justice designates the writer. When the chief justice is in the minority, the senior associate justice voting with the majority assigns the job of writing the majority opinion.

Any justice may write a separate opinion. If in agreement with the Court's decision but not with some of the reasoning in the majority opinion, the justice writes a concurring opinion giving his or her reasoning. If in disagreement with the majority, the justice writes a dissenting opinion or simply goes on record as a dissenter without an opinion. More than one justice can sign a concurring opinion or a dissenting opinion.

The amount of time between the vote on a case and the announcement of the decision varies from case to case. In simple cases where few points of law are at issue, the opinion sometimes can be written and cleared by the other justices in a week or less. In more complex cases, especially those with several dissenting or concurring opinions, the process can take six months or more. Some cases may have to be reargued or the initial decision reversed after the drafts of opinions have been circulated.

The assigning justice may consider the points made by majority justices during the conference discussion, the workload of the other justices, the need to avoid the more extreme opinions within the majority, and expertise in the particular area of law involved in a case.

The style of writing a Court opinion—majority, concurring, or dissenting—depends primarily on the individual justice. In some cases, the justice may prefer to write a restricted and limited opinion; in others, a broader approach to the subject. The decision likely is to be influenced by the need to satisfy the other justices in the majority.

When a justice is satisfied that the written opinion is conclusive or "unanswerable," it goes into print. Draft opinions are circulated, revised, and printed on a computerized typesetting system. The circulation of the drafts—whether computer-to-computer or on paper—provokes further discussion in many cases. Often the suggestions and criticisms require the writer to juggle opposing views. To retain a majority, the author of the draft opinion frequently feels obliged to make major emendations to satisfy justices who are unhappy with the initial draft. Some opinions have to be rewritten several times.

One reason for the secrecy surrounding the circulation of drafts is that some of the justices who voted with the majority may find the majority draft opinion so unpersuasive—or one or more of the dissenting drafts so convincing—that they change their vote. If enough justices alter their votes, the majority may shift, so that a former dissent becomes the majority opinion. When a new majority emerges from this process, the task of writing, printing, and circulating a new majority draft begins all over again.

When the drafts of an opinion—including dissents and concurring views—have been written, circulated, discussed, and revised, if necessary, the final versions then are printed. Before the opinion is produced the reporter of decisions adds a "headnote" or syllabus summarizing the decision and a "lineup" showing how the justices voted.

Two hundred copies of the "bench opinion" are made. As the decision is announced in Court, the bench opinion is distributed to journalists and others in the public information office. Another copy, with any necessary corrections noted on it, is sent to the U.S. Government Printing Office, which prints 3,397 "slip" opinions, which are distributed to federal and state courts and agencies. The Court receives 400 of these, and they are available to the public free through the Public Information Office as long as supplies last. The Government Printing Office also prints the opinion for inclusion in *United States Reports,* the official record of Supreme Court opinions.

The public announcement of opinions in Court probably is the Court's most dramatic function. It may also be the most expendable. Depending on who delivers the opinion and how, announcements can take a considerable amount of the Court's time. Opinions are given simultaneously to the public information officer for distribution. Nevertheless, those who are in the courtroom to hear the announcement of a ruling are participating in a very old tradition. The actual delivery may be tedious or exciting, depending on the nature of the case, the eloquence of the opinion, and the style of its oral delivery.

Brief Biographies

William Hubbs Rehnquist

Born October 1, 1924, Milwaukee, Wisconsin.

Education Stanford University, B.A., Phi Beta Kappa, and M.A., 1948; Harvard University, M.A., 1949; Stanford University Law School, LL.B., 1952.

Family Married Natalie Cornell, 1953; died, 1991; two daughters, one son.

Career Law clerk to Justice Robert H. Jackson, U.S. Supreme Court, 1952-1953; practiced law, 1953-1969; assistant U.S. attorney general, Office of Legal Counsel, 1969-1971.

Supreme Court Service Nominated as associate justice of the U.S. Supreme Court by President Richard Nixon, October 21, 1971; confirmed December 10, 1971; nominated as chief justice of the United States by President Ronald Reagan, June 17, 1986; confirmed September 17, 1986.

President Reagan's appointment of William H. Rehnquist as chief justice in 1986 was a clear indication that the president was hoping to shift the Court to the right. Since his early years as an associate justice in the 1970s, Rehnquist has been one of the Court's most conservative justices.

Rehnquist, the fourth associate justice to become chief, argues that the original intent of the Framers of the Constitution and the Bill of Rights is the proper standard for interpreting those documents today. He also takes a literal approach to individual rights. These beliefs have led him to dissent from the Court's rulings protecting a woman's privacy-based right to abortion, to argue that no constitutional barrier exists to school prayer, and to side with police and prosecutors on questions of criminal law. In 1991 he wrote the Court's decision upholding an administration ban on abortion counseling at publicly financed clinics and in 1992 vigorously dissented from the Court's affirmation of *Roe v. Wade,* the 1973 opinion that made abortion legal nationwide.

Born in Milwaukee, Wisconsin, October 1, 1924, Rehnquist attended Stanford University, where he earned both a B.A. and M.A. He received a second M.A. from Harvard before returning to Stanford for law school. His classmates there recalled him as an intelligent student with already well-entrenched conservative views.

After graduating from law school in 1952, Rehnquist came to Washington, D.C., to serve as a law clerk to Supreme Court justice Robert H. Jackson. There, he wrote a memorandum that later would come back to haunt him during his Senate confirmation hearings. In the memo, Rehnquist favored separate but equal schools for blacks and whites. Asked about those views by the Senate Judiciary Committee in 1971, Rehnquist repudiated them, declaring that they were Justice Jackson's—not his own, although Jackson was a moderate.

Following his clerkship, Rehnquist decided to practice law in the Southwest. He moved to Phoenix and immediately became immersed in Arizona Republican politics. From his earliest days in the state, he was associated with the party's conservative wing. A 1957 speech denouncing the liberalism of the Warren Court typified his views at the time.

During the 1964 presidential race, Rehnquist campaigned ardently for Barry Goldwater. It was then that Rehnquist met and worked with Richard G. Kleindienst, who later, as President Richard Nixon's deputy attorney general, would appoint Rehnquist to head the Justice Department's Office of Legal Counsel as an assistant attorney general. In 1971 Nixon nominated him to the Supreme Court.

Controversy surrounded Rehnquist's 1986 nomination as chief justice. He was accused of harassing voters and challenging their right to vote years earlier when he was a GOP poll watcher in Phoenix. Accusations of racial bias also were raised against him. His views on civil rights were questioned, and he was found to have accepted anti-Semitic restrictions in a property deed to a Vermont home.

Before Clarence Thomas's 1991 nomination battle, more votes were cast against Rehnquist for chief justice (thirty-three nays to sixty-five ayes) than against any other successful Supreme Court nominee in the twentieth century. In 1971 Rehnquist had tied for the second-highest number of negative votes (twenty-six nays to sixty-eight ayes) when he was confirmed as an associate justice.

Rehnquist was married to Natalie Cornell, who died in 1991. They had two daughters and a son.

Harry Andrew Blackmun

Born November 12, 1908, Nashville, Illinois.

Education Harvard College, B.A., Phi Beta Kappa, 1929; Harvard University Law School, LL.B., 1932.

Family Married Dorothy E. Clark, 1941; three daughters.

Career Law clerk to John Sanborn, U.S. Court of Appeals for the Eighth Circuit, St. Paul, 1932-1933; practiced law, Minneapolis, 1934-1950; resident counsel, Mayo Clinic, Rochester, Minnesota, 1950-1959; judge, U.S. Court of Appeals for the Eighth Circuit, 1959-1970.

Supreme Court Service Nominated as associate justice of the U.S. Supreme Court by President Richard Nixon, April 14, 1970; confirmed May 12, 1970.

During his first years on the Court, Harry A. Blackmun frequently was described as one of the "Minnesota Twins" along with the Court's other Minnesota native, Chief Justice Warren E. Burger. Blackmun and Burger, who retired in 1986, were friends who initially voted together on important decisions.

However, Blackmun, who originally impressed observers as a modest, even meek, addition to the Court's conservative bloc, has written some of the Court's most controversial, liberally oriented decisions, among them its 1973 ruling upholding a woman's right to an abortion. He since has become the liberal pole.

Blackmun was born in Nashville, Illinois, November 12, 1908, but spent most of his early years in St. Paul, Minnesota, where his father was in business. His lifelong friendship with Burger began in grade school.

Blackmun went east after high school to attend Harvard College on a scholarship. He majored in mathematics and toyed briefly with the idea of becoming a physician. But he chose the law instead. After graduating from Harvard in 1929, Phi Beta Kappa, Blackmun entered Harvard Law School and received his degree in 1932. During his law school years, Blackmun supported himself with a variety of odd jobs, including tutoring in math and driving the launch for the college crew team.

Following law school Blackmun returned to St. Paul, where he served for a year and a half as a law clerk to United States Circuit Court judge John B. Sanborn, whom Blackmun succeeded twenty years later. He left the clerkship at the end of 1933 and joined a law firm in Minneapolis, where he specialized in taxation, trusts and estates, and civil litigation. At the same time he taught for a year at Burger's alma mater, the St. Paul College of Law (since renamed the William Mitchell College of Law). In addition to his practice, Blackmun taught for two years during the 1940s at the University of Minnesota Law School.

In 1950 he accepted a post as "house counsel" for the world-famous Mayo Clinic in Rochester, Minnesota. Among his colleagues there, Blackmun quickly developed a reputation as a serious man, totally engrossed in his profession. The reputation followed him to the bench of the U.S. Court of Appeals for the Eighth Circuit, to which Blackmun was appointed by President Dwight D. Eisenhower in 1959. As a judge, Blackmun was known for his scholarly and thorough opinions.

Blackmun's total devotion to the law leaves little time for outside activities. He is an avid reader, delving primarily into judicial tomes. Over the years he also has been active in Methodist church affairs. Before he developed knee problems, Blackmun was a proficient squash and tennis player.

It was on the tennis court that Blackmun met his wife, Dorothy E. Clark. They were married in 1941 and have three daughters.

John Paul Stevens

Born April 20, 1920, Chicago, Illinois.

Education University of Chicago, B.A., Phi Beta Kappa, 1941; Northwestern University School of Law, J.D., 1947.

Family Married Elizabeth Jane Sheeren, 1942; three daughters, one son; divorced 1979; married Maryan Mulholland Simon, 1980.

Career Law clerk to Justice Wiley Rutledge, U.S. Supreme Court, 1947-1948; practiced law, Chicago, 1949-1970; judge, U.S. Court of Appeals for the Seventh Circuit, 1970-1975.

Supreme Court Service Nominated as associate justice of the U.S. Supreme Court by President Gerald R. Ford, November 28, 1975; confirmed December 17, 1975.

When President Gerald R. Ford nominated federal appeals court judge John Paul Stevens to the Supreme Court seat vacated by veteran liberal William O. Douglas in 1975, Court observers struggled to pin an ideological label on the new nominee. The consensus that finally emerged was that Stevens was neither a doctrinaire liberal nor conservative, but a judicial centrist. His subsequent opinions bear out this description, although in recent years he has leaned more toward the liberal side.

Stevens is a soft-spoken, mild-mannered man who occasionally sports a bow tie under his judicial robes. A member of a prominent Chicago family, he had a long record of excellence in scholarship, graduating Phi Beta Kappa from the University of Chicago in 1941. After a wartime stint in the Navy, during which he earned the Bronze Star, he returned to Chicago to enter Northwestern University Law School, from which he graduated magna cum laude in 1947. From there, Stevens left for Washington, where he served as a law clerk to Supreme Court justice Wiley Rutledge. He returned to Chicago to join the prominent law firm of Poppenhusen, Johnston, Thompson & Raymond, which specialized in antitrust law. Stevens developed a reputation as a preeminent antitrust lawyer, and after three years with Poppenhusen he left in 1952 to form his own firm, Rothschild, Stevens, Barry & Myers. He remained there, engaging in private practice and teaching part time at Northwestern and the University of Chicago law schools, until his appointment by President Richard Nixon in 1970 to the U.S. Court of Appeals for the Seventh Circuit.

Stevens developed a reputation as a political moderate during his undergraduate days at the University of Chicago, then an overwhelmingly liberal campus. Although he is a registered Republican, he has never been active in partisan politics. Nevertheless, Stevens served as Republican counsel in 1951 to the House Judiciary Subcommittee on the Study of Monopoly Power. He also served from 1953 to 1955, during the Eisenhower administration, as a member of the attorney general's committee to study antitrust laws.

In 1942 Stevens married Elizabeth Jane Sheeren. They have four children. They were divorced in 1979. Stevens subsequently married Maryan Mulholland Simon, a longtime neighbor in Chicago.

Sandra Day O'Connor

Born March 26, 1930, El Paso, Texas.

Education Stanford University, B.A., 1950; Stanford University Law School, LL.B., 1952.

Family Married John J. O'Connor III, 1952; three sons.

Career Deputy county attorney, San Mateo, California, 1952-1953; assistant attorney general, Arizona, 1965-1969; Arizona state senator, 1969-1975; Arizona Senate majority leader, 1972-1975; judge, Maricopa County Superior Court 1974-1979; judge, Arizona Court of Appeals, 1979-1981.

Supreme Court Service Nominated as associate justice of the U.S. Supreme Court by President Ronald Reagan August 19, 1981; confirmed September 21, 1981.

Sandra Day O'Connor was the Court's first woman justice, and in 1992, after a decade on the Court, she emerged as a coalition builder in the Court's legal doctrine on abortion and other controversial issues.

Pioneering came naturally to O'Connor. Her grandfather left Kansas in 1880 to take up ranching in the desert land that eventually would become the state of Arizona. O'Connor, born in El Paso, Texas, where her mother's parents lived, was raised on the Lazy B Ranch, the 198,000-acre spread that her grandfather founded in southeastern Arizona near Duncan. She spent her school years in El Paso, living with her grandmother. She graduated from high school at age sixteen and then entered Stanford University.

Six years later, in 1952, Sandra Day had won degrees, with great distinction, both from the university, in economics, and from Stanford Law School. At Stanford, she met John J. O'Connor III, her future husband, and William H. Rehnquist, a future colleague on the Supreme Court. While in law school, Sandra Day was an editor of the *Stanford Law Review* and a member of Order of the Coif, both reflecting her academic leadership.

Despite her outstanding law school record, she found securing a job as an attorney difficult in 1952 when relatively few women were practicing law. She applied, among other places, to the firm in which William French Smith—first attorney general in the Reagan administration—was a partner, only to be offered a job as a secretary.

After she completed a short stint as deputy county attorney for San Mateo County (California) while her new husband completed law school at Stanford, the O'Connors moved with the U.S. Army to Frankfurt, Germany. There Sandra O'Connor worked as a civilian attorney for the Army, while John O'Connor served his tour of duty. In 1957 they returned to Phoenix, where, during the next eight years, their three sons were born. O'Connor's life was a mix of parenthood, homemaking, volunteer work, and some "miscellaneous legal tasks" on the side.

In 1965 she resumed her legal career full time, taking a job as an assistant attorney general for Arizona. After four years in that post she was appointed to fill a vacancy in the state Senate, where she served on the judiciary committee. In 1970 she was elected to the same body and two years later was chosen its majority leader, the first woman in the nation to hold such a post. O'Connor was active in Republican party politics, serving as co-chairman of the Arizona Committee for the Re-election of the President in 1972.

In 1974 she was elected to the Superior Court for Maricopa County, where she served for five years. Then in 1979 Gov. Bruce Babbitt—acting, some said, to remove a potential rival for the governorship—appointed O'Connor to the Arizona Court of Appeals. It was from that seat that President Reagan chose her as his first nominee to the Supreme Court, succeeding Potter Stewart, who had retired. Reagan described her as "a person for all seasons."

By a vote of 99-0 the Senate confirmed O'Connor September 21, 1981, and she became the first woman associate justice of the U.S. Supreme Court.

Antonin Scalia

Born March 11, 1936, Trenton, New Jersey.

Education Georgetown University, A.B., 1957; Harvard University Law School, LL.B., 1960.

Family Married Maureen McCarthy, 1960; five sons, four daughters.

Career Practiced law, Cleveland, 1960-1967; taught at the University of Virginia, 1967-1971; general counsel, White House Office of Telecommunications Policy, 1971-1972; chairman, Administrative Conference of the United States, 1972-1974; head, Justice Department Office of Legal Counsel, 1974-1977; taught at the University of Chicago Law School, 1977-1982; judge, U.S. Court of Appeals for the District of Columbia, 1982-1986.

Supreme Court Service Nominated as associate justice of the U.S. Supreme Court by President Ronald Reagan June 17, 1986; confirmed September 17, 1986.

After Warren E. Burger retired from the Court and Ronald Reagan named William H. Rehnquist to succeed him as chief justice, the president's next move—appointing Antonin Scalia as associate justice—was not surprising. On issues dear to Reagan, Scalia clearly met the president's tests for conservatism. Scalia, whom Reagan had named to the U.S. Court of Appeals for the District of Columbia in 1982, became the first Supreme Court justice of Italian ancestry. A Roman Catholic, he opposes abortion. He also has expressed opposition to "affirmative action" preferences for minorities.

Deregulation, which Reagan pushed as president, was a subject of considerable interest to Scalia, a specialist in administrative law. From 1977 to 1982 he was editor of the magazine *Regulation,* published by the American Enterprise Institute for Public Policy Research.

In contrast to the hours of floor debate over Rehnquist's nomination as chief justice, only a few brief speeches were given in opposition to the equally conservative Scalia before he was confirmed, 98-0. He has since become the scourge of some members of Congress because of his suspicion of committee reports, floor speeches, and other artifacts of legislative history that courts traditionally rely on to interpret a statute.

Born in Trenton, New Jersey, March 11, 1936, Scalia grew up in Queens, New York. His father was a professor of Romance languages at Brooklyn College, and his mother was a schoolteacher. Scalia graduated from Georgetown University in 1957 and from Harvard Law School in 1960. He worked for six years for the firm of Jones, Day, Cockley & Reavis in Cleveland and then taught contract, commercial, and comparative law at the University of Virginia Law School.

Scalia served as general counsel of the White House Office of Telecommunications Policy from 1971 to 1972. He then headed the Administrative Conference of the United States, a group that advises the government on questions of administrative law and procedure. From 1974 through the Ford administration he headed the Justice Department's Office of Legal Counsel, a post Rehnquist had held three years earlier. Scalia then returned to academia, to teach at the University of Chicago Law School.

Scalia showed himself to be a hard worker, an aggressive interrogator, and an articulate advocate. On the appeals court he was impatient with what he saw as regulatory or judicial overreaching. In 1983 he dissented from a ruling requiring the Food and Drug Administration (FDA) to consider whether drugs used for lethal injections met FDA standards as safe and effective. The Supreme Court agreed, reversing the appeals court in 1985.

Scalia was thought to be the principal author of an unsigned decision in 1986 that declared major portions of the Gramm-Rudman-Hollings budget-balancing act unconstitutional. The Supreme Court upheld the decision later in the year.

Anthony McLeod Kennedy

Born July 23, 1936, Sacramento, California.

Education Stanford University, A.B., Phi Beta Kappa, 1958; Harvard University Law School, LL.B., 1961.

Family Married Mary Davis, 1963; two sons, one daughter.

Career Practiced law, San Francisco, 1961-1963, Sacramento, 1963-1975; professor of constitutional law, McGeorge School of Law, University of the Pacific, 1965-1988; judge, U.S. Court of Appeals for the Ninth Circuit, 1975-1988.

Supreme Court Service Nominated as associate justice of the U.S. Supreme Court by President Ronald Reagan November 11, 1987; confirmed February 3, 1988.

Quiet, scholarly Anthony M. Kennedy, President Reagan's third choice for his third appointment to the Supreme Court, made all the difference when the Court's conservative majority began coalescing in 1989.

Kennedy proved to be a crucial fifth vote for the Court's conservative wing in civil rights cases, a firm supporter of state authority over defendants' rights in criminal cases, and a strict constructionist in the mode of Chief Justice William H. Rehnquist in most cases. Kennedy's presence effectively ushered in a new era on the Court. Reagan's earlier appointees, Sandra Day O'Connor and Antonin Scalia, had moved the Court somewhat to the right. But when Kennedy succeeded Lewis F. Powell, Jr., a moderate conservative and a critical swing vote, the balance of power shifted. On a range of issues where Powell often joined the Court's four liberals, Kennedy has gone the other way. Kennedy, however, broke with the hardline conservatives in 1992. He voted to disallow prayer at public school graduations and to uphold a woman's right to abortion.

Before Kennedy's nomination in November 1987, the Senate and the country had agonized through Reagan's two unsuccessful attempts to replace Powell, first with Robert H. Bork and then with Douglas H. Ginsburg. The Senate rejected Bork's nomination after contentious hearings, and Ginsburg withdrew his name amid controversy about his qualifications and admitted past use of marijuana.

A quiet sense of relief prevailed when Reagan finally selected a nominee who could be confirmed without another wrenching confrontation. Later, Republicans would note the irony in Kennedy's tipping the balance of the Court because anti-Bork Democrats had so willingly embraced him as a moderate.

Kennedy spent twelve years as a judge on the U.S. Court of Appeals for the Ninth Circuit. But unlike Bork, who wrote and spoke extensively for twenty years, Kennedy's record was confined mostly to his approximately five hundred judicial opinions. His views thus were based in large part on issues that were distilled at the trial level and further refined by legal and oral arguments. Furthermore, Kennedy sought to decide issues narrowly instead of using his opinions as a testing ground for constitutional theories. He continued this approach in the decisions he has written on the high Court.

A native Californian, Kennedy attended Stanford University from 1954 to 1957 and the London School of Economics from 1957 to 1958. He received an A.B. from Stanford in 1958 and an LL.B. from Harvard Law School in 1961. Admitted to the California bar in 1962, he was in private law practice until 1975, when President Gerald R. Ford appointed him to the appeals court. From 1965 to 1988 he taught constitutional law at McGeorge School of Law, University of the Pacific. Confirmed by the Senate, 97-0, February 3, 1988, Kennedy was sworn in as an associate justice of the Supreme Court February 18.

He and his wife, the former Mary Davis, have three children.

David Hackett Souter

Born September 17, 1939, Melrose, Massachusetts.

Education Harvard College, B.A., 1961; Rhodes scholar, Oxford University, 1961-1963; Harvard University Law School, LL.B., 1966.

Family Unmarried.

Career Private law practice, Concord, New Hampshire, 1966-1968; assistant attorney general, New Hampshire, 1968-1971; deputy attorney general, New Hampshire, 1971-1976; attorney general, New Hampshire, 1976-1978; associate justice, New Hampshire Superior Court, 1978-1983; associate justice, New Hampshire Supreme Court, 1983-1990; judge, U.S. Court of Appeals for the First Circuit, 1990.

Supreme Court Service Nominated as associate justice of the U.S. Supreme Court by President George Bush July 23, 1990; confirmed October 2, 1990.

At first, the Senate did not know what to make of David H. Souter, a cerebral, button-down nominee who was President Bush's first appointment to the Court. Souter was little known outside of his home state of New Hampshire, where he had been attorney general, a trial judge, and a state supreme court justice.

Unlike Antonin Scalia and Anthony M. Kennedy, his immediate predecessors on the Court, Souter had virtually no scholarly writings to dissect and little federal court experience to scrutinize. Only three months earlier Bush had appointed him to the U.S. Court of Appeals for the First Circuit. Souter had yet to write a legal opinion on the appeals court.

During his confirmation hearings, the Harvard graduate and former Rhodes scholar demonstrated intellectual rigor and a masterly approach to constitutional law. Souter was able to recognize where a particular questioner was headed and to deflect most tough inquiries. He took refuge in the history of legal principles. His earlier work as state attorney general and as a New Hampshire Supreme Court justice had a conservative bent, but during the hearings Souter came across as more moderate, winning over both Democrats and Republicans with his knowledge of judicial precedent.

Souter was approved by the Senate 90-9; dissenting senators cited his reluctance to take a stand on abortion. During his confirmation hearings, Souter refused to say how he would vote if the question of overruling *Roe v. Wade* arose. Senators predicted he would be a swing vote, but in his first year that was not the case.

Instead, Souter remained a mystery. He was a tenacious questioner during oral argument but reserved in the opinions he wrote. However, he could be counted on to side with the conservative wing of the Court. In the 1989-1990 term, before Souter replaced Justice William J. Brennan, Jr., one-third of the Court's decisions were 5-4 rulings. In the 1990-1991 term, only one-fifth were so narrowly decided, and many controversial disputes were settled by 6-3 votes.

Souter, in the 1991-1992 term, staked out a more middle ground with Justices Sandra Day O'Connor and Kennedy. The three joined to write the majority opinion in an abortion case and declined to overturn *Roe v. Wade*. In the 1992-1993 term, Souter took liberal positions in a number of civil rights, church-state, and criminal law cases. Overall, however, he continued to vote more often with the conservatives than with the liberals.

Souter is known for his intensely private, ascetic life. He was born September 17, 1939, in Melrose, Massachusetts. An only child, he moved with his parents to Weare, New Hampshire, at age eleven. Except for college, he had lived in Weare since.

Graduating from Harvard College in 1961, Souter attended Oxford University on a Rhodes Scholarship from 1961 to 1963, then returned to Cambridge for Harvard Law School. Graduating in 1966, he worked for two years in a Concord law firm. In 1968 he became an assistant attorney general, rose to deputy attorney general in 1971, and in 1976 was appointed attorney general. Under conservative governor Meldrim Thomson, Jr., Attorney General Souter defended a number of controversial orders, including the lowering of state flags to half-staff on Good Friday to observe the death of Jesus. He prosecuted Jehovah's Witnesses who obscured the state motto "Live Free or Die" on their license plates.

Souter served as attorney general until 1978, when he was named to the state's trial court. Five years later, Gov. John H. Sununu appointed Souter to the state Supreme Court. Sununu was Bush's chief of staff when Souter was named to the U.S. Supreme Court.

Souter, a bachelor, is a nature enthusiast and avid hiker.

Clarence Thomas

Born June 23, 1948, Savannah, Georgia.

Education Immaculate Conception Seminary, 1967-1968; Holy Cross College, B.A., 1971; Yale University Law School, J.D., 1974.

Family Married Kathy Grace Ambush, 1971; one son; divorced 1984; married Virginia Lamp, 1987.

Career Assistant attorney general, Missouri, 1974-1977; attorney, Monsanto Co., 1977-1979; legislative assistant to Sen. John C. Danforth, R-Mo., 1979-1981; assistant secretary of education for civil rights, 1981-1982; chairman, Equal Employment Opportunity Commission, 1982-1990; judge, U.S. Court of Appeals for the District of Columbia, 1990-1991.

Supreme Court Service Nominated as associate justice of the U.S. Supreme Court by President George Bush July 1, 1991; confirmed October 15, 1991.

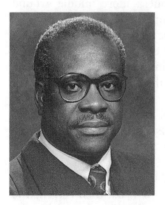

The Senate's 52-48 vote on Clarence Thomas was the closest Supreme Court confirmation vote in more than a century and followed a tumultuous nomination process that culminated in accusations against Thomas of sexual harassment. The charges, brought out in nationally televised hearings, were never proved and led the nominee to accuse the Senate of a "high-tech lynching."

Thomas, who took his judicial oath on October 23, 1991, succeeded Thurgood Marshall, the Court's last consistent liberal and a man whose six-decade legal career shaped the country's civil rights struggle. Marshall was the first black justice, and Thomas became the second.

Thomas also was the fifth conservative appointment by a Republican president in ten years, a historic record that raised the stakes for the Democratically controlled Senate and led in part to the politics surrounding the confirmation. Thomas was only forty-three when President Bush nominated him, and senators noted that Thomas likely would be affecting the outcome of major constitutional rulings well into the twenty-first century. His confirmation also solidified the conservative majority on the Court that began asserting itself in the late 1980s.

Most difficult for Thomas were the eleventh-hour allegations from a former employee that he had sexually harassed her when he was assistant secretary of education for civil rights and then chairman of the Equal Employment Opportunity Commission (EEOC). In an unprecedented move, senators abruptly postponed a scheduled confirmation vote and reconvened hearings to take testimony from accuser Anita F. Hill, a University of Oklahoma law professor, Thomas, and witnesses for both.

In the end, most senators said Hill's charges and Thomas's defense— a categorical denial—were inconclusive. Senators fell back on their previous positions based on Thomas's judicial philosophy or his determined character and rise from poverty in rural Georgia.

In Thomas's first two years on the Court, he voted most often with Antonin Scalia. Thomas was with dissenting justices when the Court upheld a constitutional right to abortion and prohibited prayer at public school graduations.

Thomas graduated from Yale Law School in 1974. He worked as an assistant attorney general of Missouri and later was a staff attorney for Monsanto Company. He worked for Sen. John C. Danforth, R-Mo., as a legislative assistant and served in the Department of Education as assistant secretary for civil rights for one year before being named chairman of the EEOC.

Ruth Bader Ginsburg

Born March 15, 1933, Brooklyn, New York.

Education Cornell University, B.A., 1954; attended Harvard University Law School, 1956-1958; graduated Columbia Law School, J.D., 1959.

Family Married Martin D. Ginsburg, 1954; one daughter, one son.

Career Law clerk to U.S. District Court Judge Edmund L. Palmieri, 1959-1961; Columbia Law School Project on International Procedure, 1961-1963; taught at Rutgers University School of Law, 1963-1972; director, Women's Rights Project, American Civil Liberties Union, 1972-1980; professor, Columbia Law School, 1972-1980; judge, U.S. Court of Appeals for the District of Columbia, 1980-1993.

Supreme Court Service Nominated as associate justice of the U.S. Supreme Court by President Bill Clinton, June 22, 1993; confirmed August 3, 1993.

Ruth Bader Ginsburg's path to the U.S. Supreme Court is a classic American story of overcoming obstacles and setbacks through intelligence, persistence, and quiet hard work. Her achievements as a student, law teacher, advocate, and judge came against a background of personal adversity and institutional discrimination against women. Ginsburg not only surmounted those hurdles for herself, but also charted the legal strategy in the 1970s that helped broaden opportunities for women by establishing constitutional principles limiting sex discrimination in the law.

Born into a Jewish family of modest means in Brooklyn, Ruth Bader was greatly influenced by her mother Celia, who imparted a love of learning and a determination to be independent. Celia Bader died of cancer on the eve of her daughter's high school graduation in 1948.

Ruth Bader attended Cornell University, where she graduated first in her class and met her future husband, Martin Ginsburg, who became a tax lawyer and later a professor at Georgetown University Law Center in Washington.

At Harvard Law School, Ruth Bader Ginsburg made law review, cared for an infant daughter, and then helped her husband complete his studies after he was diagnosed with cancer. He recovered, graduated, and got a job in New York, and she transferred to Columbia for her final year of law school.

Although she was tied for first place in her class when she graduated, Ginsburg was unable to land a Supreme Court clerkship or job with a top New York law firm. Instead, she won a two-year clerkship with a federal district court judge. She then accepted a research position at Columbia that took her to Sweden, where she studied civil procedure and began to be stirred by feminist feelings. Ginsburg taught at Rutgers University Law School in New Jersey from 1963 to 1972. She also worked with the New Jersey affiliate of the American Civil Liberties Union (ACLU), where her caseload included several early sex discrimination complaints. In 1972 Ginsburg became the first woman to be named to a tenured position on the Columbia Law School faculty. As director of the national ACLU's newly established Women's Rights Project, she also handled the cases that over the course of several years led the Supreme Court to require heightened scrutiny of legal classifications based on sex. Ginsburg won five of the six cases she argued before the court.

President Jimmy Carter named Ginsburg to the U.S. Court of Appeals for the District of Columbia in 1980. There, she earned a reputation as a judicial moderate on a sharply divided court. Although she is prochoice, she stirred controversy among abortion rights groups by criticizing some aspects of the way the Supreme Court's landmark abortion case, *Roe v. Wade*, was decided.

When Justice Byron R. White announced plans for his retirement in March 1993, Ginsburg was among the large field of candidates President Bill Clinton considered for the vacancy. Clinton passed over two other leading candidates for the position before deciding to interview Ginsburg. White House aides told reporters later that Clinton had been especially impressed with Ginsburg's life story. Reaction to the nomination was overwhelmingly positive. On Capitol Hill, Ginsburg won the support of some pivotal Republican senators, including Minority Leader Robert Dole of Kansas.

In three days of confirmation hearings before the Senate Judiciary Committee, Ginsburg depicted herself as an advocate of judicial restraint, but also said courts sometimes had a role to play in bringing about social change. On specific issues, she strongly endorsed abortion rights, equal rights for women, and the constitutional right to privacy. But she declined to give her views on many other issues, including capital punishment. Some senators said that she had been less than forthcoming, but the committee voted unanimously to recommend her for confirmation.

The full Senate confirmed her four days later by a vote of 96-3. Three conservative Republicans cast the only negative votes. Ginsburg was sworn in August 10, 1993, as the court's second female justice—joining Justice Sandra Day O'Connor—and the first Jewish justice since 1969.

Byron Raymond White (Retired)

Born June 8, 1917, Fort Collins, Colorado.

Education University of Colorado, B.A., Phi Beta Kappa, 1938; Rhodes scholar, Oxford University; Yale University Law School, LL.B., 1946.

Family Married Marion Stearns, 1946; one son, one daughter.

Career Law clerk to Chief Justice Fred M. Vinson, U.S. Supreme Court, 1946-1947; practiced law, Denver, 1947-1960; U.S. deputy attorney general, 1961-1962.

Supreme Court Service Nominated as associate justice of the U.S. Supreme Court by President John F. Kennedy March 30, 1962; confirmed April 11, 1962; retired June 28, 1993.

Byron R. White was born June 8, 1917, in Fort Collins, Colorado, and grew up in Wellington, a small town in a sugar beet growing area of the state. Ranking first in his high school class, White won a scholarship to the University of Colorado, which he entered in 1934.

At the university White earned a reputation as an outstanding scholar-athlete. He was first in his class, a member of Phi Beta Kappa, and the winner of three varsity letters in football, four in basketball, and three in baseball. By the end of his college career in 1938 he had been nicknamed "Whizzer" for his outstanding performance as a football player, a performance that earned him not only a national reputation but also a one-year contract with the Pittsburgh Pirates (now the Steelers). White already had accepted a coveted Rhodes Scholarship for study at Oxford but decided to postpone his year in England.

Despite his success as a professional player, at the end of the football season White sailed for England to attend Oxford. When the European war broke out in September 1939, White returned to the United States and entered Yale Law School. But during 1940 and 1941 he alternated law study with playing football for the Detroit Lions.

After the United States entered the war, White served in the Navy in the South Pacific. There he renewed an old acquaintance with John F. Kennedy, whom he had met in England and who later would nominate him to the Supreme Court. After the war, White returned to Yale, earning his law degree magna cum laude in 1946. Following graduation, White served as law clerk to U.S. Chief Justice Fred M. Vinson. In 1947 White returned to his native Colorado, where for the next fourteen years he practiced law with the Denver law firm of Lewis, Grant & Davis.

White renewed his contact with Kennedy during the 1960 presidential campaign, leading the nationwide volunteer group Citizens for Kennedy. After the election, Kennedy named White to the post of deputy attorney general, a position he held until his Supreme Court appointment in 1962.

As a justice, White was noted for his quick and precise legal mind and his incisive legal questioning. He dissented from many of the Warren Court's liberal rulings on criminal procedures and then helped form pro-law-enforcement majorities in the Burger and Rehnquist eras. He also took conservative positions on First Amendment issues, but sided with liberals in most civil rights cases.

White has been married since 1946 to Marion Stearns. They have one son and one daughter.

Glossary of Legal Terms

Accessory. In criminal law, a person not present at the commission of an offense who commands, advises, instigates, or conceals the offense.

Acquittal. A person is acquitted when a jury returns a verdict of not guilty. A person also may be acquitted when a judge determines that insufficient evidence exists to convict him or that a violation of due process precludes a fair trial.

Adjudicate. To determine finally by the exercise of judicial authority, to decide a case.

Affidavit. A voluntary written statement of facts or charges affirmed under oath.

A fortiori. With stronger force, with more reason.

Amicus curiae. A friend of the court; a person, not a party to litigation, who volunteers or is invited by the court to give his views on a case.

Appeal. A legal proceeding to ask a higher court to review or modify a lower court decision. In a civil case, either the plaintiff or the defendant can appeal an adverse ruling. In criminal cases, a defendant can appeal a conviction, but the Double Jeopardy Clause prevents the government from appealing an acquittal. In Supreme Court practice, an appeal is a case that falls within the Court's mandatory jurisdiction as opposed to a case that the Court agrees to review under the discretionary writ of certiorari. With the virtual elimination of the Court's mandatory jurisdiction in 1988, the Court now hears very few true appeals, but petitions for certiorari are often referred to imprecisely as appeals.

Appellant. The party who appeals a lower court decision to a higher court.

Appellee. One who has an interest in upholding the decision of a lower court and is compelled to respond when the case is appealed to a higher court by an appellant.

Arraignment. The formal process of charging a person with a crime, reading that person the charge, asking whether he pleads guilty or not guilty, and entering the plea.

Attainder, Bill of. A legislative act pronouncing a particular individual guilty of a crime without trial or conviction and imposing a sentence.

Bail. The security, usually money, given as assurance of a prisoner's due appearance at a designated time and place (as in court) to procure in the interim the prisoner's release from jail.

Bailiff. A minor officer of a court usually serving as an usher or a messenger.

Brief. A document prepared by counsel to serve as the basis for an argument in court, setting out the facts of and the legal arguments in support of the case.

Burden of proof. The need or duty of affirmatively providing a fact or facts that are disputed.

Case law. The law as defined by previously decided cases, distinct from statutes and other sources of law.

Cause. A case, suit, litigation, or action, civil or criminal.

Certiorari, Writ of. A writ issued from the Supreme Court, at its discretion, to order a lower court to prepare the record of a case and send it to the Supreme Court for review.

Civil law. Body of law dealing with the private rights of individuals, as distinguished from criminal law.

Class action. A lawsuit brought by one person or group on behalf of all persons similarly situated.

Code. A collection of laws, arranged systematically.

Comity. Courtesy, respect; usually used in the legal sense to refer to the proper relationship between state and federal courts.

Common law. Collection of principles and rules of action, particularly from unwritten English law, that derive their authority from longstanding usage and custom or from courts recognizing and enforcing these customs. Sometimes used synonymously with case law.

Consent decree. A court-sanctioned agreement settling a legal dispute and entered into by the consent of the parties.

Contempt (civil and criminal). Civil contempt arises from a failure to follow a court order for the benefit of another party. Criminal contempt occurs when a person willfully exhibits disrespect for the court or obstructs the administration of justice.

Conviction. Final judgment or sentence that the defendant is guilty as charged.

Criminal law. The branch of law that deals with the enforcement of laws and the punishment of persons who, by breaking laws, commit crimes.

Declaratory judgment. A court pronouncement declaring a legal right or interpretation but not ordering a specific action.

De facto. In fact, in reality.

Defendant. In a civil action, the party denying or defending itself against charges brought by a plaintiff. In a criminal action, the person indicted for commission of an offense.

De jure. As a result of law, as a result of official action.

De novo. Anew; afresh; a second time.

Deposition. Oral testimony from a witness taken out of court in response to written or oral questions, committed to writing, and intended to be used in the preparation of a case.

Dicta. *See* Obiter dictum.

Dismissal. Order disposing of a case without a trial.

Docket. A calendar prepared by the clerks of the court listing the cases set to be tried.

Due process. Fair and regular procedure. The Fifth and Fourteenth Amendments guarantee persons that they will not be deprived of life, liberty, or property by the government until fair and usual procedures have been followed.

Error, Writ of. A writ issued from an appeals court to a lower court requiring it to send to the appeals court the record of a case in which it has entered a final judgment and which the appeals court will review for error.

Ex parte. Only from, or on, one side. Application to a court for some ruling or action on behalf of only one party.

Ex post facto. After the fact; an ex post facto law makes an action a crime after it already has been committed, or otherwise changes the legal consequences of some past action.

Ex rel. Upon information from; usually used to describe legal proceedings begun by an official in the name of the state, but at the instigation of, and with information from, a private individual interested in the matter.

Grand jury. Group of twelve to twenty-three persons impanelled to hear, in private, evidence presented by the state against an individual or persons accused of a criminal act and to issue indictments when a majority of the jurors find probable cause to believe that the accused has committed a crime. Called a "grand" jury because it comprises a greater number of persons than a "petit" jury.

Grand jury report. A public report, often called "presentments," released by a grand jury after an investigation into activities of public officials that fall short of criminal actions.

Guilty. A word used by a defendant in entering a plea or by a jury in returning a verdict, indicating that the defendant is legally responsible as charged for a crime or other wrongdoing.

Habeas corpus. Literally, "you have the body"; a writ issued to inquire whether a person is lawfully imprisoned or detained. The writ demands that the persons holding the prisoner justify the detention or release the prisoner.

Immunity. A grant of exemption from prosecution in return for evidence or testimony.

In camera. In chambers. Refers to court hearings in private without spectators.

In forma pauperis. In the manner of a pauper, without liability for court costs.

In personam. Done or directed against a particular person.

In re. In the affair of, concerning. Frequent title of judicial proceedings in which there are no adversaries, but instead where the matter itself—such as a bankrupt's estate—requires judicial action.

In rem. Done or directed against the thing, not the person.

Indictment. A formal written statement, based on evidence presented by the prosecutor, from a grand jury. Decided by a majority vote, an indictment charges one or more persons with specified offenses.

Information. A written set of accusations, similar to an indictment, but filed directly by a prosecutor.

Injunction. A court order prohibiting the person to whom it is directed from performing a particular act.

Interlocutory decree. A provisional decision of the court before completion of a legal action that temporarily settles an intervening matter.

Judgment. Official decision of a court based on the rights and claims of the parties to a case that was submitted for determination.

Jurisdiction. The power of a court to hear a case in question, which exists when the proper parties are present and when the point to be decided is within the issues authorized to be handled by the particular court.

Juries. *See* Grand jury; Petit jury.

Magistrate. A judicial officer having jurisdiction to try minor criminal cases and conduct preliminary examinations of persons charged with serious crimes.

Mandamus. "We command." An order issued from a superior court directing a lower court or other authority to perform a particular act.

Moot. Unsettled, undecided. A moot question also is one that no longer is material; a moot case is one that has become hypothetical.

Motion. Written or oral application to a court or a judge to obtain a rule or an order.

Nolo contendere. "I will not contest it." A plea entered by a defendant at the discretion of the judge with the same legal effect as a plea of guilty, but it may not be cited in other proceedings as an admission of guilt.

Obiter dictum. Statements by a judge or justice expressing an opinion and included with, but not essential to, an opinion resolving a case before the court. Dicta are not necessarily binding in future cases.

Parole. A conditional release from imprisonment under conditions that, if the prisoner abides by the law and other restrictions that may be imposed, the prisoner will not have to serve the remainder of the sentence.

Per curiam. "By the court." An unsigned opinion of the court, or an opinion written by the whole court.

Petit jury. A trial jury, originally a panel of twelve persons who tried to reach a unanimous verdict on questions of fact in criminal and civil proceedings. Since 1970 the Supreme Court has upheld the legality of state juries with fewer than twelve persons. Fewer persons serve on a "petit" jury than on a "grand" jury.

Petitioner. One who files a petition with a court seeking action or relief, including a plaintiff or an appellant. But a petitioner also is a person who files for other court action where charges are not necessarily made; for example, a party may petition the court for an order requiring another person or party to produce documents. The opposite party is called the respondent.

      When a writ of certiorari is granted by the Supreme Court, the parties to the case are called petitioner and respondent in contrast to the appellant and appellee terms used in an appeal.

Plaintiff. A party who brings a civil action or sues to obtain a remedy for injury to his rights. The party against whom action is brought is termed the defendant.

Plea bargaining. Negotiations between a prosecutor and the defendant aimed at exchanging a plea of guilty from the defendant for concessions by the prosecutor, such as reduction of charges or a request for leniency.

Pleas. *See* Guilty; Nolo contendere.

Presentment. *See* Grand jury report.

Prima facie. At first sight; referring to a fact or other evidence presumably sufficient to establish a defense or a claim unless otherwise contradicted.

Probation. Process under which a person convicted of an offense, usually a first offense, receives a suspended sentence and is given freedom, usually under the guardianship of a probation officer.

Quash. To overthrow, annul, or vacate; as to quash a subpoena.

Recognizance. An obligation entered into before a court or magistrate requiring the performance of a specified act—usually to appear in court at a later date. It is an alternative to bail for pretrial release.

Remand. To send back. When a decision is remanded, it is sent back by a higher court to the court from which it came for further action.

Respondent. One who is compelled to answer the claims or questions posed in court by a petitioner. A defendant and an appellee may be called respondents, but the term also includes those parties who answer in court during actions where charges are not necessarily brought or where the Supreme Court has granted a writ of certiorari.

Seriatim. Separately, individually, one by one.

Stare decisis. "Let the decision stand." The principle of adherence to settled cases, the doctrine that principles of law established in earlier judicial decisions should be accepted as authoritative in similar subsequent cases.

Statute. A written law enacted by a legislature. A collection of statutes for a particular governmental division is called a code.

Stay. To halt or suspend further judicial proceedings.

Subpoena. An order to present oneself before a grand jury, court, or legislative hearing.

Subpoena duces tecum. An order to produce specified documents or papers.

Tort. An injury or wrong to the person or property of another.

Transactional immunity. Protects a witness from prosecution for any offense mentioned in or related to his testimony, regardless of independent evidence against the witness.

Use immunity. Protects a witness from the use of his testimony against the witness in prosecution.

Vacate. To make void, annul, or rescind.

Writ. A written court order commanding the designated recipient to perform or not perform specified acts.

United States Constitution

We the People of the United States, in Order to form a more perfect Union, establish Justice, insure domestic Tranquility, provide for the common defence, promote the general Welfare, and secure the Blessings of Liberty to ourselves and our Posterity, do ordain and establish this Constitution for the United States of America.

Article I

Section 1. All legislative Powers herein granted shall be vested in a Congress of the United States, which shall consist of a Senate and House of Representatives.

Section 2. The House of Representatives shall be composed of Members chosen every second Year by the People of the several States, and the Electors in each State shall have the Qualifications requisite for Electors of the most numerous Branch of the State Legislature.

No Person shall be a Representative who shall not have attained to the age of twenty five Years, and been seven Years a Citizen of the United States, and who shall not, when elected, be an Inhabitant of that State in which he shall be chosen.

[Representatives and direct Taxes shall be apportioned among the several States which may be included within this Union, according to their respective Numbers, which shall be determined by adding to the whole Number of free Persons, including those bound to Service for a Term of Years, and excluding Indians not taxed, three fifths of all other Persons.][1] The actual Enumeration shall be made within three Years after the first Meeting of the Congress of the United States, and within every subsequent Term of ten Years, in such Manner as they shall by Law direct. The Number of Representatives shall not exceed one for every thirty Thousand, but each State shall have at Least one Representative; and until such enumeration shall be made, the State of New Hampshire shall be entitled to chuse three, Massachusetts eight, Rhode-Island and Providence Plantations one, Connecticut five, New-York six, New Jersey four, Pennsylvania eight, Delaware one, Maryland six, Virginia ten, North Carolina five, South Carolina five, and Georgia three.

When vacancies happen in the Representation from any State, the Executive Authority thereof shall issue Writs of Election to fill such

Vacancies.

The House of Representatives shall chuse their Speaker and other Officers; and shall have the sole Power of Impeachment.

Section 3. The Senate of the United States shall be composed of two Senators from each State, [chosen by the Legislature thereof,][2] for six Years; and each Senator shall have one Vote.

Immediately after they shall be assembled in Consequence of the first Election, they shall be divided as equally as may be into three Classes. The Seats of the Senators of the first Class shall be vacated at the Expiration of the second Year, of the second Class at the Expiration of the fourth Year, and of the third Class at the Expiration of the sixth Year, so that one third may be chosen every second Year; [and if Vacancies happen by Resignation, or otherwise, during the Recess of the Legislature of any State, the Executive thereof may make temporary Appointments until the next Meeting of the Legislature, which shall then fill such Vacancies.][3]

No Person shall be a Senator who shall not have attained to the Age of thirty Years, and been nine Years a Citizen of the United States, and who shall not, when elected, be an Inhabitant of that State for which he shall be chosen.

The Vice President of the United States shall be President of the Senate, but shall have no Vote, unless they be equally divided.

The Senate shall chuse their other Officers, and also a President pro tempore, in the Absence of the Vice President, or when he shall exercise the Office of President of the United States.

The Senate shall have the sole Power to try all Impeachments. When sitting for that Purpose, they shall be on Oath or Affirmation. When the President of the United States is tried, the Chief Justice shall preside: And no Person shall be convicted without the Concurrence of two thirds of the Members present.

Judgment in Cases of Impeachment shall not extend further than to removal from Office, and disqualification to hold and enjoy any Office of honor, Trust or Profit under the United States: but the Party convicted shall nevertheless be liable and subject to Indictment, Trial, Judgment and Punishment, according to Law.

Section 4. The Times, Places and Manner of holding Elections for Senators and Representatives, shall be prescribed in each State by the Legislature thereof; but the Congress may at any time by Law make or alter such Regulations, except as to the Places of chusing Senators.

The Congress shall assemble at least once in every Year, and such Meeting shall [be on the first Monday in December],[4] unless they shall by Law appoint a different Day.

Section 5. Each House shall be the Judge of the Elections, Returns and Qualifications of its own Members, and a Majority of each shall constitute a Quorum to do Business; but a smaller Number may adjourn from day to day, and may be authorized to compel the Attendance of absent Members, in such Manner, and under such Penalties as each House may provide.

Each House may determine the Rules of its Proceedings, punish its Members for disorderly Behaviour, and, with the Concurrence of two thirds, expel a Member.

Each House shall keep a Journal of its Proceedings, and from time to time publish the same, excepting such Parts as may in their Judgment require Secrecy; and the Yeas and Nays of the Members of either House on any question shall, at the Desire of one fifth of those Present, be entered on the Journal.

Neither House, during the Session of Congress, shall, without the Consent of the other, adjourn for more than three days, nor to any other Place than that in which the two Houses shall be sitting.

Section 6. The Senators and Representatives shall receive a Compensation for their Services, to be ascertained by Law, and paid out of the Treasury of the United States. They shall in all Cases, except Treason, Felony and Breach of the Peace, be privileged from Arrest during their Attendance at the Session of their respective Houses, and in going to and returning from the same; and for any Speech or Debate in either House, they shall not be questioned in any other Place.

No Senator or Representative shall, during the Time for which he was elected, be appointed to any civil Office under the Authority of the United States, which shall have been created, or the Emoluments whereof shall have been encreased during such time; and no Person holding any Office under the United States, shall be a Member of either House during his Continuance in Office.

Section 7. All Bills for raising Revenue shall originate in the House of Representatives; but the Senate may propose or concur with Amendments as on other Bills.

Every Bill which shall have passed the House of Representatives and the Senate, shall, before it become a Law, be presented to the President of the United States; If he approve he shall sign it, but if not he shall return it, with his Objections to that House in which it shall have originated, who shall enter the Objections at large on their Journal, and proceed to reconsider it. If after such Reconsideration two thirds of that House shall agree to pass the Bill, it shall be sent, together with the Objections, to the other House, by which it shall likewise be reconsidered, and if approved by two thirds of that House, it shall become a Law. But in all such Cases the Votes of both Houses shall be determined by yeas and Nays, and the Names of the Persons voting for and against the Bill shall be entered on the Journal of each House respectively. If any Bill shall not be returned by the President within ten Days (Sundays excepted) after it shall have been presented to him, the Same shall be a Law, in like Manner as if he had signed it, unless the Congress by their Adjournment prevent its Return, in which Case it shall not be a Law.

Every Order, Resolution, or Vote to which the Concurrence of the Senate and House of Representatives may be necessary (except on a question of Adjournment) shall be presented to the President of the United States; and before the Same shall take Effect, shall be approved by him, or being disapproved by him, shall be repassed by two thirds of the Senate and House of Representatives, according to the Rules and Limitations prescribed in the Case of a Bill.

Section 8. The Congress shall have Power To lay and collect Taxes, Duties, Imposts and Excises, to pay the Debts and provide for the common Defence and general Welfare of the United States; but all Duties, Imposts and Excises shall be uniform throughout the United States;

To borrow Money on the credit of the United States;

To regulate Commerce with foreign Nations, and among the several States, and with the Indian Tribes;

To establish an uniform Rule of Naturalization, and uniform Laws on the subject of Bankruptcies throughout the United States;

To coin Money, regulate the Value thereof, and of foreign Coin, and fix the Standard of Weights and Measures;

To provide for the Punishment of counterfeiting the Securities and current Coin of the United States;

To establish Post Offices and post Roads;

To promote the Progress of Science and useful Arts, by securing for limited Times to Authors and Inventors the exclusive Right to their respective Writings and Discoveries;

To constitute Tribunals inferior to the supreme Court;

To define and punish Piracies and Felonies committed on the high Seas, and Offences against the Law of Nations;

To declare War, grant Letters of Marque and Reprisal, and make Rules concerning Captures on Land and Water;

To raise and support Armies, but no Appropriation of Money to that Use shall be for a longer Term than two Years;

To provide and maintain a Navy;

To make Rules for the Government and Regulation of the land and naval Forces;

To provide for calling forth the Militia to execute the Laws of the Union, suppress Insurrections and repel Invasions;

To provide for organizing, arming, and disciplining, the Militia, and for governing such Part of them as may be employed in the Service of the United States, reserving to the States respectively, the Appointment of the Officers, and the Authority of training the Militia according to the discipline prescribed by Congress;

To exercise exclusive Legislation in all Cases whatsoever, over such District (not exceeding ten Miles square) as may, by Cession of particular States, and the Acceptance of Congress, become the Seat of the Government of the United States, and to exercise like Authority over all Places purchased by the Consent of the Legislature of the State in which the Same shall be, for the Erection of Forts, Magazines, Arsenals, dock-Yards, and other needful Buildings;—And

To make all Laws which shall be necessary and proper for carrying into Execution the foregoing Powers, and all other Powers vested by this Constitution in the Government of the United States, or in any Department or Officer thereof.

Section 9. The Migration or Importation of such Persons as any of the States now existing shall think proper to admit, shall not be prohibited by the Congress prior to the Year one thousand eight hundred and eight, but a Tax or duty may be imposed on such Importation, not exceeding ten dollars for each Person.

The Privilege of the Writ of Habeas Corpus shall not be suspended, unless when in Cases of Rebellion or Invasion the public Safety may require it.

No Bill of Attainder or ex post facto Law shall be passed.

No Capitation, or other direct, Tax shall be laid, unless in Proportion to the Census or Enumeration herein before directed to be taken.[5]

No Tax or Duty shall be laid on Articles exported from any State.

No Preference shall be given by any Regulation of Commerce or Revenue to the Ports of one State over those of another; nor shall Vessels bound to, or from, one State, be obliged to enter, clear, or pay Duties in another.

No Money shall be drawn from the Treasury, but in Consequence of Appropriations made by Law; and a regular Statement and Account of the Receipts and Expenditures of all public Money shall be published from time to time.

No Title of Nobility shall be granted by the United States: And no Person holding any Office of Profit or Trust under them, shall, without the Consent of the Congress, accept of any present, Emolument, Office, or Title, of any kind whatever, from any King, Prince, or foreign State.

Section 10. No State shall enter into any Treaty, Alliance, or Confederation; grant Letters of Marque and Reprisal; coin Money; emit

Bills of Credit; make any Thing but gold and silver Coin a Tender in Payment of Debts; pass any Bill of Attainder, ex post facto Law, or Law impairing the Obligation of Contracts, or grant any Title of Nobility.

No State shall, without the Consent of the Congress, lay any Imposts or Duties on Imports or Exports, except what may be absolutely necessary for executing it's inspection Laws: and the net Produce of all Duties and Imposts, laid by any State on Imports or Exports, shall be for the Use of the Treasury of the United States; and all such Laws shall be subject to the Revision and Controul of the Congress.

No State shall, without the Consent of Congress, lay any Duty of Tonnage, keep Troops, or Ships of War in time of Peace, enter into any Agreement or Compact with another State, or with a foreign Power, or engage in War, unless actually invaded, or in such imminent Danger as will not admit of delay.

Article II

Section 1. The executive Power shall be vested in a President of the United States of America. He shall hold his Office during the Term of four Years, and, together with the Vice President, chosen for the same Term, be elected, as follows

Each State shall appoint, in such Manner as the Legislature thereof may direct, a Number of Electors, equal to the whole Number of Senators and Representatives to which the State may be entitled in the Congress: but no Senator or Representative, or Person holding an Office of Trust or Profit under the United States, shall be appointed an Elector.

[The Electors shall meet in their respective States, and vote by Ballot for two Persons, of whom one at least shall not be an Inhabitant of the same State with themselves. And they shall make a List of all the Persons voted for, and of the Number of Votes for each; which List they shall sign and certify, and transmit sealed to the Seat of the Government of the United States, directed to the President of the Senate. The President of the Senate shall, in the Presence of the Senate and House of Representatives, open all the Certificates, and the Votes shall then be counted. The Person having the greatest Number of Votes shall be the President, if such Number be a Majority of the whole Number of Electors appointed; and if there be more than one who have such Majority, and have an equal Number of Votes, then the House of Representatives shall immediately chuse by Ballot one of them for President; and if no Person have a Majority, then from the five highest on the list the said House shall in like Manner chuse the President. But in chusing the President, the Votes shall be taken by States, the Representation from each State having one Vote; A quorum for this Purpose shall consist of a Member or Members from two thirds of the States, and a Majority of all the States shall be necessary to a

Choice. In every Case, after the Choice of the President, the Person having the greatest Number of Votes of the Electors shall be the Vice President. But if there should remain two or more who have equal Votes, the Senate shall chuse from them by Ballot the Vice President.][6]

The Congress may determine the Time of chusing the Electors, and the Day on which they shall give their Votes; which Day shall be the same throughout the United States.

No Person except a natural born Citizen, or a Citizen of the United States, at the time of the Adoption of this Constitution, shall be eligible to the Office of President; neither shall any Person be eligible to that Office who shall not have attained to the Age of thirty five Years, and been fourteen Years a Resident within the United States.

In Case of the Removal of the President from Office, or of his Death, Resignation, or Inability to discharge the Powers and Duties of the said Office,[7] the Same shall devolve on the Vice President, and the Congress may by Law provide for the Case of Removal, Death, Resignation or Inability, both of the President and Vice President, declaring what Officer shall then act as President, and such Officer shall act accordingly, until the Disability be removed, or a President shall be elected.

The President shall, at stated Times, receive for his Services, a Compensation, which shall neither be encreased nor diminished during the Period for which he shall have been elected, and he shall not receive within that Period any other Emolument from the United States, or any of them.

Before he enter on the Execution of his Office, he shall take the following Oath or Affirmation:—"I do solemnly swear (or affirm) that I will faithfully execute the Office of President of the United States, and will to the best of my Ability, preserve, protect and defend the Constitution of the United States."

Section 2. The President shall be Commander in Chief of the Army and Navy of the United States, and of the Militia of the several States, when called into the actual Service of the United States; he may require the Opinion, in writing, of the principal Officer in each of the executive Departments, upon any Subject relating to the Duties of their respective Offices, and he shall have Power to grant Reprieves and Pardons for Offences against the United States, except in Cases of Impeachment.

He shall have Power, by and with the Advice and Consent of the Senate, to make Treaties, provided two thirds of the Senators present concur; and he shall nominate, and by and with the Advice and Consent of the Senate, shall appoint Ambassadors, other public Ministers and Consuls, Judges of the supreme Court, and all other Officers of the United States, whose Appointments are not herein otherwise provided for, and which shall be established by Law: but the Congress may by Law vest the Appointment of such inferior Officers, as they think proper, in the President alone, in the Courts of Law, or in the Heads of Departments.

The President shall have Power to fill up all Vacancies that may happen during the Recess of the Senate, by granting Commissions which shall expire at the End of their next Session.

Section 3. He shall from time to time give to the Congress Information of the State of the Union, and recommend to their Consideration such Measures as he shall judge necessary and expedient; he may, on extraordinary Occasions, convene both Houses, or either of them, and in Case of Disagreement between them, with Respect to the Time of Adjournment, he may adjourn them to such Time as he shall think proper; he shall receive Ambassadors and other public Ministers; he shall take Care that the Laws be faithfully executed, and shall Commission all the Officers of the United States.

Section 4. The President, Vice President and all civil Officers of the United States, shall be removed from Office on Impeachment for, and Conviction of, Treason, Bribery, or other high Crimes and Misdemeanors.

Article III

Section 1. The judicial Power of the United States, shall be vested in one supreme Court, and in such inferior Courts as the Congress may from time to time ordain and establish. The Judges, both of the supreme and inferior Courts, shall hold their Offices during good Behaviour, and shall, at stated Times, receive for their Services, a Compensation, which shall not be diminished during their Continuance in Office.

Section 2. The judicial Power shall extend to all Cases, in Law and Equity, arising under this Constitution, the Laws of the United States, and Treaties made, or which shall be made, under their Authority;—to all Cases affecting Ambassadors, other public Ministers and Consuls;—to all Cases of admiralty and maritime Jurisdiction;—to Controversies to which the United States shall be a Party;—to Controversies between two or more States;—between a State and Citizens of another State;[8]—between Citizens of different States;—between Citizens of the same State claiming Lands under Grants of different States, and between a State, or the Citizens thereof, and foreign States, Citizens or Subjects.[8]

In all Cases affecting Ambassadors, other public Ministers and Consuls, and those in which a State shall be Party, the supreme Court shall have original Jurisdiction. In all the other Cases before mentioned, the supreme Court shall have appellate Jurisdiction, both as to Law and

Fact, with such Exceptions, and under such Regulations as the Congress shall make.

The Trial of all Crimes, except in Cases of Impeachment, shall be by Jury; and such Trial shall be held in the State where the said Crimes shall have been committed; but when not committed within any State, the Trial shall be at such Place or Places as the Congress may by Law have directed.

Section 3. Treason against the United States, shall consist only in levying War against them, or in adhering to their Enemies, giving them Aid and Comfort. No Person shall be convicted of Treason unless on the Testimony of two Witnesses to the same overt Act, or on Confession in open Court.

The Congress shall have Power to declare the Punishment of Treason, but no Attainder of Treason shall work Corruption of Blood, or Forfeiture except during the Life of the Person attainted.

Article IV

Section 1. Full Faith and Credit shall be given in each State to the public Acts, Records, and judicial Proceedings of every other State. And the Congress may by general Laws prescribe the Manner in which such Acts, Records and Proceedings shall be proved, and the Effect thereof.

Section 2. The Citizens of each State shall be entitled to all Privileges and Immunities of Citizens in the several States.

A Person charged in any State with Treason, Felony, or other Crime, who shall flee from Justice, and be found in another State, shall on Demand of the executive Authority of the State from which he fled, be delivered up, to be removed to the State having Jurisdiction of the Crime.

[No Person held to Service or Labour in one State, under the Laws thereof, escaping into another, shall, in Consequence of any Law or Regulation therein, be discharged from such Service or Labour, but shall be delivered up on Claim of the Party to whom such Service or Labour may be due.][9]

Section 3. New States may be admitted by the Congress into this Union; but no new State shall be formed or erected within the Jurisdiction of any other State; nor any State be formed by the Junction of two or more States, or Parts of States, without the Consent of the Legislatures of the States concerned as well as of the Congress.

The Congress shall have Power to dispose of and make all needful Rules and Regulations respecting the Territory or other Property belonging to the United States; and nothing in this Constitution shall be so construed as to Prejudice any Claims of the United States, or of any particular State.

Section 4. The United States shall guarantee to every State in this Union a Republican Form of Government, and shall protect each of them against Invasion; and on Application of the Legislature, or of the Executive (when the Legislature cannot be convened) against domestic Violence.

Article V

The Congress, whenever two thirds of both Houses shall deem it necessary, shall propose Amendments to this Constitution, or, on the Application of the Legislatures of two thirds of the several States, shall call a Convention for proposing Amendments, which, in either Case, shall be valid to all Intents and Purposes, as Part of this Constitution, when ratified by the Legislatures of three fourths of the several States, or by Conventions in three fourths thereof, as the one or the other Mode of Ratification may be proposed by the Congress; Provided [that no Amendment which may be made prior to the Year One thousand eight hundred and eight shall in any Manner affect the first and fourth Clauses in the Ninth Section of the first Article; and][10] that no State, without its Consent, shall be deprived of its equal Suffrage in the Senate.

Article VI

All Debts contracted and Engagements entered into, before the Adoption of this Constitution, shall be as valid against the United States under this Constitution, as under the Confederation.

This Constitution, and the Laws of the United States which shall be made in Pursuance thereof; and all Treaties made, or which shall be made, under the Authority of the United States, shall be the supreme Law of the Land; and the Judges in every State shall be bound thereby, any Thing in the Constitution or Laws of any State to the Contrary notwithstanding.

The Senators and Representatives before mentioned, and the Members of the several State Legislatures, and all executive and judicial Officers, both of the United States and of the several States, shall be bound by Oath or Affirmation, to support this Constitution; but no religious Test shall ever be required as a Qualification to any Office or public Trust under the United States.

Article VII

The Ratification of the Conventions of nine States, shall be sufficient for the Establishment of this Constitution between the States so ratifying the Same.

Done in Convention by the Unanimous Consent of the States present the Seventeenth Day of September in the Year of our Lord one thousand seven hundred and Eighty seven and of the Independence of the United States of America the Twelfth. IN WITNESS whereof We have hereunto subscribed our Names,

George Washington,
President and
deputy from Virginia.

New Hampshire:	John Langdon, Nicholas Gilman.
Massachusetts:	Nathaniel Gorham, Rufus King.
Connecticut:	William Samuel Johnson, Roger Sherman.
New York:	Alexander Hamilton.
New Jersey:	William Livingston, David Brearley, William Paterson, Jonathan Dayton.
Pennsylvania:	Benjamin Franklin, Thomas Mifflin, Robert Morris, George Clymer, Thomas FitzSimons, Jared Ingersoll, James Wilson, Gouverneur Morris.
Delaware:	George Read, Gunning Bedford Jr., John Dickinson, Richard Bassett, Jacob Broom.
Maryland:	James McHenry, Daniel of St. Thomas Jenifer, Daniel Carroll.

Virginia: John Blair,
                          James Madison Jr.

North Carolina: William Blount,
                          Richard Dobbs Spaight,
                          Hugh Williamson.

South Carolina: John Rutledge,
                          Charles Cotesworth Pinckney,
                          Charles Pinckney,
                          Pierce Butler.

Georgia: William Few,
                          Abraham Baldwin.

[The language of the original Constitution, not including the Amendments, was adopted by a convention of the states on September 17, 1787, and was subsequently ratified by the states on the following dates: Delaware, December 7, 1787; Pennsylvania, December 12, 1787; New Jersey, December 18, 1787; Georgia, January 2, 1788; Connecticut, January 9, 1788; Massachusetts, February 6, 1788; Maryland, April 28, 1788; South Carolina, May 23, 1788; New Hampshire, June 21, 1788.

Ratification was completed on June 21, 1788.

The Constitution subsequently was ratified by Virginia, June 25, 1788; New York, July 26, 1788; North Carolina, November 21, 1789; Rhode Island, May 29, 1790; and Vermont, January 10, 1791.]

Amendments

Amendment I

(First ten amendments ratified December 15, 1791.)

Congress shall make no law respecting an establishment of religion, or prohibiting the free exercise thereof; or abridging the freedom of speech, or of the press; or the right of the people peaceably to assemble, and to petition the Government for a redress of grievances.

Amendment II

A well regulated Militia, being necessary to the security of a free State, the right of the people to keep and bear Arms, shall not be infringed.

Amendment III

No Soldier shall, in time of peace be quartered in any house, without the consent of the Owner, nor in time of war, but in a manner to be prescribed by law.

Amendment IV

The right of the people to be secure in their persons, houses, papers, and effects, against unreasonable searches and seizures, shall not be violated, and no Warrants shall issue, but upon probable cause, supported by Oath or affirmation, and particularly describing the place to be searched, and the persons or things to be seized.

Amendment V

No person shall be held to answer for a capital, or otherwise infamous crime, unless on a presentment or indictment of a Grand Jury, except in cases arising in the land or naval forces, or in the Militia, when in actual service in time of War or public danger; nor shall any person be subject for the same offence to be twice put in jeopardy of life or limb; nor shall be compelled in any criminal case to be a witness against himself, nor be deprived of life, liberty, or property, without due process of law; nor shall private property be taken for public use, without just compensation.

Amendment VI

In all criminal prosecutions, the accused shall enjoy the right to a speedy and public trial, by an impartial jury of the State and district wherein the crime shall have been committed, which district shall have been previously ascertained by law, and to be informed of the nature and cause of the accusation; to be confronted with the witnesses against him; to have compulsory process for obtaining witnesses in his favor, and to have the Assistance of Counsel for his defence.

Amendment VII

In Suits at common law, where the value in controversy shall exceed twenty dollars, the right of trial by jury shall be preserved, and no fact tried by a jury, shall be otherwise re-examined in any Court of the United States, than according to the rules of the common law.

Amendment VIII

Excessive bail shall not be required, nor excessive fines imposed, nor cruel and unusual punishments inflicted.

Amendment IX

The enumeration in the Constitution, of certain rights, shall not be construed to deny or disparage others retained by the people.

Amendment X

The powers not delegated to the United States by the Constitution, nor prohibited by it to the States, are reserved to the States respectively, or to the people.

Amendment XI

(Ratified February 7, 1795)

The Judicial power of the United States shall not be construed to extend to any suit in law or equity, commenced or prosecuted against one of the United States by Citizens of another State, or by Citizens or Subjects of any Foreign State.

Amendment XII

(Ratified June 15, 1804)

The Electors shall meet in their respective states and vote by ballot for President and Vice-President, one of whom, at least, shall not be an inhabitant of the same state with themselves; they shall name in their ballots the person voted for as President, and in distinct ballots the person voted for as Vice-President, and they shall make distinct lists of all persons voted for as President, and of all persons voted for as Vice-President, and of the number of votes for each, which lists they shall sign and certify, and transmit sealed to the seat of the government of the United States, directed to the President of the Senate;—The President of the Senate shall, in the presence of the Senate and House of Representatives, open all the certificates and the votes shall then be counted;— The person having the greatest number of votes for President, shall be the President, if such number be a majority of the whole number of

Electors appointed; and if no person have such majority, then from the persons having the highest numbers not exceeding three on the list of those voted for as President, the House of Representatives shall choose immediately, by ballot, the President. But in choosing the President, the votes shall be taken by states, the representation from each state having one vote; a quorum for this purpose shall consist of a member or members from two-thirds of the states, and a majority of all the states shall be necessary to a choice. [And if the House of Representatives shall not choose a President whenever the right of choice shall devolve upon them, before the fourth day of March next following, then the Vice-President shall act as President, as in the case of the death or other constitutional disability of the President.—][11] The person having the greatest number of votes as Vice-President, shall be the Vice-President, if such number be a majority of the whole number of Electors appointed, and if no person have a majority, then from the two highest numbers on the list, the Senate shall choose the Vice-President; a quorum for the purpose shall consist of two-thirds of the whole number of Senators, and a majority of the whole number shall be necessary to a choice. But no person constitutionally ineligible to the office of President shall be eligible to that of Vice-President of the United States.

Amendment XIII

(Ratified December 6, 1865)

Section 1. Neither slavery nor involuntary servitude, except as a punishment for crime whereof the party shall have been duly convicted, shall exist within the United States, or any place subject to their jurisdiction.

Section 2. Congress shall have power to enforce this article by appropriate legislation.

Amendment XIV

(Ratified July 9, 1868)

Section 1. All persons born or naturalized in the United States, and subject to the jurisdiction thereof, are citizens of the United States and of the State wherein they reside. No State shall make or enforce any law which shall abridge the privileges or immunities of citizens of the United States; nor shall any State deprive any person of life, liberty, or property, without due process of law; nor deny to any person within its jurisdiction the equal protection of the laws.

Section 2. Representatives shall be apportioned among the several States according to their respective numbers, counting the whole number of persons in each State, excluding Indians not taxed. But when the right to vote at any election for the choice of electors for President and Vice President of the United States, Representatives in Congress, the Executive and Judicial officers of a State, or the members of the Legislature thereof, is denied to any of the male inhabitants of such State, being twenty-one years of age,[12] and citizens of the United States, or in any way abridged, except for participation in rebellion, or other crime, the basis of representation therein shall be reduced in the proportion which the number of such male citizens shall bear to the whole number of male citizens twenty-one years of age in such State.

Section 3. No person shall be a Senator or Representative in Congress, or elector of President and Vice President, or hold any office, civil or military, under the United States, or under any State, who, having previously taken an oath, as a member of Congress, or as an officer of the United States, or as a member of any State legislature, or as an executive or judicial officer of any State, to support the Constitution of the United States, shall have engaged in insurrection or rebellion against the same, or given aid or comfort to the enemies thereof. But Congress may by a vote of two-thirds of each House, remove such disability.

Section 4. The validity of the public debt of the United States, authorized by law, including debts incurred for payment of pensions and bounties for services in suppressing insurrection or rebellion, shall not be questioned. But neither the United States nor any State shall assume or pay any debt or obligation incurred in aid of insurrection or rebellion against the United States, or any claim for the loss or emancipation of any slave; but all such debts, obligations and claims shall be held illegal and void.

Section 5. The Congress shall have power to enforce, by appropriate legislation, the provisions of this article.

Amendment XV

(Ratified February 3, 1870)

Section 1. The right of citizens of the United States to vote shall not be denied or abridged by the United States or by any State on account of race, color, or previous condition of servitude.

Section 2. The Congress shall have power to enforce this article by appropriate legislation.

Amendment XVI

(Ratified February 3, 1913)

The Congress shall have power to lay and collect taxes on incomes, from whatever source derived, without apportionment among the several States, and without regard to any census or enumeration.

Amendment XVII

(Ratified April 8, 1913)

The Senate of the United States shall be composed of two Senators from each State, elected by the people thereof, for six years; and each Senator shall have one vote. The electors in each State shall have the qualifications requisite for electors of the most numerous branch of the State legislatures.

When vacancies happen in the representation of any State in the Senate, the executive authority of such State shall issue writs of election to fill such vacancies: *Provided,* That the legislature of any State may empower the executive thereof to make temporary appointments until the people fill the vacancies by election as the legislature may direct.

This amendment shall not be so construed as to affect the election or term of any Senator chosen before it becomes valid as part of the Constitution.

[Amendment XVIII

(Ratified January 16, 1919)

Section 1. After one year from the ratification of this article the manufacture, sale, or transportation of intoxicating liquors within, the importation thereof into, or the exportation thereof from the United States and all territory subject to the jurisdiction thereof for beverage purposes is hereby prohibited.

Section 2. The Congress and the several States shall have concurrent power to enforce this article by appropriate legislation.

Section 3. This article shall be inoperative unless it shall have been ratified as an amendment to the Constitution by the legislatures of the several States, as provided in the Constitution, within seven years from the date of the submission hereof to the States by the Congress.][13]

Amendment XIX

(Ratified August 18, 1920)

The right of citizens of the United States to vote shall not be denied or abridged by the United States or by any State on account of sex.

Congress shall have power to enforce this article by appropriate legislation.

Amendment XX

(Ratified January 23, 1933)

Section 1. The terms of the President and Vice President shall end at noon on the 20th day of January, and the terms of Senators and Representatives at noon on the 3d day of January, of the years in which such terms would have ended if this article had not been ratified; and the terms of their successors shall then begin.

Section 2. The Congress shall assemble at least once in every year, and such meeting shall begin at noon on the 3d day of January, unless they shall by law appoint a different day.

Section 3.[14] If, at the time fixed for the beginning of the term of the President, the President elect shall have died, the Vice President elect shall become President. If a President shall not have been chosen before the time fixed for the beginning of his term, or if the President elect shall have failed to qualify, then the Vice President elect shall act as President until a President shall have qualified; and the Congress may by law provide for the case wherein neither a President elect nor a Vice President elect shall have qualified, declaring who shall then act as President, or the manner in which one who is to act shall be selected, and such person shall act accordingly until a President or Vice President shall have qualified.

Section 4. The Congress may by law provide for the case of the death of any of the persons from whom the House of Representatives may choose a President whenever the right of choice shall have devolved upon them, and for the case of the death of any of the persons from whom the Senate may choose a Vice President whenever the right of choice shall have devolved upon them.

Section 5. Sections 1 and 2 shall take effect on the 15th day of October following the ratification of this article.

Section 6. This article shall be inoperative unless it shall have been ratified as an amendment to the Constitution by the legislatures of three-fourths of the several States within seven years from the date of its submission.

Amendment XXI

(Ratified December 5, 1933)

Section 1. The eighteenth article of amendment to the Constitution of the United States is hereby repealed.

Section 2. The transportation or importation into any State, Territory, or possession of the United States for delivery or use therein of intoxicating liquors, in violation of the laws thereof, is hereby prohibited.

Section 3. This article shall be inoperative unless it shall have been ratified as an amendment to the Constitution by conventions in the several States, as provided in the Constitution, within seven years from the date of the submission hereof to the States by the Congress.

Amendment XXII

(Ratified February 27, 1951)

Section 1. No person shall be elected to the office of the President more than twice, and no person who has held the office of President, or acted as President, for more than two years of a term to which some other person was elected President shall be elected to the office of the President more than once. But this Article shall not apply to any person holding the office of President when this Article was proposed by the Congress, and shall not prevent any person who may be holding the office of President, or acting as President, during the term within which this Article become operative from holding the office of President or acting as President during the remainder of such term.

Section 2. This article shall be inoperative unless it shall have been ratified as an amendment to the Constitution by the legislatures of three-fourths of the several States within seven years from the date of its submission to the States by the Congress.

Amendment XXIII

(Ratified March 29, 1961)

Section 1. The District constituting the seat of Government of the United States shall appoint in such manner as the Congress may direct:

A number of electors of President and Vice President equal to the whole number of Senators and Representatives in Congress to which the District would be entitled if it were a State, but in no event more than the least populous State; they shall be in addition to those appointed by the States, but they shall be considered, for the purposes of the election of President and Vice President, to be electors appointed by a State; and they shall meet in the District and perform such duties as provided by the twelfth article of amendment.

Section 2. The Congress shall have power to enforce this article by appropriate legislation.

Amendment XXIV

(Ratified January 23, 1964)

Section 1. The right of citizens of the United States to vote in any primary or other election for President or Vice President, for electors for President or Vice President, or for Senator or Representative in Congress, shall not be denied or abridged by the United States or any State by reason of failure to pay any poll tax or other tax.

Section 2. The Congress shall have power to enforce this article by appropriate legislation.

Amendment XXV

(Ratified February 10, 1967)

Section 1. In case of the removal of the President from office or of his death or resignation, the Vice President shall become President.

Section 2. Whenever there is a vacancy in the office of the Vice President, the President shall nominate a Vice President who shall take office upon confirmation by a majority vote of both Houses of Congress.

Section 3. Whenever the President transmits to the President pro tempore of the Senate and the Speaker of the House of Representatives his written declaration that he is unable to discharge the powers and duties of his office, and until he transmits to them a written declaration to the contrary, such powers and duties shall be discharged by the Vice President as Acting President.

Section 4. Whenever the Vice President and a majority of either the principal officers of the executive departments or of such other body as Congress may by law provide, transmit to the President pro tempore of the Senate and the Speaker of the House of Representatives their written declaration that the President is unable to discharge the powers and duties of his office, the Vice President shall immediately assume the powers and duties of the office as Acting President.

Thereafter, when the President transmits to the President pro tempore of the Senate and the Speaker of the House of Representatives his written declaration that no inability exists, he shall resume the powers and duties of his office unless the Vice President and a majority of either the principal officers of the executive department or of such other body as Congress may by law provide, transmit within four days to the President pro tempore of the Senate and the Speaker of the House of Representatives their written declaration that the President is unable to discharge the powers and duties of his office. Thereupon Congress shall decide the issue, assembling within forty-eight hours for that purpose if not in session. If the Congress, within twenty-one days after receipt of the latter written declaration, or, if Congress is not in session, within twenty-one days after Congress is required to assemble, determines by two-thirds vote of both Houses that the President is unable to discharge the powers and duties of his office, the Vice President shall continue to discharge the same as Acting President; otherwise, the President shall resume the powers and duties of his office.

Amendment XXVI

(Ratified July 1, 1971)

Section 1. The right of citizens of the United States, who are eighteen years of age or older, to vote shall not be denied or abridged by the United States or by any State on account of age.

Section 2. The Congress shall have power to enforce this article by appropriate legislation.

Amendment XXVII

(Ratified May 7, 1992)

No law varying the compensation for the services of the Senators and Representatives shall take effect, until an election of Representatives shall have intervened.

Notes

1. The part in brackets was changed by section 2 of the Fourteenth Amendment.
2. The part in brackets was changed by the first paragraph of the Seventeenth Amendment.
3. The part in brackets was changed by the second paragraph of the Seventeenth Amendment.
4. The part in brackets was changed by section 2 of the Twentieth Amendment.
5. The Sixteenth Amendment gave Congress the power to tax incomes.
6. The material in brackets has been superseded by the Twelfth Amendment.
7. This provision has been affected by the Twenty-fifth Amendment.
8. These clauses were affected by the Eleventh Amendment.
9. This paragraph has been superseded by the Thirteenth Amendment.
10. Obsolete.
11. The part in brackets has been superseded by section 3 of the Twentieth Amendment.
12. See the Nineteenth and Twenty-sixth Amendments.
13. This Amendment was repealed by section 1 of the Twenty-first Amendment.
14. See the Twenty-fifth Amendment.

Source: House Committee on the Judiciary, *The Constitution of the United States of America, as Amended,* H. Doc. 100-94, 100th Cong., 1st sess., 1987.

Index

Herrera, Raul, Sr., 36, 120
Herrera v. Collins, Director, Texas Department of Criminal Justice, Institutional Division (1993), 35-38, 56-57, 118-133. *See also* Capital punishment
Hicks, Melvin, 26, 167-174
Hill, Anita F., 251
Holder v. Hall, 221
Holmes, Oliver Wendell, Jr., 13
Home offices (taxation), 51
Housing and Urban Development Dept., 72-73
Hudson v. McMillian (1992), 66
Human rights suits, 17
Hunt v. McNair (1973), 139

Idaho
  capital punishment, 56
  water rights, 97
Illinois
  capital punishment, 220
  damage suits, 86
  habeas corpus, 63-64
Immigration law, 17, 27-29, 81-82, 153-166
Immigration and Nationality Act of 1952, 28, 154, 156, 158, 159
Immigration and Naturalization Service (INS), 82
Immunity (Puerto Rico), 94
Impeachment, 75-76
Indian Health Service, 77
Indian Major Crimes Act (1885), 70
Indigents, 54-55
Individual rights, 19, 83-89, 223-225
  abortion, 5, 16-17, 23-25, 83-89, 101-118, 213, 215, 223
  affirmative action, 83-84
  age discrimination, 84
  attorneys' fees, 84-85
  damage suits, 85-87
  international law, 88-89
  job discrimination, 17, 25-27, 88, 167-174, 223-224
  mental health law, 87-88
Individuals With Disabilities Education Act (IDEA), 30, 144, 145, 148,

150-151. *See also* Disability rights
Insurance law, 48-49
INS. *See* Immigration and Naturalization Service
INS v. Doherty (1992), 163
Internal Revenue Service (IRS), 50-52, 54, 90
International law, 88-89
Interstate Agreement on Detainers, 58
Interstate Commerce Commission (ICC), 75
IRS. See Internal Revenue Service
Itel Containers International Corp. v. Huddleston, Commissioner of Revenue of Tennessee (1993), 95

J.E.B. v. T.B., 219
Jackson, Michael, 215
Jackson, Robert H., 240
Jackson v. Virginia (1979), 122, 126
Jails and Prisons. *See* Prisons and Jails
Jehovah's Witnesses, 31
Jipping, Thomas, 19
Job discrimination, 17, 25-27, 88, 167-174, 223-224
Johnson, Dorsie, 57
Johnson v. De Grandy, 221
Johnson v. Mississippi (1988), 127-128
Johnson v. Texas (1993), 57, 64
Jones Act, 165
Judiciary Act of 1925, 231
"Junk science." *See* Scientific evidence
Juries, 65-66
Jury selection (Alabama), 219
Juveniles, Alien, 82

Kaiser Steel Corporation, 92
Kawakita v. United States (1952), 165
Keene Corp. v. United States (1993), 54
Kennedy, Anthony McLeod, 5, 30
  on abortion, 108
  antitrust decisions, 44-45
  biography, 246-248
  on capital punishment, 9, 37, 57, 125
  as a centrist, 19